Communicating Literature

An Introduction to Oral Interpretation

Fourth Edition

Todd V. Lewis

Biola University

KENDALL/HUNT PUBLISHING COMPANY

4050 Westmark Drive   Dubuque, Iowa 52002

Graphic Design for Cover and Illustrations: Jonathan W.R. Price

The photographs of the Hummel figurines, "Honor Student" and "Once Upon a Time" on the cover are used by permission. M.I. HUMMEL ®, HUMMEL ® AND M.I. HUMMEL CLUB ®, in signature and/or block forms, are registered trademarks of W. Goebel Porzellanfabrik, GmbH & Co. KG, Germany. M.I. Hummel figurines, plates and bells are copyrighted products. © Goebel 2003. Picture © ARS AG.

This edition is dedicated to my wife, Ginny.

Contents

Chapter 7   **Preparation for Oral Interpretation: Rehearsals and Performance 81**

Chapter 8   **Oral Interpretation of Prose 93**

Chapter 9   **Oral Interpretation of Drama: Solo and Duo 111**

Chapter 10   **Oral Interpretation of Poetry 127**

Chapter 11   Readers Theatre and Other Group Forms of Interpretation 149

Chapter 12   Evaluating Oral Interpretation Performances 165

Chapter 13   Specialized Forms and Outlets for Oral Interpretation 173

Appendix **Evaluation Critique Sheets 189**

Index   225

Preface

Communicating Literature: An Introduction to Oral Interpretation—4th Edition features a new, yet old, approach to the performance of literature. The history of scholarship in this area reveals a concentration on the communicative aspects of literature that lately has been relegated to a secondary status. The emphasis in this text suggests that the focus of performance studies needs to return to communicative intent in literature. Each performance text should have an argument, a thesis, a premise, a theme, a communicative center. Identifying this communicative center and making performance choices that justify the message is what this text is all about.

Lower division courses in oral interpretation, storytelling, and performance studies should find this text helpful. The writing style is personal and direct. At the end of each chapter you will find assignment suggestions and occasional exercises to assist you in comprehending issues and concepts. Assignments provide new professors with semester course objectives and performance ideas.

This edition of the textbook is unique from previous beginning oral interpretation texts in several areas. Chapter 1 offers a communication-oriented definition of oral interpretation, a basic rudimentary statement of oral interpretation essentials and a link between oral interpretation and acting. The fourth edition expands the discussion on stage fright, offering outlets and suggestions for coping with the normal anxiety found in public performances. Chapter 2 has been separated out in this edition as a brief history of oral interpretation (with unique references to the Judeo-Christian influence on recitation). Chapter 3 offers a new model of the communicative process of oral interpretation, current practices in introductory preparations, and theoretical prescriptions for viewing performance as persuasion.

Chapter 4 has expanded references to nonverbal gestures and codified means to analyze involuntary nonverbal responses. Chapter 5 not only discusses vocal factors in performance, but suggests exercises to learn how changes in voice can assist the performer and his/her perceived behaviors. Especially noteworthy in this edition is the exercise section at the end of the chapter which humorously looks at regional dialects as well as words spelled the same but requiring different pronunciations. Chapters 6 and 7 are key chapters, calling upon performers to study and analyze all texts before a performance and learn how to rehearse. Commentaries concerning focus points and audience adaptation are practical and useful.

Although literature samples are purposely kept to a minimum in this textbook, this fourth edition has a few more samples to illustrate chapter perspectives. This text is comparatively "long" on description and explication of concepts and "short" on literary examples. Chapters 8, 9, and 10 have helpful lists of possible literary selections. Experience shows that most students skip over samples of literature if they become excessive and lengthy. The samples included in this text are brief excerpts, generally, and are productive in illustrating concepts and genres.

Chapter 8 provides expanded notions of literature classified as prose. Chapter 9 introduces *solo* and *duo* formats for the performance of drama. New to this fourth edition is a section on the reading performance of Shakespeare. Chapter 10 expands poetry categories to include the interpretation of song lyrics. Chapter 11 introduces Readers Theatre, Chamber Theatre, and choral reading styles. Chapter 13 suggests optional performance formats with novel ideas for original material and religious scripture offerings. A new section on multicultural interpretation and expanded notions about competing in forensics tournament has also been included. Career opportunities and community service outlets figure prominently in this concluding chapter.

Chapter 12 links with the Appendix to suggest not only standards for evaluation, but also provides perforated evaluation sheets for in-class assignments as well as out-of-class observations. New to this edition and requested by many previous users is an accompanying Instructor's Manual with possible classroom assignments and sample test questions from each chapter. Finally, a CD-ROM accompanies each textbook with examples of original and public domain student presentations to illustrate various genre public performances with oral interpretation. The CD-ROM will also have downloadable evaluation sheets, such as the ones at the end of this book.

This oral interpretation text suggests that competitive forensics and noncompetitive festivals provide meaningful outlets for the performance of literature. Hopefully, this text serves as a bridge between performance studies scholars and coaches in the speech and debate activity. Both camps should be pleased at the attention and balance of theory, textual analysis, and practice. This text particularly reaches out to a neglected group of teachers and students: the community colleges. Community college instructors and students will find a mix of description and practical advice for performance in this text. Also, this text serves courses in speech education, preparing future teachers for elective courses in speech/drama/debate at the secondary education levels.

I would like to thank the following colleagues who gave specific and insightful comments for this fourth edition: Diane Conrad, Riverside City College—Moreno Valley Campus; Marcia Berry, Azusa Pacific University; Thomas Carmody, Vanguard University; Diana Crossman, El Camino College; Rozilyn Miller, University of Central Oklahoma; and Karla Bassett, Snow College. I wanted to express a special word of appreciation to my oldest son, Jonathan Price, who reconfigured the cover design as well as the graphic elements of the models and figures in this fourth edition. Thanks, Jon, your ideas make the graphics easier to understand. I would also like to indicate my appreciation to Janice Samuells, Associate Editor, and Billee Jo Hefel, Senior Developmental Editor, with Kendall/Hunt Publishers for their help and assistance in this project. Carrie Kulak of the M.I. Hummel Club was particularly helpful arranging for the photographic use of the two Hummel figures on the cover of this text. Finally, I would like to thank the hundreds of students I have had in classes and on the Biola University Forensics Team over the past thirty years for teaching me about literature and performance.

As you read on, you may wish to laugh or shudder or ponder. The text should provide you with a semester or quarter of marvelous performance experiences. Ultimately, this text seeks to open your eyes to the vast wealth of literary and communicative encounters that will shape you for years to come.

Todd V. Lewis

Permissions

Copyright © 1944 by Robert Frost. Reprinted by permission of Henry Holt and Company, Inc.

112-113   from Dean Koontz, *One Door Away From Heaven.* Copyright © 2001. Published by Bantam Books, New York.

129-130   Excerpt from "The City" by Ray Bradbury in *The Illustrated Man* by Ray Bradbury. © 1951 by Ray Bradbury. Renewed © 1979 by Ray Bradbury.

137-138   "The Peacelike Mongoose." Copyright © 1956 James Thurber. Copyright © 1984 Helen Thurber. Reprinted by special permission of Rosemary Thurber. from *Further Fables For Our Time,* published by Simon & Schuster, New York.

139   Excerpt from the Editorial Page, *Los Angeles Times* (June 6, 2003):B16.

140-141   Excerpt from John Irving, *A Prayer For Owen Meany.* Copyright © 1989. Published by Ballantine Books, New York.

141-142   "Two Monks" by Irmgard Schloegel/The Wisdom of Zen Masters. Excerpted from Jack Canfield and Mark Victor Hansen, *Chicken Soup for the Soul.* Copyright © 1993 by Jack Canfield and Mark Victor Hansen. Published by Health Communications, Inc., Deerfield Beach, FL.

143-145   From *Trinity* by Leon Uris. Copyright © 1976 by Leon Uris. Used by permission of Doubleday, a division of Bantam Doubleday Dell Publishing Group, Inc., 666 Fifth Avenue, New York, NY 10103.

146-147   Excerpt from "I Have a Dream" by Martin Luther King, Jr. Copyright © 1963 by Martin Luther King, Jr. Copyright renewed © 1991 by Coretta Scott King. Reprinted by arrangement with The Heirs to the Estate of Martin Luther King, Jr. c/o Writers House, Inc. as agent for the proprietor.

148-150   from Steve Andreas, "Napoleon and the Furrier," adapted by Jack Canfield and Mark Victor Hansen, *A 2nd Helping of Chicken Soup for the Soul.* Copyright © 1995 by Jack Canfield and Mark Victor Hansen. Published by Health Communications, Inc., Deerfield Beach, FL.

151-154   "Garbage Scan" from *Dave Barry Talks Back* by Dave Barry. Copyright © 1991 by Dave Barry. Reprinted by permission of Crown Publishers, Inc.

168-170   from *The Man In The Glass Booth* by Robert Shaw. Reprinted by permission of International Creative Management, Inc. © 1968 by Robert Shaw.

191-193   "For Grandma (& You)" by Charles Kerns. Reprinted by permission of Jane Kerns.

193-195   "Bit Part" by Charles Kerns. Reprinted by permission of Jane Kerns.

199-201   "I Dreamed A Dream" from the musical *"Les Misérables"* by Alain Boublil and Claude-Michel Schönberg. Music by Claude-Michel Schönberg. Lyrics by

_____ **CHAPTER 1**

Introduction to Oral Interpretation ———

Oral Interpretation as "Synergism"

Webster's dictionary defines the concept of *synergism* as the "interaction of discrete agencies such that the total effect is greater than the sum of the individual effects."[1] You would be more likely to discover this word in a science class, but its application in the arts generates new and exciting challenges as well. Such is the case for the course most frequently entitled ORAL INTERPRETATION OF LITERATURE. It is also possible that at your institution the course may be named INTRODUCTION TO PERFORMANCE STUDIES. Whatever its name a course in the performance of literature calls on you to amalgamate different "agencies" to create a unique artform.

Most college students sign up for the "O.I." course because it meets a general education public communication requirement or it is a curricular requirement for speech, drama, or English majors. Perhaps you signed up for the course because you were petrified at the thought of giving speeches or arguing a debate proposition. Regardless of your reasons, you are about to discover a course of study that is a synergism of the skills of literary appreciation and criticism, persuasive communication, and theatrical performance.

There are many useful and fascinating approaches for the student of performance. One can engage in "performance art" or "political performance" or "ethnographic performance" or even basic "storytelling." However, in this particular approach toward the performance of literature the emphasis will focus on "performance as argument." You will have an awesome responsibility to find literary texts and prepare these texts for oral presentation. You will seek to discover the inherent "message" of the particular text and perform it before an audience, sharing your own personal experience and insights by means of your voice and body. In a very real sense you as "performer" make a literary "text" a creative rendering of what you believe the text to be stating as a form of "message." A musical metaphor may help you understand your role. A composer writes down notes on a page, but a performer makes choices to render those notes accurately and precisely, but with an interpretive range of nuances to bring the musical composition to life and vitality. Even though the notes in a Beethoven sonata are played exactly the same by two pianists, the rendering of those performances can be very different, revealing levels and expressive choices to influence and entertain an audience.

When you sign into a course such as "American Literature," you expect to study and analyze the content and style of such noted authors as Walt Whitman, Mark Twain, Emily Dickinson,

John Steinbeck, and Willa Cather. When you sign up for a beginning speech class, you expect to learn how to research a topic and offer well-reasoned arguments to persuade audience members to become organ donors or to establish limits for genetic engineering research. When you decide to join a beginning acting course, you expect to learn how to portray characters singly and in groups before a watchful audience. As you will soon discover, by signing up for a course in the oral performance of literature these three "skills" synergize to create a unique and intriguing art form.

Definition

Oral interpretation of literature seeks to fuse three functions into a composite artform. First, *textual analysis* leads to the discovery of possible choices and clues for interpreting the purpose and intent of a literary agent's work. A close scrutiny and study of a text help one discover a tone, a mood, and a justification for performance variables. Second, *communicative intent* consists of the performer's choices galvanized into a rhetorical or persuasive message with the literature providing an analog to "evidence" in an argument. Performers "argue" by allowing literature to *speak* a message. The messages can be related to raising consciousness concerning an issue or personality or merely to entertain or give pleasure. Finally, *performance skills* are practiced and refined to become the channel for the oral/aural comprehension and understanding of literature. Thus, *oral interpretation of literature becomes the art of presenting literature so that textual analysis, communicative intent, and performance skills synergize to arouse a meaningful audience response.*

Experiences in Literature

Oral Interpretation is unlike any other course in literature appreciation. Your peers will introduce you to hundreds of literary selections. You will determine the choices of literature to study and consider. Although you and your professor hope that you will not have to "repeat" this course for academic "deficiencies," the reality is that if that were to occur the content of the course would dramatically change. Obviously, there are basic lecture notes and objective criteria to consider, but the "performance" aspects of the class would change because people would choose to perform different choices of literature. This class should never be "boring" for you or your instructor because you and your friends in the class actively determine the content. Hopefully, you will gain an understanding and appreciation of literature that supersedes a mere "silent" reading of a text. You make the decision to share an author's recorded work because it has initially made an impact on you. You must choose wisely, however, because the performer must also anticipate the specific audience that will come together to observe the presentation. The performer wants to assure that a "meaningful audience response" is due largely to sensitive preparation and audience adaptation. Certainly, the performer of literature wants to impress an audience with the literary choices, but we also desire to gain respect and admiration from our immediate audience.

Classification by Genres

Your in-class performances will consist of various literary genres. This text divides the genres of literature into three types: prose, drama, and poetry. (Sub-categories or specialized aspects of each genre will also be suggested.) *Prose* consists of: (1) narrative fictional literature, composed in story form, written in sentence/paragraph structure, and varying in verb tense (usually past or present); (2) nonfiction works of observation or hypotheses. Examples of prose work include: short stories, novels, letters, prayers, diaries, essays, newspaper editorials, some children's literature, speeches, biographies and autobiographies, and historical descriptions. *Drama* literature is narrowly defined as a play or script, written in prose or verse style, that has characters and expositional discussion revealed by action or dialogue. The original intent for most dramatic pieces is performance by actors before a microphone, on a stage or in front of a camera. Virtually all tense in drama is present-tense. Examples of drama include: one-act plays, full-length plays, musicals, skits, monologues, radio plays, television and film scripts, and role-play. *Poetry* is characterized by condensed language and phrasing, atypical imagery, syntax, and figures of speech. Conventional/traditional poetry has rhyming features, but free verse poetry does not, usually. Most poetry has a definite rhythm or discernible beat. Examples of poetry include: sonnets, limericks, odes, elegies, song lyrics, epic poems, some verse plays, some children's literature, prayers, "slam poetry," and free-standing, self-contained poems.

Authors who write "prose poems" or "dramatic novels" sometimes blur the categories above. Some authors defy categorization. The genre descriptions will help discern distinctions, but need not be prohibitively prescriptive.

Confronting Your Fear of Performance

No matter which genre of literature you choose to present, you will gain an understanding of the power of literature to change and alter your perceptions and values. No doubt you will have to read many more literary pieces than you could possibly present. You will find yourself attracted to some selections more than others. Why? Perhaps the primary "voice" in the selection makes statements you wish you had said. The "voice" may be funny or sensitive or angry or depressed. You may find yourself identifying with the circumstances or feelings embodied in the selection. Performing literature allows you to share known and unknown personal experiences. Performing literature can also aid you in overcoming a common fear that affects many people.

Are you petrified at the thought of standing before an audience of observers/critics? You are not alone; everyone has performance "jitters" or "butterflies in one's stomach." Speech anxiety, or "stage fright," is one of the most widely researched variables in the study of basic communication and performance practices. Studies on "phobias" (fears) continue to replicate the findings that the number one fear of the average human being is "public speaking or performance." Comedian Jerry Seinfeld humorously reminds us that death is the number two "phobia" on the list, thus reminding us that "to the average person, if you have to go to a funeral you're better off in the casket than giving the eulogy."[2] A certain amount of nervousness helps generate a creativity that brings out uninhibited behaviors or emotional outbursts in a character "voice" or narrative. A performer who loses the nervous anxiety at a performance loses the edge of understanding the literary "voice" and the tension of the piece. A performer that is too "cocky" or overconfident may present an inferior rendition of the selection. With each public performance you gain experience and confidence in your abilities to bring to life these "voices" from a silent page of literature. So what is the best way to respond to performance anxiety?

Prepare adequately ahead of time, channel the anxiety into your presentation, and be grateful you have some anxiety. Anticipation of possible negative outcomes in a performance is much more of a problem that the actual performance itself. Think rationally and ask yourself, "Why am I so afraid of doing this reading today?" If the answer is, "I believe I will lose my place in my script." That can be easily prevented through practice that mentally reminds you where to look on a portion of a reading script for your next line. What if your answer is, "I know my hands will shake, my voice might crack, and I will have involuntary leg twitches." That physical response is usually modified by repetitive experiences that lessen the negative anticipation of the unknown reaction. Although you may not state it exactly this way, some people have a fear of performance because "I know it won't be perfect." Get used to the fact that no performance is perfect; in fact, adapting to the unexpected and the unforeseen makes for a more credible presentation in most cases.

That sounds too easy. You're saying to yourself, "It doesn't matter how much time I prepare for this presentation because I know that I'm still going to get so nervous that I know I'll fail." You won't fail if you approach the performance with a sense of bringing the literature to life. You chose the piece because it had qualities that you found exciting or entertaining or interesting. If you merely chose a piece because time ran out and you had to choose something, you probably deserve to be a little bit nervous. You can alleviate much of the anticipated anxiety by beginning with a selection of literature that you truly appreciate. The next step is obvious: you must practice the selection by yourself and possibly before a willing (or possibly a "bribed") spectator. (Tell your roommate that you are owed this favor.) If you read out loud a short selection at least five to seven times, you will notice that you are becoming so familiar with the text that you can feel comfortable to look up out of the printed text. You can establish eye contact with the audience and be able to go back to the portion of the page where the text continues without an obvious lapse in timing or phrasing. You do not have to memorize word for word each line for an in-class performance, but the more familiar you are with the text (i.e. approaching memorization) the more comfortable you should be. And if you forget a word or short phrase you can always look down at the text. Like a practiced golf swing, your eyes learn to go back to the part of the page you left when you looked up and out at the audience. You will feel less anxious once you have a significant familiarity with the text.

But you say, "You don't understand. I get so nervous that I break out in hives or I stutter or I have involuntary muscle twitches or . . . (fill in the blank)." Some campus health facilities are capable of helping students with physical relaxation therapies or tension release mechanisms. Books and audio tapes/CDs are available with exercises to assist you in learning these relaxation techniques. One particular organization offers seminars, "camps," and biofeedback mechanisms to assist you if the "fear factor" is inhibiting any form of your self-expression.[3] Still, you might help yourself by choosing a literary selection with a character that speaks and sounds and acts just like you feel. If the thought of performance in public still induces spasms of fear, look for a literary selection where the primary "voice" is nervous, self-conscious, and anxious. As you read it aloud, let your natural feelings come out as a character. You know you can duplicate the sound of "nervousness" because that isn't going to be "acting" for you. You may be surprised to find that the audience was overwhelmed by your rendition of the character, so much so that you could hear comments such as, "You sure sounded believable," or "Wow! That nervous twitch and the beet red face were SO well done. How did you ever do it?" Inside you chuckle and say to yourself, "That's because *I* was so nervous." By transferring your own feelings to the literary "voice," you take the first step toward developing a sensitivity to performing any literary message.

It is quite impossible to gain poise, confidence, self-esteem, stronger vocal and nonverbal skills without public performances. And anxiety about a public performance can and should be your ally, not your undoing. Even though you practice and have a selection near-memorized, you will need to develop a sensitivity to the actual performance "moment" that allows you to adjust or alter your voice, speed up or slow down, pause longer, or pause less frequently. This is the "good" result of being anxious; performance anxiety can keep you on the "edge," and highly sensitive to how you need to perform a word or line or phrase so that the audience will understand it better. The cocky or overly-prepared performer can become static or stiff or even sound as "programmed" as a robot. People in audiences tend to "tune out" the performer who sounds too perfect or too calculating. Let a small amount of performance anxiety keep you alert and ready to perform at your best level. So what if you tell yourself, "No one will be able to understand me because of my accent." Frequently, an accent that is natural and distinct draws an audience to your performance because it is different and in many cases fascinating and captivating. Audiences listen more intently at times if the spoken word requires more attention.

Since this is a group performance-oriented art form, you will also gain critical and performance option skills from watching or listening to other performers. Believe it or not, performance anxiety can be reduced once you discover that everyone who is any good at performing suffers some level of nervousness. Maybe you are nervous because you are dreading the "oral comments" from the teacher and worse, your peers. Constructive criticism from a professor or a classmate should never be viewed as a personal attack. Criticism that suggests behavioral alterations or skill development can help you immensely. You should be able to notice clear improvement in your performance skills with each presentation. You also will incorporate performance skills from watching and listening to others that have abilities you have not yet mastered. Your own personal performance style will evolve from experimentation and observation of others inside and outside of class.

If all else fails, you can at least experience a good joke by going online to and note *www.fear.com* the hundreds of items, people, situations, and circumstances that cause people extreme fear and leave your comment for others at this humorous site. Remember: Learning to select literature for presentation, discovering relaxation therapies and self-help mechanisms, channeling performance anxiety, and maturing as a performer by involvement in group participation are significant means to assist you in achieving success in a course based on the oral interpretation of literature.

Interpretation and Acting

In the early to middle part of this century many of the academic instructors of oral interpretation attempted to argue for the distinction of oral interpretation as performance. They set up a chasm between oral interpretation and acting that would separate the art forms. Recent scholarship has wisely spanned the gulf and argued for a more inclusive view of performance studies. In this text oral interpretation and acting are viewed as similar performance arts but unique in cognitive emphasis.

In this chapter you will discover theoretical distinctions in the cognitive roles of acting and interpretation. But it is the perspective of this author that the preparation for the performance of literature is the same for actors and interpreters.

A favorite expression for some performance practitioners is that "one must *become* the character in a text." We have called this speaker in a text a "voice" or "character," but a more accurate term is *persona*. Every literary piece has a persona(e) that is imbued by an author with feelings, nuances, characteristics, and perspectives. The actor and interpreter must study the persona(e) in the literature and decide how to present their choices. A knowledge of your own feelings, a keen eye and ear for observing others, and the ability to make the presentational choices credible bring a persona to life. But do all performers literally *become* another persona? No. You do not have to *become* psychopathic to perform as the persona of the serial-killer, Charles Manson. Performers who seek to lose their own independent identity in a character run the risk of deep psychological trauma if they cannot leave the persona in a text or on a stage when the performance has ended. Are you expected to *become* a persona to perform literature? No, you are not.

But you are expected to *match* a persona with a text and perceived author's intent. What is the difference between *matching* and *becoming*? *Matching is a process of study, practice, and textual analysis wherein you amalgamate your experiences and associations with the choices available to you as you understand the persona.* This process should be different for every persona you present. In matching a persona, you find yourself analyzing and rehearsing vocal mannerisms, body language, tone, and attitude and fusing these qualities with your own personality. Matching is not necessarily impersonation, either. Suggesting a characteristic can make a persona as credible as an exact impersonation. However, if you have abilities as a mimic, you may choose to explore aspects of impersonation, attempting to emphasize such factors as speech patterns, motions and mannerisms, habits, and even physical stances. Where do you learn to pick out these persona elements? You observe people, you listen to the sound of accents and ethnic distinctiveness, and you attempt to duplicate the sounds fairly and without disdain. Useful "laboratories" for studying people and what they sound like include restaurants, airport terminals, school admissions lines, television shows, and movies. But how close are you expected to *match* before you *become*?

Consider the following selection:

> So for you people who are filled with the fear that I might someday be released: breathe easy, I don't see it happening. And for you people who are victims of all the hype that portrays me as a charismatic cult leader, guru, lover, pied piper or another Jesus, I want you to know I've got everything in the world, and beyond, right here. My eyes are

cameras. My mind is tuned to more television channels than exist in your world. And it suffers no censorship. Through it, I have a world and the universe as my own. So, save your sympathy and know that only a body is in prison. At my will, I walk your streets and am right out there among you.

As Nuel Emmons indicated in his interview book, Charles Manson is a complex man, a deeply troubled and psychologically distressed felon.[4] To prepare to perform the preceding excerpt, a performer need not *become* a mass murderer like Charles Manson, but the *matching process* would identify characteristics to be represented: paranoia, megalomania, depression, hardness, cynicism, non-rehabilitation, etc. Does Charles Manson have a discernible accent or vocal patterning? Can facial expressions or posture share an evil overtone? Reading the excerpt in its context and Emmons' editorial comments about the Manson interviews will help give the performer the creative elements, which, added with one's personal choices will find the match between the performer and the persona of Charles Manson.

The actor seeks to match the choices so closely that with make-up, costuming, and theatrical stage area the viewing audience suspends belief and actually sees Charles Manson before them. The interpreter seeks to match the choices so closely that with an economy of overt theatrical accouterments the viewing audience *imagines* that the performer is Charles Manson. The differences between acting and interpretation are thus degrees of *actualization* versus economical pointers to one's *imagination*.

The actor physically *acts* (i.e., sits, stands, fights, runs, etc.); the interpreter can *suggest* movements by mime or slight literalization. The actor asks an audience primarily to *observe* the performance; the interpreter asks an audience primarily to *recreate* the text in the theater of their own minds.

Gratefully, we have moved from the stultifying view that oral interpretation is only from the neck up. The performer of literature offers a complete vocal and physical suggestion of a literary text. Both the actor and the interpreter need to analyze a text. Both performers prepare to present persona(e) with accuracy and credibility. Both performers seek the same audience reactions: to please, to entertain, to provoke, to communicate. Hugh Morrison provides wise advice for both the actor and the interpreter when he says that

> The actor suffers and enjoys his character's experiences, and to do so believably must understand his own and other people's emotions, having no inhibitions about expressing the deepest and most private feelings. He or she must also possess the ability to relate people sympathetically.[5]

Arbitrary comments that "This is acting" and "That is interpretation" are based on outmoded proscriptive rules that only serve to hamper the creativity, performance, and maturity of the performance study discipline. It is not exclusively acting if you see a tear fall from a performer's face, but the oral interpreter need not cry in order for the audience member to "feel" the emotionality of a selection. Ideally, the performer of literature wants to facilitate the audience member who desires to cry or laugh or get angry or respond in any number of emotional ways.

Presenting Your First Reading

One of the recommended first activities for this course as listed at the back of this chapter is a preliminary reading of about two or three minutes. Your instructor will allow you to choose a short poem or brief essay to "read" to the class, but without receiving a grade. The "lack of a grade" should relieve some of your anxiety initially, but it should not give you a license to treat this performance lightly.

As part of your preparation for any reading, you will need to attempt to understand what the purpose or intent of the literary selection is. Some authors do not tell you their intent, nor do they wish to have others tell you what it specifically means. In a post-modern world, one might be led to think that all literature can mean anything to anyone and any "interpretation of text" is equally valid. While literature can be multi-layered with meaning, a text has "good" and "better" choices as to intent and meaning. Certainly all interpretations of any text can find someone who can justify an approach toward meaning. But as is true with so much of our existence, we have "choices." Choices for meaning or intent are on a scale of "acceptable" to "better or best." It would be incorrect for anyone to say that a text "cannot mean this or that." It is permissible to analyze a text for meaning and intent and decide that some meanings are "better." This value judgment does not negate anyone's creativity, but it can enhance the probative analytical quest that any performer must make. "Choices" are the vanguard of any actor worth his/her "salt" and it is what separates the "good" performers from the "best" performers.

Deciding what a "text" means will be discussed with greater detail in later chapters. For the present, you should read and re-read a chosen text, attempting to discover what the author is trying to communicate. You should be able to encapsulate this thought in a complete sentence that will become your *performance thesis.* You will present this thesis as part of preliminary remarks that will set the scene for your performance. These preliminary remarks are what constitute your *introduction.*

INTRODUCTIONS/TEASERS/TRANSITIONS

Introductions prepare an audience for what they are about to witness. They should be delivered in a conversational, extemporized fashion. You may be tempted to write out your introduction and paste it on the front of your reading notebook, but you should avoid this. Deliver the introduction in a conversational, off-the-cuff, natural manner. If you have a manuscript present, offer the introduction with manuscript closed. Why? The open manuscript or text symbolizes and points to the text as the source of the spoken word. When you are uttering your own words, a closed manuscript suggests that the words are those of the performer.

You should include specific informational aspects in every introduction. Performers vary the order of the information to show creativity. Remember to include:

1. Author's name.
2. The title of the text selection.
3. Sentences where a *theme* or *thesis* is stated (Avoid cliches such as: "I want to read for you today . . . ." or "I will now present . . . .").

4. A demeanor (e.g., happy, somber, energetic) which will set the tone for the selection.
5. Direct audience eye contact.
6. Background information about personae, scene, context, time frame, or author.
7. Conversationality (You are yourself, not a persona; do not over-act).
8. Statements which will tell an audience how to listen to the piece (what to expect).
9. Vocabulary clearly understandable to your audience.
10. A concluding statement or pause that clearly indicates the end of the introduction and the beginning of textual performance.

Introductions can also be presented once you have caught the attention of the audience members with a brief (thirty seconds to a minute) reading of the actual text. Serving as a *transition* from the "capture your attention" motif, this approach makes use of what is called a *teaser*. It attempts to "tease" an audience with a brief segment, followed by the original introduction that now serves as an extended type of transition.

Transitions are also originally-composed statements and occur most frequently in multiple-selection presentations or to explain passage of time and events in a single work. Closing the manuscript text for a transition signifies that the following words are original and not part of the text. Transitions need to link one segment with another by means of chronology (what happened and what is to come) or theme (i.e., the texts share a common or contrasting viewpoint). Too many transitions can break up the atmosphere created or the mood of a piece, so you will want to use them sparingly if at all.

Introductions, transitions, and teasers help the reader to translate the communication message by: (1) preparing the audience to appreciate the text selection; (2) focusing the theme and message for the performer; (3) allowing the audience to get to know the performer; and (4) clarifying the communicative message as unfolding in the text.

For your first reading in class, your instructor will inform you if you can read from the actual text or require you to read from a three-ring binder notebook with the text reproduced within it. Generally, it is easier for you as a performer to have a notebook that has a hard cover that can lie out flat in your hands. It is wise to re-type a text with a font size that is easy for you to read and double-spaced to help prevent "losing your place." Many readers prefer to purchase 5" X 7" binder notebooks because they cradle easier in your hands. Do whatever works best for you and will enhance your performance of the literary text.

Once you have completed your first class reading, you will be amazed at how much less anxiety and stress you experience. You are now ready to enjoy a fun-filled and certainly educational experience as you enter the exciting world of literature. As you will discover in chapter two, the oral performance of literature has a rich historical tradition. Courses in colleges and universities continue to attract students. Oral interpretation categories abound in high school and collegiate forensics contests. Religious groups offer performances of literature as liturgy or substitutes for homilies or sermons. The oral traditions from non-English speaking and non-Western sources infuse oral performances with vitality and consciousness-raising. Oral Interpretation is a creative and evolving art form that provides ever-expanding opportunities to comprehend the universe of ideas, stories, and personal narratives.

Assignments

1. Discuss the following poem in class:

Do Not Go Gentle Into That Good Night
Dylan Thomas

Do not go gentle into that good night,
    Old age should burn and rave at close of day;
Rage, rage against the dying of the light.
Though wise men at their end know dark is right,
    Because their words had forked no lightning they
Do not go gentle into that good night.
Good men, the last wave by, crying how bright
    Their frail deeds might have danced in a green bay,
Rage, rage against the dying of the light.
Wild men who caught and sang the sun in flight,
    And learn, too late, they grieved it on its way,
Do not go gentle into that good night.
Grave men, near death, who see with blinding sight
    Blind eyes could blaze like meteors and be gay,
Rage, rage against the dying of the light.
And you, my father, there on the sad height,
    Curse, bless, me now with your fierce tears, I pray.
Do not go gentle into that good night.
    Rage, rage against the dying of the light.

Which of the following "introductions" represents the better choice of focus for communicative intent of the text? Why?:

(Sample One) "When I was growing up, I enjoyed visiting my mom's mother—my grandmother. She was always enthusiastic about life, fun to be with, energetic. But after a freak falling accident in the bathroom and a trip to the hospital that revealed a growing cancer, not just cuts and bruises, it became apparent overnight that she was dying. I loved my grandmother. I didn't want her to die. I wanted her to fight death. I wanted to say to her,— 'Do Not Go Gentle Into That Good Night' by Dylan Thomas. . . ."

(Sample Two) "How can you love and hate someone at the same time? If you are a victim of child abuse and neglect, you know the answer to that question: you just do.

Dylan Thomas was a brilliant Welsh poet, but he died of acute alcoholism—a form of self-abuse that had destroyed his father some years before. As he watched his father deteriorate, mixed emotions seemed at cross purposes. He remembered the personal abuse, but he also remembered the love. It was as if he said, 'I love you! I hate you!' in the same breath. Hear Dylan Thomas wrestle with these feelings as he addresses his father in— 'Do Not Go Gentle Into That Good Night' . . . ."

2.   You are now ready for your first in-class reading. To counteract some of your initial nervousness, this reading will not be graded, but you will receive constructive criticism from the professor and perhaps your classmates.

Choose a poem or brief prose selection, approximately three to five minutes in length. Compose an original introduction. Deliver it with your manuscript closed. Open the manuscript to present your text.

What did you feel after your own performance? Did any other classmates choose a text that you particularly liked? Why? Can you adopt and adapt any specific performance skills from observing others in class? What will you do differently in the initial graded assignment?

References

Adler, Ronald B. and Rodman, George. *Understanding Human Communication—8th Ed.* New York: Oxford University Press, 2003.

Gottlieb, Marvin R. *Oral Interpretation.* New York: McGraw-Hill Book Co., 1980.

Lee, Charlotte and Gura, Timothy. *Oral Interpretation—10th Ed.* Boston: Houghton Mifflin Company, 2001.

Sprague, Jo and Stuart, Douglas. *The Speaker's Handbook—6th Ed.* Belmont, CA: Wadsworth/Thomson Learning Inc., 2003.

Notes

1. *Webster's Ninth New Collegiate Dictionary,* (1988), s.v. "Synergism."
2. As cited by Ronald B. Adler and George Rodman in *Understanding Human Communication—8th Ed.* (New York: Oxford Unviersity Press, 2003), 382.
3. The Speech Improvement Company, Inc., 1614 Beacon Street, Boston (Brookline), MA 02446 can be reached by mail or by phone at: (617) 739-3330 or by fax at (617) 232-9430 or e-mail at <www.fearofspeaking.com>. One day "camp" seminars are available. An audiotape version of the book, *No Fear Speaking* by Dr. Dennis Becker, comes in a six tape soft-pack pouch and can be ordered from the company. The Speech Improvement Company, Inc. has forty years of training experience and specializes in public speaking, speech coaching, fear of speaking modification, corporate communications, customer service, accent reduction, and telephone skills.
4. *Manson In His Own Words,* told to Nuel Emmons (New York: Grove Press, 1986), 227.
5. Hugh Morrison, *Acting Skills* (New York: Theatre Arts Books, Routledge, 1992), 6.

CHAPTER 2

A History of Oral Interpretation

This introduction to the study of oral interpretation is also best understood when placed in a historical context. The oral interpretation of literature has a rich heritage that can be seen in major epochs.

It would be most presumptive to call the following paragraphs "*The* History of Oral Interpretation." Instead, "*A* History Of Oral Interpretation" seeks to highlight a chain of events and performers from ancient Greece and the oral traditions of the Judeo-Christian era, through the Roman period, the Middle Ages, the Renaissance, to the English traditions in Great Britain and Ireland, extending to America, and twentieth-century performance examples.

Greece

A history of oral interpretation of literature naturally begins in an ancient culture where literature was perceived as a thing to be heard or said, rather than read. Books were rare and tedious to compose. But the spoken word—the literature of oral tradition and tales—was a living vital incarnation of human thought and expression.

This high view of spoken literature is in direct contrast to our own era. Ancient Greeks preferred "verbal agreements" to "black and white" signed agreements. While a written agreement might be ignored or dissolved, a verbal agreement between parties seemed bound by the perceived power of *speaking* the agreement.

While most literature today is intended for silent reading, the ancient Greeks felt literature, particularly poetry and drama, required oral delivery. As far back as the eighth century BC, itinerant performers called *minstrels* were invited to "sing" their original poetry in royal courts as well as rural villages. Originally, all Greek verse was accompanied by music. The actual presentation would probably resemble the "talk song" format of many contemporary musical comedy stars.[1] The instrument used to serve as chorded introduction was a harp-like *lyre* or *cithara*. By the time of Plato, the instrumental link to recitation had dissipated, however.

A particular performer emerged in the Ionian district. Historians disagree whether Homer was a single person or pseudonymous authors of collected tales of mythology. The performers who told stories of gods, goddesses, and harrowing tales of adventure were called *rhapsodes*. Roughly translated as "song-stitcher," the rhapsodes took individualized verses or episodes and made them into connected stories. Unlike the minstrels, the rhapsodes of the Platonic era frequently recited the works of other known poets. The rhapsodes were also the first performers to link the performance of literature to public contests, with winners receiving victory wreaths or other awards. In many of these contests the competitors had to recite from only the *Iliad* and the *Odyssey.* Characterized by their rather flamboyant theatrical gesturing and broad vocal inflections, the rhapsodes endured as performers until the time of Christ.

Other performers saw oral interpretation as a means to further their business ventures. Booksellers at market places such as the Acropolis would stand on elevated platforms near their stalls and recite passages from books, drawing crowds and customers to purchase their products.

Ancient Israel

As the Greek culture emerged and developed, an independent progression of oral recitation tradition materialized, but in the religious context of the ancient Hebrews. Archaeological discoveries in the Mesopotamian area show descriptions of group chants, praises, and prayers that evolved into established patterns for worship services. *Antiphony,* a recitative device wherein groups of people would respond as choral echo or question/response, is described in biblical references to the Israelite judges Deborah and Barak (Judges Chapter 5) and kings Saul and David (I Samuel 18:7).

In the sixth century BC, the nation of Israel was captured and the Babylonian Empire took the entire nation as prisoners and slaves. Though the exile was relatively brief (70 years), the captivity forced a change in liturgical format in a setting that was devoid of most major shrines and altars. The synagogue replaced the larger, more ornate Temple in Jerusalem as the center of corporate worship. In the synagogues a specially designated performer *(Precentor)* led the recitation of scripture and liturgy. To be asked to serve as the Precentor was deemed an honor, second only to the reverence accorded to the rabbi. Various references in the Four Gospels imply that Jesus not only led synagogue recitations, but also amplified the recitations with original teachings.

After the Romans destroyed the rebuilt Jerusalem temple in 70 AD, the synagogue liturgy became a more ritualized service. The format has not deviated much from those early days to the present. A solo reader/reciter intoned "Barechu et adonai ha-mevorach" ("Bless ye the Lord, the One who is blessed"). This was followed by a group recitation called *Shema* (from Deuteronomy 6:4, "Hear, O Israel, the Lord Our God is One Lord"). Sometimes this recitation occurred antiphonally, as reader and congregation answered one another. Other recitative features included the *Kaddish,* the *Tefillah,* an *Amen* response, and a rabbinical homily, followed by a chanted choral benediction.

The uses of solo reader/reciter and choral respondents serve as a legacy for not only Jewish religious worship, but group dramatic recitation in secular settings as well.

Rome

As with so much of the Greek culture, Rome absorbed and further promoted the Greek custom of recitation. The Romans understood that soldiers required entertainment as a respite from battle. The poet Ennius accompanied Scipio on various military excursions. In performances that foreshadowed Bob Hope's USO tours, Ennius enlivened the drudgeries of war with his verses.

Recitations of poetry constituted a primary means of entertainment in private homes and in small groups. Many of the major literary figures of the Augustan Age (including Virgil, Pliny, Horace, and Ovid) performed their own works for royalty and commoner alike.

The ancients believed that the spoken word could also serve therapeutic values. A Roman physician Celsus prescribed reading as a cure for such ailments as stomach disorders, indigestion, and whooping cough. The mentally ill were treated by memorizing poetry or storytelling. Contemporary health officials still use oral reading as a form of treatment or care in many nursing homes and hospitals today.

The Romans believed that reading aloud was essential in the education of citizens. Rhetorical theorists such as Cicero and Quintilian emphasized that the experience of comprehending an author's intent and attitude must precede an effective oral presentation of literature. Their insights continue to focus contemporary scholarship and teaching on the importance of analyzing a text.

Early Christian Era

The initial followers and disciples of Jesus Christ were Jewish. After the death of Christ, the message, form, and worship practices of these early Christians changed from synagogue recitation formats as Jews and Gentiles created a new institution—the Church.

Reflecting their Jewish heritage, early Christian worship practices demonstrate the close connection between the Church and synagogue. Christians moved the worship day to Sunday to honor the day of the week when Christ arose from the dead. To prevent interruption and possible persecution, Christians met in private homes, probably at night. A remarkable fragment of antiquity, a letter written about 112 AD from Pliny the Younger, Roman governor of Bithynia, to Emperor Trajan, reveals certain group recitation practices in these home services: "They [the Christians] were in the habit of meeting on a certain fixed day . . . and reciting an antiphonal hymn to Christ as God . . ."[2]

The apostle Paul penned multiple letters to members of these early home-churches. A reader first presented the teachings of these letters, perhaps the homeowner or an elder in the congregation. Though copies were eventually made and canonized as part of the New Testament, the initial presentation was featured as an oral interpretation of literature. As worship services evolved into a patterned liturgy, the oral readings of the writings of the apostles and prophets became known as *lections*.

Following the edict of Theodosius in 380 AD proclaiming Christianity as the state religion of the Roman Empire, the Church grew too large to continue meeting in homes or in the Roman catacombs. Immense cathedrals called *basilicas* were built to house the crowds. Due to the difficulty in sound comprehension by a solo reader, group lections or recitations were introduced. By the fifth century a standardized liturgy had evolved and was called *The Catholic Missa* or *Mass*. Varying little from its early roots, the Mass includes such solo and group recitation elements as the *Introit,* the *Kyrie Eleison* ("Lord, have mercy"), *Gloria in Excelsis* ("Glory to God in the highest"), *Deo Gratias* ("Thanks be to God"), *Alleluia,* the *Canon,* the *Eucharist* (Communion), and *Benediction.*

Though ritualized in a specific format, the legacy of oral reading and recitation within all Christian churches continues to this day. Some liturgical churches today use the lections as a significant portion of the actual religious service, while others merely have a brief reading or congregational response. It is significant that this heritage reminds us that the oral interpretation of literature by one or many performers should be audience-centered as well as idea-centered.

Middle Ages

As monastic orders appeared to become the guardians of the educational and literary heritage, the primary figures expressing opinions about the values of oral reading were Church saints. Jerome and Augustine advocated oral reading to improve diction, knowledge of literature, and especially a comprehension of texts from the Bible.

Benedict of Nursia formed a guild of monks dedicated to preserving the Christian faith and particularly the practice of reading aloud. Even while cloistered, the Benedictine monks practiced reading aloud privately.

When Christianity was introduced to Britain and Ireland, the early missionaries encountered a secular tradition of oral recitation, based on the Celtic heritage. The *scop* was a reciter of poetry, usually attached to a kingdom as a court entertainer. The *gleeman* was more likely to be an itinerant chanter of other people's works. In Ireland, the *fili* (feel-ee), like their English counterparts, were poets who memorized the sagas and myths of the Celts. They were highly respected, learned, and articulate historians as well. Many of the major myths such as *Beowulf* and the tales of *Cuchulain* may well have been originally composed by these performers.

In 1066 with the Norman Invasion of England, the Celtic heritage joined with the culture of southern Europe. The Normans encouraged the growth and development of *minstrels* or *trouveres,* which formed schools and guilds to pass on their talents of recitation. Some wandered the countryside, plying their trade; others became permanent members of a royal court. By the twelfth and thirteenth centuries, these minstrels regaled audiences with their tales of Gawain, Tristan, Lancelot, Charlemagne, and Roland. Some barely eked out a basic existence, while others became "well-to-do gentlemen" supported by wealthy patrons. A few texts survive today indicating performance notations by these minstrels, but unfortunately none of the texts indicate any musical notation for the combination of declamation and song. Many "court jesters" (*gestours*) combined bawdy and humorous entertainment for a nobleman with serious performances of narrative stories and song.[3]

While the art of oral interpretation was flourishing in Anglo-Saxon England, a German figure who stands as a herald for modern Readers Theatre practices was writing original plays to be read aloud, not acted out. Hroswitha was a nun who came to live in a southern German convent in the tenth century. Six of her plays are extant. All were composed in Latin, following a secular format of Roman plays, but religious in character and theme. Strangely, Hroswitha called her plays "comedies," but they seemed quite gruesome. A Christian saint would be tortured for his or her faith, die, but proceed into Heaven at the conclusion of the play. Much evidence suggests that these plays were cast for readers, not actors, and read before guests and clergy at the Gandersheim convent.[4] Hroswitha's plays compelled her audience to use their imaginations and in so doing left a historical legacy that we now call "Readers Theatre."

The masterpiece of English medieval literature is no doubt *The Canterbury Tales* by Geoffrey Chaucer. The characters in this fourteenth-century-pilgrimage adventure tell stories, and the tales have an innate quality of being recited and orally composed.

The Renaissance and Elocutionary Periods

The work of the medieval monks in saving and copying ancient secular and religious texts did not go unnoticed or unappreciated. By the end of the fourteenth century, a "renaissance" of interest in classical literature and classical expressions of art occurred among wealthy and aristocratic patrons.

Beginning in Italy and eventually making its way to England, this renewed classical interest provided oral interpretation opportunities in schools and colleges. Educational curriculum centered on memorizing and reciting a vast number of poetic pieces.

The Protestant Reformation and the invention of the printing press made the Bible as well as other books more readily available. Some Renaissance scholars amplified the treatises of Quintilian and others by emphasizing the physical aspects of delivery and use of gestures. John Bulwer's *Chirologia* (1644) anticipated the fervent interest in stylistic delivery extensively taught in the eighteenth and nineteenth century. Bulwer's work affected oral performance because of its emphasis on the communicative power of nonverbal elements, particularly hand gestures.

Scholars assigned the task of translating the Bible into the ever-popular King James Version stopped at intervals, reading aloud their translations. Subsequent criticism led to rewrites and an overall unity of text that was enabled by the oral reading exercise.

The reawakened interest in classical literature and education established a foundation for theorists and practitioners who would make the eighteenth and nineteenth centuries an epoch of mechanical delivery patterns. Treatises began to stray from the study of texts to the study of *elocutio,* a portion of the ancient rhetorical canon that emphasized style and verbal/nonverbal delivery. *The Elocutionary Movement* began with an emphasis on proper speaking and reading skills, but eventually degenerated into a prescriptive and stilted artificial performance mode.

The clergy were criticized for their boring and lulling attempts to read scripture and sermons. Essays in the popular press asked ministers to find effective role models and emulate, even imitate, their speaking habits. Others claimed that effective reading skills would occur if only the performer would give in to his emotions and be "natural." The mechanical expression school emerged in the eighteenth century, calling for rules, uniformity, imitation, and duplication.

If music notation could allow duplication of a Mozart piano concerto, then why could not a "vocal" notation allow duplication of the speaking style of famous English actors? Joshua Steele taught his students by superimposing a symbolic graph above literary lines so that readers would orate as David Garrick, the famous actor.

Prescriptive rules began to dominate the teaching of expression: punctuation marks were to be held for specific beats; different emotions could only be shared by position and action of body parts; gestures should be practiced in front of mirrors; and gestures should be modified and reduced when reading. Famous teachers and practitioners of the eighteenth-century Elocutionary Movement included Thomas Sheridan, John Walker, and James Burgh.

As the Elocutionary Movement spread to the fledgling United States, the curriculum began to emphasize the excesses of the movement. Gilbert Austin, an Englishman, published *Chironomia* (1806) and immediately became a popular proponent of degrees of gesture. Levels of anguish required a performer to alter gestures accordingly. James Rush attempted to balance the mechanical and natural approaches to elocution in his significant treatise, *The Philosophy of the Human Voice* (1827). Many of the skills Rush discussed are still an important part of the teaching of performance today: pause, force, pitch, vocal quality, and rate.

A Frenchman named Francois Delsarte supplanted Rush's influence in America. Though he never visited America, Delsarte and his disciples spread the "gospel" of the Delsarte System of Oratory, a combination of religious mysticism, body part division, emotions, and aesthetic gesture practice. He claimed that the practice of exercising and gesturing would develop poise, grace, attractiveness, and good physical health. It is humorous to relate that the study of oral interpretation and the modern physical education movement (with calisthenics) owe much to Delsarte. The next time you watch the movie or see the musical play, *The Music Man,* notice the Grecian urn dance sequence with the town women. They refer to this "cultural" activity as a "Delsarte." Delsarte's histrionic gestures made their final appearances in the silent films of the early twentieth century.

It would be unfair to characterize the Elocutionary Movement as merely excessive and too mechanical to study. To an extent every beginning oral interpreter must be taught with some elocutionary remnants to establish a personal style and sensitivity to performance factors. But excesses only lead to poor performances and minimal credibility.

The Storyteller

The Irish have long been known as a people who revel in the oral tradition of stories about ghosts, and fairies, pookas, and leprechauns.[5] The legacy of the Irish fili continued into the eighteenth and nineteenth centuries with the *seanchai* (shann-uh-kee). The seanchai was normally a member of a particular family in a village who was given the task of remembering and retelling stories, myths, legends, and local and national history. He was generally supported financially by the community and was revered as a community leader. One of the most famous of the seanchais was James Berry (1842-1914). Berry was a farm laborer in the Connemara region of Ireland. He collected folktales and invented stories, originally publishing them in *The Mayo News.* Berry was a typical performer of the time, making his rounds to pubs and different houses. Although Berry wrote and published many of his stories, other seanchais passed the stories on to a chosen son for oral tradition links to the past generations. The seanchais were known as vivid and emotional performers and their tradition unfortunately died out in the early years of the twentieth century as various mass media replaced the need for a community storyteller.[6]

Lecture Circuits

In the mid to late nineteenth century, an educational movement materialized paralleling the Elocutionary Movement but emphasizing the cultural legacy of authors, texts, and performances. Beginning first with the *Lyceum,* founded in 1826, and the *Chautauqua,* begun in 1874, Americans in small, mid-size, and urban cities came out to local churches or auditoriums to see famous authors lecture or perform readings of their works. The Chautauqua concept led to independent circuits that paved the way for "mass-mediated entertainment forms, especially in (the) creation and emphasis of celebrity."[7] Such American authors as Ralph Waldo Emerson, Harriet Beecher Stowe, and Mark Twain regaled local audiences with abbreviated versions of their larger works. Twain, in particular, studied audiences' reactions and adapted his performance skills accordingly while he read from his published works or lectured about important social issues.[8] Englishman Charles Mathews (1776-1835) was the most famous comedian of his day, but his reputation as a performer was based primarily on one-man shows known as "At Homes." These presentations consisted "of a mixture of narrative, impersonation, and song."[9] Mathews was undoubtedly the single most important influence on the public performance career of the noted author Charles Dickens. Dickens apparently attended many of Mathews' London performances during his youth and never forgot the exciting format of directly addressing a theatrical audience. During his lifetime Dickens gave 472 public readings, 75 of which were in America from 1867 to 1868. Dickens traveled the American lecture circuit, with manuscripts adapted for public reading, and was extremely popular:

Figure 2.1 Mr. Charles Dickens' last reading*

> Facing his public, he stood on the stage with a plain dark curtain behind him and with only an open desk and a book as props, thus creating a setting which allowed nothing to distract the attention of his audience from the delivery of his spoken words.[10]

*Reproduced by courtesy of The Dickens House, 48 Doughty Street, London WC1N2LF England

Dickens, himself a frustrated actor,

> knew that he was good at reading, and was not so self-denying as to abstain from parading his skills in public. Moreover he was justly proud of what he had written, and loved giving an oral interpretation of his own work which could enhance its meaning, for his audiences.[11]

In the nineteenth century oral interpretation of literature served to entertain, lead in religious worship, and educate in aesthetics and culture. But in the twentieth century, new technological discoveries would return oral interpretation to a concentration on the personality and intent of the author's text as well as psychological nuances in performing a text.

The Twentieth Century and Beyond

The Lyceum and Chautauqua circuits encouraged the establishment of schools to further one's education. Many schools of speech, begun in the nineteenth century, joined nearby colleges and universities in the twentieth century. These schools eventually evolved into our modern collegiate departments of speech, communication, and theater.

Advances in psychology and the social sciences affected the teaching of oral interpretation. Instructors asked performers to study, analyze, and brood over the inner motivations of personae and authors. Overt elocution waned and textual analysis took its place.

Oral interpretation became a sister discipline to public speaking and emerged in separate course offerings in colleges and universities. In 1914, a new professional academic organization formed as the National Association of Academic Teachers of Public Speaking, known today as the NCA, the National Communication Association. The NCA continues to support oral performance as a major field of study and presentational outlet to this day. Each November the NCA National Convention hosts numerous programs and academic papers that reveal the contemporary directions for oral performance of any text.

New channels for oral expression evolved with each technological advance. Radio provided avenues for performers to bring to life dramatic and comedic stories. Still today, certain radio stations throughout the United States periodically replay old recordings of radio broadcasts, reminding us of this oral reading outlet. Even though radio has moved toward specialized formats today, the oral interpretation of drama continues in such syndicated examples as The CBS Radio Mystery series, Garrison Keillor's "A Prairie Home Companion," and the *Star Wars* adapted scripts for National Public Radio. Television still offers programs where dramatic reading is emphasized, primarily on Public Broadcast System stations. The highly acclaimed motion picture *Dead Poets' Society* proclaims the aesthetic joys and intellectual pleasures found in the oral interpretation of poetry. The underlying premise of the offbeat and funny motion picture, *The Princess Bride,* is that the events that are portrayed are brought to life by a kindly grandfather, played by Peter Falk, who reads a story aloud to a skeptical, but nevertheless enthralled ten year old, played by Fred Savage.

One-person shows continue to be popular as well-known actors recreate the Lyceum and Chautauqua circuit programs. In the late 1970s James Whitmore established a "tour de force" in his one-man show about the life and times of former President Harry S. Truman ("Give 'Em Hell, Harry!"). Noteworthy performers of solo performances also include Hal Holbrook as Mark Twain, Emlyn Williams as Charles Dickens, and Julie Harris as Emily Dickinson.[12] Beginning in the late 1990s, Patrick Stewart has performed an annual rendition of Dickens' *A Christmas Carol* in which he portrays more than thirty distinct characters and voices with minimal staging and sensational performance.

Although its format has antecedents that can be traced back to the Greeks and medieval mystery plays, the term "readers theatre" was probably first used in 1945 to describe a New York production of *Oedipus Rex* that apparently relied on stationary performers reading from behind lecterns.[13] Readers Theatre (RT) developed in the early 1950s as a multiple performer theatrical alternative to proscenium staging. In 1951, a production of George Bernard Shaw's *Don Juan in Hell* was offered as a group reading on the Broadway stage. RT emphasized the traditional "Theatre of the Mind" presentational format, asking readers and audience members to imagine scenes and confrontations. Stephen Vincent Benet's epic poem, *John Brown's Body,* proved that nondramatic literature could be transformed into a "group reading" format and be viable on Broadway. Its initial run on Broadway, beginning in 1953, was revived on Broadway during the 1968-69 and 1971-72 seasons.[14] HopKins and Bouldin remind us also that "productions of nondramatic literature no longer stand out as oddments in the theatrical scene. As 'traditional' plays become increasingly flexible in their treatment of time and place, as scenery and set properties become increasingly minimal, as a kind of visual realism recedes, plays increasingly resemble, at least in presentational form, the productions of scripts adapted from fiction, poetry, and non-fictional literature."[15] In the last forty years, Readers Theatre techniques and uses of readers or characters who play multiple roles and directly address the audience have been observed in such diverse Broadway productions as *You're A Good Man, Charlie Brown* (1999), *Godspell,* and *Evita.* The Royal Shakespeare Company's version of *Nicholas* Nickleby (1980), adapted from the original Dickens' novel by David Edgar, employed 39 performers, who played approximately 123 speaking parts in 95 scenes. The subsequent Broadway production in 1981 required two tickets per person for subsequent portions of the eight-hour play version.[16] A recent touring production of A.R. Gurney's two-person play, *Love Letters,* has been called a "staged reading" with numerous actors and actresses performing from notebooks with minimal staging and Readers Theatre trappings. Frank Galati's readers theatre-like adaptation of John Steinbeck's novel, *The Grapes of Wrath,* won a Tony Award for its director/adapter in 1990. During the 1993 theatrical season in London, a stage adaptation of Graham Greene's 1969 novel, *Travels With My Aunt* won Olivier Awards (England's equivalent to the Tony Award) for "Best Entertainment" and "Comedy Performance." The staging and adaptation were essentially Readers Theatre/Chamber Theatre with four male performers, identically dressed, performing multiple character roles, both male and female personae (and even a dog), while using direct audience eye contact as well as onstage attention. The Royal Shakespeare Company recently developed a "readers theatre-like" staging of Homer's epic poem, *The Odyssey,* and compelled the audience to imagine the epic dreams from a bare stage with minimal props.[17] The distinction for the longest-running production in the history of Readers Theatre must go to the Stephen Mallatratt adaptation of *The Woman In Black,* a two act compilation of spine-tingling ghost stories, still running as of this publication in the London theater district after 15 years.[18]

In 1975 a group of professional actors, writers, educators and singers created the first professional Readers Theatre ensemble called *The Open Book.* This group combines traditional acting with methods drawn from traditional oral interpretation and Readers Theatre, plus "antiphonal devices such as the controlled dynamics and multiple rhythms generally associated with chamber or choral music. Each year this group fosters a national readers theatre playwriting contest and publishes as well as performs the winning selections."[19]

Current trends have opened up the traditions of oral interpretation and have led to new nomenclature. *Performance Studies* is the operative term that now describes a wide range of activities. People purchase "oral" renditions of popular novels in cassette or CD formats to have someone else "read" to them in the privacy of their own automobiles or living rooms. The "audiobooks" industry now takes in $2 billion annually, with one in five American households having listened to an audiobook in the previous year.[20] Ethnographic selections of literature reveal the world-views and rich experiences of cultures and sub-cultures. Minority and activist political writers offer opportunities to perform feminist, gay/lesbian, and counter-to-the-mainstream cultural messages. As Judy Yordan states, "The definitions of both 'text' and 'performance' have expanded to include non-literary materials and everyday life events."[21]

Arthur Lerner, a clinical psychologist and poet, helped organize the National Association for Poetry Therapy in the 1960s. Lerner re-discovered what the ancient Greeks and Romans had practiced regularly, the use of writing and reciting poetry as a means to achieve better mental health. Lerner often asked patients to write as well as read aloud or listen to poems. Despite his death in 1998, Lerner's work continues as poetry therapy sessions that "awaken memories and feelings in patients suffering from Alzheimer's, Parkinson's, heart disease and stroke. Poetry could not cure them, he said, but could increase their awareness of their surrounding and improve their quality of life."[22]

Whether oral performance is seen as entertainment, education, advocacy, or therapy, the future bodes well for oral performance outlets. As new performance venues emerge to give us new "texts" and new "performance" options, the tradition seems alive and well and capable of evolving, yet retaining its connection to a rich heritage. Long after you have finished this academic course you will continue to see how the performance of literature/text emerges in every aspect of human existence.

References

Adams, William. *Institute Book of Readers Theatre: A Practical Guide for School, Theater, & Community.* San Diego, CA: Institute for Readers Theatre, 2003.

Bahn, Eugene, and Bahn, Margaret L. *A History of Oral Interpretation.* Minneapolis: Burgess Publishing Co., 1970.

Gentile, John S. *Cast Of One: One-Person Shows From The Chautauqua Platform To The Broadway Stage.* Urbana and Chicago: University of Illinois Press, 1989.

Gray, Paul H., and VanOosting, James. *Performance in Life and Literature.* Boston: Allyn and Bacon, 1996.

Lewis, Todd V. "Traditions of Group Reading in Religious Worship." Master's Thesis, Ohio State University, 1974.

Lewis, Todd V. "Historical Antecedents of Readers Theatre in Jewish Worship Services." *Readers Theatre News* 9 (Spring/Summer 1981): 26-29.

Lewis, Todd V. "Historical Antecedents: Early Christian Reading/Recitation Practices," *Readers Theatre News* 10 (Fall/Winter 1982): 28-29, 36.

Neill, Kenneth. *The Irish People.* New York: Mayflower Books, 1979.

Post, Robert M. " 'To Read as a Poet': Major Performances of Edith Sitwell," *Text and Performance Quarterly* 2 (April 1991): 128-140.

Sonkowsky, Robert P. "Oral Performance and Ancient Greek Literature." and "Oral Interpretation of Classical Latin Literature." In *Performance of Literature in Historical Perspectives,* 1-30, 31-65. Edited by David W. Thompson. Lanham, MD: University Press of America, Inc., 1983.

Warman, Edward B. "Gestures and Attitudes" (1892). In *How To Be An Absolutely Smashing Public Speaker.* Edited by David Hoffman and Kristi Witker. New York: American Heritage Press, 1970.

Notes

1. Donald E. Hargis, "The Rhapsode," *Quarterly Journal of Speech* 56 (December 1970), 388-390.
2. *Epistles of Pliny,* X, 33-34, trans. and cited by F.F. Bruce, *The Spreading Flame* (Grand Rapids, MI: Eerdmans, 1958), 170.
3. Christopher Page, "Secular Music" in Boris Ford, ed., *Medieval Britain—The Cambridge Cultural History of Britain.* Volume II. (Cambridge: Cambridge University Press, 1992), 243-244.

4. Todd Lewis, "Hroswitha: Precursor of Religious Readers Theatre," *Religious Communication Today* 7 (September 1984): 35-39.

5. Frank O'Connor, "The Storyteller" in Frank O'Connor, ed., *A Book Of Ireland* (Belfast: The Blackstaff Press Limited, 1991), 216-220.

6. D.J. Hickey and J.E. Doherty, *A Dictionary of Irish History 1800-1980* (Dublin: Gill and Macmillan, 1980), 32, 523.

7. Richard Bello, "The Contemporary Rise of Louisiana Voices and Other Neo-Chautauquas: A Return to Oral Performance," *Text and Performance Quarterly* 17 (1997): 183.

8. Randall Knoper, *Acting Naturally: Mark Twain In The Culture Of Performance.* (Berkeley: University of California Press, 1995) and Marlene B. Vallin, "Mark Twain, Platform Artist: A Nineteenth-Century Preview of Twentieth-Century Performance Theory," *Text and Performance Quarterly* 9 (1989), 322-323.

9. Paul Schlicke, *Dickens And Popular Entertainment* (London: Unwin Hyman Limited, 1988), 234.

10. Schlicke, 231.

11. Philip Collins, ed., *Charles Dickens' Sikes And Nancy And Other Public Readings* (New York: Oxford University Press, 1983), viii.

12. John S. Gentile, "Early Examples of the Biographical One-Person Show Genre: *Emlyn Williams as Charles Dickens* and Hal Holbrook's *Mark Twain Tonight!*" *Literature in Performance* 6 (1985): 42-53.

13. Judy E. Yordon, "Preface," in Marvin Kaye, *From Page to Stage* (Garden City, NY: The Fireside Theatre, 1996), vii.

14. Mary Francis HopKins and Brent Bouldin, "Professional Group Performance of Nondramatic Literature in New York," in David W. Thompson, Ed. *Performance of Literature in Historical Perspectives.* (Lanhma, MD: University Press of America, 1983, 699.

15. HopKins and Bouldin, 716.

16. William Adams, *Institute Book of Readers Theatre: A Practical Guide for School, Theater, & Community.* (San Diego: Institute for Readers Theatre, 2003), 239.

17. Judy E. Yordon, *Experimental Theatre: Creating and Staging Texts* (Prospect Heights, IL: Waveland Press, Inc., 1997), 12.

18. Adams, 257.

19. Marvin Kaye, ed., *Readers Theatre* (Newark, NJ: Wildside Press, 1995), 11.

20. Patricia Ward Biederman, "Readers Find Voice With Audiobooks," *Los Angeles Times* (June 11, 2001), B3.

21. Yordon, "Preface," x-xi.

22. Myrna Oliver, "Obituaries: Arthur Lerner; Promoted Use of Poetry in Therapy," *Los Angeles Times* (April 8, 1998).

CHAPTER 3

Communicating Literature: Theory and Perceptions

Communicative Intent in the Performance of Literature

The three functions of oral interpretation (textual analysis, communicative intent, and performance skills) sometimes divide scholars along demarcation lines. Textual analysis proponents stress the over-riding importance of understanding how a text feels and of interpretive choices. Communicative intent advocates view literature as a means to share and ultimately influence performers and audiences with intrinsic messages. Performance skill supporters emphasize the nuances and levels of character portrayal as paramount. All three functions require balance and mutual dependency, but without neglecting the other two functions this text centers on the importance of performing literature so that an oral text becomes a communicative message.

Scholars generally agree that *oral interpretation is simultaneously an art as well as a communicative act.* Wallace Bacon acknowledges the special use of performance:

> It [oral interpretation] may be given a specific rhetorical or forensics slant; it may select one dominant attitude from a piece and emphasize that . . . to make a particular point a reader or a program may wish to stress.[1]

But he speaks for other scholars in cautioning rhetorical performers to remember that, "For the interpreter, the literary text lives, *is,* it does not only *say;* it does not only *tell.*"[2] Bacon's point is clear: while looking for a text's rhetorical message, do not neglect the aesthetics of form and composition—the text itself.

Assuming an underlying commitment to balancing textual analysis and performance skills, why should a "communicative theory" of performance predominate? First, *the performance of texts provides perceptual alternatives in attitudes.* Exposure to a variety of textual perspectives can raise consciousness, effect attitude-change or maintenance, and possibly result in behavior alteration. Second, specialized formats such as prose and drama *can influence due to the innate human affinity for narrativity.*[3] We move away from or reinforce our value systems with continued exposure to narrative opportunities. And third, *when literature is performed there is measurably greater comprehension, empathic response, and the achievement of cognitive and behavioral changes.*[4]

| Advantages of Communicative Perspective |
| To Oral Performance of Literature |

1. Provides perceptual alternatives in attitudes.

2. Influence due to human affinity for narrativity.

3. Greater comprehension, empathetic responses, and achievement of cognitive and behavioral changes.

Figure 3.1

One should not wholeheartedly embrace the communicative intent perspective without recognizing its potential for abuse. No performer should *force* a text to communicate a message it is not saying. Performers should avoid isolating features of a text and claiming that the isolated message indicates the entire text. And no performer has the right to re-write significant portions of another author's text to conform to the chosen communicative intent.

What Constitutes a "Text"?

Most people think of a "text" as a written published example of literature. Recent changes in the perception and choices of performance venues have forced us to expand our notion of the nature of "text." The study of "performance" has provided vast newly discovered examples of "text." A text may include a personal narrative, a folk or fairy tale, an elaborate myth, a ritual, a ceremony, or a symbolic representation of an important message (e.g., the National Vietnam Veterans Memorial in Washington, D.C., the "Wall of Prayers" at Bellevue Hospital in New York City [following the 9/11 catastrophe], or a Picasso sculpture). A text may draw on both oral and written histories.

A "text" such as this one you hold in your hands cannot claim to guide you to an introduction to all "texts" in the course of one quarter or semester of study. Thus, this "text" focuses on the performance of *literary* texts, originally written or printed as novels, short stories, poems, song lyrics, plays, essays, speeches, or reports. This course in oral interpretation can merely introduce you to the performance of literary texts. However, you should always be open to exploring the wider expanses of "text" which include oral texts as well as written ones.

You must continually commit yourself to studying the "text" you choose to perform. A performance of any text without study or analysis fails to prepare you as a performer or a listening audience for the deep layers of meaning and interpretation awaiting the treasure-seeker. Kaplan and Mohrmann argue that here is clear evidence to support the notion that anticipating the audience to hear an oral performance of a literary text alters the way you "study" and "understand" a text. In their 1975 quantitative study they suggest that "the oral interpreter does, in fact, perceive literature in ways that differ from the response of a more passive participant."[5]

Maintaining a balance of perspective is paramount in understanding any theory of the oral interpretation of literature. In the next section, while borrowing an application of psychologist Fritz Heider's "Balance Theory," this interdependent balance is described.

Interdependency of: Literature/Interpreter/Observer

A rudimentary, interdependent relationship occurs in oral interpretation with the literary text, the interpreter/performer, and the observers in the audience:

Positive relationships (indicated by the "+" signs) between the literature and the interpreter occur when: (1) Pre-performance textual analysis by the interpreter isolates the choices of perspective; (2) Pre-performance textual analysis reveals a prominent rhetorical message to share; (3) Actual performance choices remain true to the text itself. Positive relationships between the interpreter and the observer are maintained when: (1) The interpreter's performance choices entertain, persuade, and provide literary elucidation; (2) The observers offer identifiable *feedback*, reactions both verbal and nonverbal to the perceived performance; (3) The interpreter adjusts, conforms, and builds upon the performance choices in view of observer feedback. And positive relationships between the observer and the literary text ensue when: (1) The text as performed is in an understandable language, with an inherent sense of uniqueness, freshness, and individuality; (2) The level of textual sophistication, use of vocabulary, and syntactical format is appropriate; (3) The text stimulates rather than offends the audience; (4) The text has an appeal due to its *universality* (i.e., it says important ideas to all people in all times).

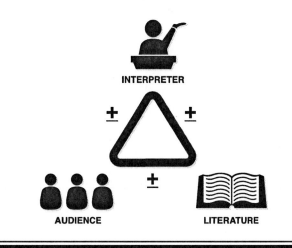

Figure 3.2

To help in understanding this relationship, consider having a discussion in class to discuss examples of *negativity* (represented by the "−" signs) in the triangular relationships. Under what circumstances does a negative relationship occur? Possible breakdowns in the relationships could occur because of: (1) Offensive literary choices; (2) Inappropriate or ill-chosen texts, due to age constraints, educational background, religious affiliation, etc.; (3) Poor performer presentational skills (e.g., too soft in volume, breaking character when reading a line in error, extreme nervousness); (4) Lack of interpreter's sensitivity to feedback and necessary adjustments; (5) Inability of observers to listen or pay attention to literary context. What other potential breakdowns might occur? What would one have to do to restore the positive relationship once it is severed?

In the next segment the three component parts are described individually. With each variable you will find helpful advice to assist you as you anticipate your first class presentations.

Literature as Message

You will need to consider the size and time constraints in the OI course when choosing a literary selection to read in class. You must be sensitive to the *length* of your selection. How long does it take to read the selection *aloud*? You may have to edit or cut out portions if you have a specific time constraint. Some pieces may have to be passed over because editing to the class time constraint is difficult or inherently destructive to the text's message.

Next, is the text *oral* (i.e., does it "sound" understandable?) and can it be read aloud? Many great works of literature are difficult to perform orally because of complexity, form, and train of thought. Choose literature for performance that is written in credible dialogue or vivid narrative or rhythmic tone.

For the text to be able to have an impact on the observer it must be appropriately chosen. By merely listening and observing, can one follow the point of the text? If it has an underlying message, moral, or theme, does the literature itself make the main point clear? A text needs *dynamic* qualities to maintain interest also: emotional range, vibrant use of descriptive language, scenes that anticipate a climax, etc.

How do you discover a communicative "message" in a literary selection? You may discover clues in the author's treatment of conflict or dialogic interplay between characters or rhetorical statements in sentences or stanzas.

Does a text have one true interpretation? If it is a complex, quality-composed piece of literature, multiple "interpretations" should be apparent. While any text may have many interpretations to choose from, not all choices for interpretation are wise. Some theorists claim that it no longer matters what a text means; a text can mean whatever the reader/performer wants. However, if you argue that a text can mean anything or everything, then you must grant that any text is meaningless since it has no unique message to share or insight to provide commonality for discussion or analysis. A more pragmatic approach to textual criticism contends that texts, while capable of multiple interpretations, have better choices for meaningful interpretation. The insightful performer scrutinizes the text for possible choices of interpretation and becomes persuaded by a rational process of critical evaluation to focus the performance on the most logical choice.[6] This choice of interpretation becomes the communicative message for the oral interpreter, but observers modify the interpretation when they witness it, due to the cognitive filters of their own experiences, associations, and interpretation of the text.

Interpreter as Translator

Before ever stepping foot in front of an audience, the oral interpreter must have a clear understanding of the chosen meaning of the performance text and the rationale for interpretive choices. It is as if the reader has said, "I've studied this text. I know some background about the author as well as some intuitive assessments from 'reading between the lines.' I know how the text makes me feel. I have decided on some performance choices that are creative but justifiable in light of my scrutiny during analysis. As I understand it, this text means this . . . ."

Now the interpreter takes on the role of *translator*. The performer reads, dramatizes, vocalizes, and nonverbally renders the text into a public presentation. As a "conduit," the performer transfers the words, nuances, and communicative aspects of the literature to an anticipatory audience. Frequently, the actual performance generates additional choices in interpretation during the presentation. While performing a text, it is as if a reader is also saying, "I am making these choices of interpretation now as I share consistently my decisions of what the text means to me. In this very moment of the actual performance, I believe my spontaneous actions and approaches are consistent as well."

Unlike a speech or debate, the performer of literature should not re-write a text with personal intrusions that blatantly offer persuasive options. The performer allows the text to influence. While it is true that as you perform a text you take ownership of that text, you must exercise responsibility along with that ownership. Responsibility must include a firm commitment to analysis of the text that should never exclude external factors in the creative process. The external factors are amalgamations of your own creative choices coupled with studied attempts to discover an author's implied intent or motivations. A performer can, however, provide a basis for evaluating the text's message and this occurs most frequently in originally composed introductions and transitions.

INTRODUCTIONS AS JUSTIFICATION FOR PERFORMANCE CHOICES

You were presented in chapter one with the necessary components of what needs to be included in an introduction. But it is essential that you realize how crucial the introduction is to the understanding of the communicative intent of an oral reading program.

Typically, beginning performers fail to establish an introduction that establishes a theme, a thesis, a communicative intent, an "argument," or information that justifies their performance choices. A communicative approach to oral interpretation stresses that any performance can be viewed in its entirety as an example of an "argument" for evaluation. Thus, an introduction which only describes a context or characters fails to provide the most important part: *when the performance is completed, you should be able to describe the primary "message" in terms of an argument for consideration and discussion.*

Sometimes a performer will approximate the "argument" or the "thesis" for the presentation by merely offering a "topic." For example, a program that purports to be a sharing of biographical information about a famous person (e.g., people's recollections who knew the notorious movie star, Mae West, coupled with her own words) may be introduced as "literature by and about a famous person (e.g., Mae West)." This "topical" connection needs to go to the next communicative level and indicate in the introduction some factor or reason to justify listening to a program "about Mae West" to create a "reason" to ascertain whether or not performance choices do in fact support a "performance thesis." A program that is about "mothers" is based on a "topic"; a program that creates the justification that "mothers suffer the most in times of war" establishes a "communicative intent" for which literary selections in the program serve as "proof" that the "thesis" is true.

Without a clearly communicative introduction the words which preface the performance become what Koeppel and Morman call "meaningless phatic introductory talk."[6] Saying something as vague as "life forces you to confront reality" is insufficient to establish a clear "thesis" or "argument" to justify your performance choices. In fact, such a statement is so vague that it could introduce virtually all literature. Construct and deliver an introduction with sufficient information to assist an audience in critical evaluation of your performance act. Your instructor should be able to ask observers in the classroom to provide in a complete sentence the "thesis" of each performance. At a minimum your fellow classmates should be able to confirm what your "topic" was, but you will have reached success if the audience comes close to stating in a sentence what you were attempting to share publicly in the oral reading. Certainly the exciting breadth of literary interpretation and perceptual data offers multiple "theses," but this is the power of literature and performance. We are made better human beings by dialoguing about the messages we hear and see performed. A fine and exciting performance should elicit commentary that focuses on a central theme or intent that can be shared by all involved.

At the end of chapter one, you discovered an exercise to find the best choice for an introduction to the Dylan Thomas poem, "Do Not Go Gentle Into That Good Night." In actuality, either introductory choice could be valid and since a text can have several meanings it would be incorrect to label one introduction or approach as "wrong." What we can "argue" however, is that some "choices" for interpretation are *better*. Your job as a performer and the audience's task as observers are to seek out the rationales for establishing better and hopefully, more creative and interesting performance choices.

Observers as Receptors/Responders/Critics

Observers, witnesses to the performance of literature, receive verbal and nonverbal stimuli to assist them in re-assembling the selected text in the arena of their imaginations. Audience members absorb the presentation and react to the intrinsic communicative message of the text in a number of ways.

An audience member may think, "I agree with this text. It matches with my own experiences and associations. I was entertained/reinforced in my own belief system." Hopefully, friendly smiles and head nods or other confirming feedback variables share the sensation of agreement.

Another audience observer may think, "I don't agree with this text's perspective. It alienated and offended me. It certainly does not reflect my own experiences and associations. I want nothing to do with even imagining such scenes." Frowns, discomfort, angry expressions, and lack of attention may imply that the text persuaded negatively.

Others in the audience seem nonplussed: "I can objectively listen to this text as a unique literary text, but I have no strong commitment to acting on its premise. You've raised my consciousness, but that's all." Polite attention is noted from these observers, but meager feedback of any kind suggests lack of commitment to an assessment of a text's communicative center.

And finally there is the observer who thinks, "What? What was that? I'm totally lost, getting bored, and will think about something else." The feedback from this member is clear enough: "The text is not interesting to me; my mind is on other matters; I don't remember anything you just read."

Each of these examples represents how a text is received. The observer also acts as evaluative critic. (More details about the role of the critic will be discussed in chapter twelve.) But why is the observer an important part of the interdependent relationships of the communicative act of oral interpretation?

It is not enough to perform; you must also observe other performers. In so doing, you learn analytical skill choices from observing how others perceived a text. You add to your own developing style as a performer by observing how others use verbal and nonverbal skills. You are introduced to authors and texts that may encourage you to look at other examples in style or authorship. You may be persuaded to sustain or reconsider values.

With previous explanations suggesting preconditions for the communicative aspects of the performance of literature, the following model delineates the relationships and persuasive nature of oral interpretation.

A Communication Model for Oral Interpretation

EXPLANATION OF THE MODEL

The term *suasion* in the model refers to various aspects of influence. Suasion urges alterations in beliefs or positions; it also strengthens previously held values. Suasion uses argument, entreaty, expostulation, even narratives to influence. In chapter one, the communicative intent of literature in performance was described as an "argument" or a "thesis." An introduction to a performance establishes a premise that is supported and sustained by the presentational choices of the performer. In this theoretical view of performance the performer is expected to offer choices that clearly support the established "theme" or "claim" offered by the literature. Jay VerLinden refers to this approach as the "metacritical model" for the performance of literature. He suggests that such communicative claims could consist of uniqueness, universality, suggestion, or philosophy. "An alternative to making a claim in the introduction about the literature is to make a claim about some aspect of life and use the literature as support for that claim."[7] Though an inherent component of the oral interpretation process, suasion is not license to force a message or idea. The interpreter who perceives the performance as merely a forum to force compliance

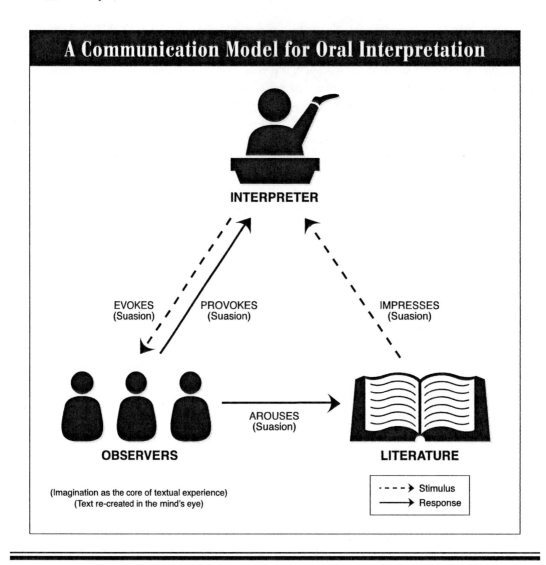

Figure 3.3 Model of the Communicative Interpretation of Literature Process

with a preset agenda no longer persuades with a text, but coerces. Coercion, although retaining some features of persuasion, distorts the communicative act by relying on forced compliance, restricted thinking, and threat. If suasion is to be productive, it should happen as a natural result of a process, not because a performer forces a message. Suasion need not result in conversion or alteration of beliefs or behaviors, either. Suasion is not based on a single act, but the cognitive decision to allow influence to occur, based on multiple suasory incidents. A performance that elicits questions concerning the message is as much an example of suasion as an observable change in behavior or beliefs.

The relationship between the literary text and the interpreter *impresses* the communicative message. In the analysis process the performer discovers the primary communicative intent of the text. The text impresses or affects the interpreter in a direct stimulus that is the initial suasion stage. Much like a stamp with ink leaves a "mark" so too does a "text" leave such an impression on the interpreter.

The interpreter and observers carry on reciprocal suasory acts in a stimulus/response pattern. Having made an analytical decision about the primary message of the text, the interpreter *evokes* or recreates imaginatively the message in a performance aimed at the observers. After absorbing the suasory attempt, the observers respond to the attempt. This feedback response *provokes* or directs attention to the initiated action, allowing the interpreter to discern how the performance and shared message are being received.

Ideally, while the stimulus/response process is going on between interpreter and observer, the text *arouses* the observer to respond to it in a suasory manner. A text may figuratively awaken an audience from sleep or boredom; a text may excite or stimulate or pique interest. Even though a performer is the means to share the text, the text becomes an integral part of the communicative influence process.

To bring to life a text, a performer must *recreate* the scene of the text initially and allow the observers to re-create the textual experience. The realm for this recreation is in the mind. Another way of understanding this is to say that the location of the literary experience is no longer merely on the page of a text being read but ultimately in the minds of the listening audience. Because of the variety of experiences and associations, the actual scenes will differ in each one's mind. It is as if separate, unique, yet shared layers of experiences and associations were superimposed over the literature, the interpreter, and the observer. And all experiences and associations validate the communicative process.

Dangers Leading to an Imbalanced View of Communication/Rhetorical Core of Interpretation

1. Forcing a text to persuade or say a message it does not intend.

2. Removing or down-playing the inherent texture and tone for the "Almighty Message."

3. Deliberate distortion of author's words by re-writing.

4. Suasion by virtue of the performer's skill rather than the text's message or observer's intellectual/emotional perceptions.

Figure 3.4

Conclusion

While a communicative approach to the performance of literature can be intriguing and stimulating, dangers of excessive commitment to discovering a rhetorical core must be avoided. Forcing a text to persuade or say a message it does not intend by deliberately misleading introductions or performance choices is a distortion of the activity. Removing, altering, or downplaying the true texture of a text in favor of an Almighty Message is misguided. Deliberate distortion of a text by extensive rewriting is a form of plagiarism or literary theft. Much care must be taken in juxtaposing several segments of texts if you compare more than one author's works. Editing, re-assembling and moving sentences and dialogue to new contexts must always be done with commitment to retaining the original author's integrity of text. Suasion by virtue of a performer's skills rather than an inherent textual message or observers' cognitive abilities short-circuits the literary appreciation objective of the performance of literature.

But as text, performer, and audience come together in a healthy, balanced relationship, suasion leads beyond a mere text. Humanity is blessed with opportunities to grow, mature, and change because of the study and performance of literature.

References

Haas, Richard and Williams, David A. *The Study of Oral Interpretation: Theory and Comment.* Indianapolis: The Bobbs-Merrill Company, Inc., 1975.

Hershey, Lewis. "The Performance of Literature as Argument." *Southern Speech Communication Journal* 53 (1988), 259-278.

Hunsinger, Paul. "A Communicative Model For Oral Interpretation," In *Studies in Interpretation*—Volume I. Edited by Esther M. Doyle and Virginia Floyd. Amsterdam: Rodopi NV, 1972.

Pelias, Ronald J. *Performance Studies: The Interpretation of Aesthetic Texts.* New York: St. Martin's Press, 1992.

Stern, Carol Simpson and Henderson, Bruce. *Performance: Text and Context.* New York: Longman Publishing Group, 1993.

Yordon, Judy E. *Roles in Interpretation*—5th Edition. Boston: McGraw Hill, 2002.

VerLinden, Jay G. "The Metacritical Model for Judging Interpretation," *The National Forensic Journal* 5 (Fall 1987), 57-66.

Notes

1. Wallace A. Bacon, *The Art of Interpretation*—3rd Edition. (New York: Holt, Rinehart and Winston, 1979), 451.
2. Bacon, "The Dangerous Shores: A Decade Later," in Richard Haas and David A. Williams, eds. *The Study of Oral Interpretation: Theory and Comment.* (Indianapolis: The Bobbs-Merrill Company, Inc., 1975), 227.
3. Walter Fisher argues from the premise that "humans as rhetorical beings are as much valuing as they are reasoning animals." ("Toward A Logic of Good Reasons," *Quarterly Journal of Speech* 64 (1978), 376). He links this valuing concept to the realm of fiction and stories in his *Narrative Paradigm* and argues that the storyteller influences and can ultimately persuade an audience to consider altering accepted values and morality. See: "Narration as a Human Communication Paradigm: The Case of Public Moral Argument," *Communication Monographs* 51 (1984), 1-22.
4. For research to support this statement, see: Kay Ellen Capo, "From Academic to Social-Political Uses of Performance," in David W. Thompson, ed., *Performance of Literature In Historical Perspectives* (Lanham, MD: University Press of America, Inc., 1983), 437-457; Gerald M. Phillips, et al., "A Preliminary Experiment in Measuring Attitude Shifts as a Result of Viewing a Dramatic Production," *Speech Monographs* 32 (1965), 209-218; David Addington, "Ego Involvement: Another Approach to Empathy," *Empirical Research in Theatre* 7 (1981), 22-31; Kristen B. Valentine, "Interpretation Trigger Scripting: An Effective Communication Strategy," *Readers Theatre News* 6 (1979), 7-8, 46-47;

Valentine and D.E. Valentine, "Facilitation of Intercultural Communication Through Performed Literature," *Communication Education* 32 (July 1983), 303-306; Kristen B. Valentine, "A Social Contexts Component For Interpretation Education," *Communication Education* 35 (October 1986), 399-405.

5. Stuart J. Kaplan and G.P. Mohrmann, "Reader, Text, Audience: Oral Interpretation and Cognitive Tuning." Paper presented at the Speech Communication Association Convention (Houston, TX), 1975, 11-13.

6. The process of applying standards to evaluate the merits for the interpretation of a text is called *hermeneutics.* See: John B. Thompson, *Critical Hermeneutics* (Cambridge: Cambridge University Press, 1981), 10.

6. Liana B. Koeppel and Mark T. Morman, "Oral Interpretation Events and Argument: Forensic Discourse or Aesthetic Entertainment?" *National Forensic Journal,* 9 (Fall 1991), 142.

7. Jay G. VerLinden, "The Metacritical Model for Judging Interpretation," *National Forensic Journal* 5 (Fall 1987), 60.

CHAPTER **4**

Nonverbal Communication and Oral Interpretation ———

This chapter and the one that follows are separate to aid you in comprehending the components and application of nonverbal and vocal performance factors. The truth is, however, "it is impossible to study either verbal or nonverbal communication as isolated structures. Rather, these systems should be regarded as a unified communication construct."[1] Chapters four and five are linked as closely as body parts, having separate but frequently overlapping functions. The oral interpreter needs to understand the power of this construct so that nonverbal and vocal factors coalesce to create understanding and meaning in any presentation.

Overview

Performers of literature intuitively discover that nonverbal communication consists of several axiomatic principles: (1) Nonverbal communication is a process of presenting and responding to behaviors without uttering words or sounds (i.e., nonverbal communication is primarily nonlinguistic); (2) Nonverbal communication is virtually anything another person does to which some other person assigns meaning (i.e., nonverbal communication tends to create meaning from analogy rather than a digital code); (3) Nonverbal communication seems to have a biological basis that displays remarkable cross-cultural similarities, though not always a one-to-one reference; (4) Nonverbal communication is the study of body language, facial expressions, physical appearance and clothing choices, space, territory, and touching behaviors, time, and the environment; and (5) Nonverbal communication is continuous, while verbal communication seems to have a beginning and end.[2] With such a broad field of knowledge how could any performer attempt a study without giving up in frustration at the seemingly impossible task of mastering the endeavor?

It is the insightful performer who admits that studying and, even to an extent, "practicing" nonverbal behaviors are parts of the continuing learning process. Nonverbal communication is "dynamic," constantly changing, and completely irreversible. Once you have indicated your feelings and attitudes in this form of communication, you live, adapt, or adjust with the consequences. The performer of literature can never forget the compelling cliche, "One cannot *not* communicate."

Scholars differ as to the percentage of meaning acquired from nonverbal communication. Estimates range from 60 to 90% indicating that nonverbal cues dominate verbal cues when paired together.[3] The percentage of weight varies due to several observable factors: (1) Children believe the "words" more than adults do; (2) When verbal and nonverbal messages conflict, nonverbal cues are deemed more powerful in guessing the meaning; (3) Nonverbal communication helps observers evaluate emotions, attitudes, relationships, and impression formations more so than verbal cues.[4]

Nonverbal communication can serve as *reinforcement;* it supports or accentuates a verbal message. Nonverbal communication can serve as *separate* communication; it supersedes any verbal utterance. Nonverbal communication can purposely sustain a *mixed* or *conflicting* message; it reveals clandestine or "hidden agenda" cues for scrutiny and understanding.

Performers must be so familiar with their bodies that they choose and consistently communicate intended meanings, based on the analytical choices they discovered in the literature. If the literature performed calls for anger, the performer must reveal tensions in the body to reinforce the verbal message and tone. If a brief pause in performing allows a performer to alter facial expressions of frustration to enjoyment or laughter, the nonverbal communication must be credible as a separate form of meaning from a verbal cue. If the true meaning of a text comes from a mixed or conflicting verbal statement of control and competency, accompanied by fidgeting nervous hand gestures, the performer must provide the well-timed cues.

All oral interpreters need to be reminded that every culture and subculture has its own nonverbal communication system. Bilingual persons must also learn to be "bi-nonverbal." To be consistent with the cultural expectations, a performer who offers a narrative of Islamic culture would read female to male dialogue portions with averted eye gaze. Why? Because the culture suggests that direct eye gaze between men and women is only for the most intimate situations; direct eye gaze between the non-married suggests lewd or lascivious intent. A performer of African narratives may discover that an ethnic preference for a "pointing" gesture is with the tongue rather than the "western" finger pointing. Even subcultures within Western culture have distinct body languages that must be learned to be shared in performance. Have you ever noticed how different television evangelists move when preaching? Have you noticed how the performers present black or specific ethnic individuals on television shows such as, *Girlfriends, The Parkers,* or *The Bernie Mac Show?* What subcultural characteristics do athletes have in nonverbal communication? Performers need to develop observational skills to attain a sensitivity to how and why cultures and subcultures communicate without words. The next time you need to go to the airport or train station take some extra time to study people, their mannerisms, their use of nonverbal communication, and remember what you see so you can use it in a later performance.

With this basic understanding of the role and impact of nonverbal communication, let us turn to a discussion of the classes of nonverbal communication. Of the hundreds of behaviors, objects, and events identified as examples of nonverbal communication, all have the potential to share meaning with an observer. To aid the performer of literature these examples are divided into the following classifications: kinesics, oculesics, physical appearance and clothing choices, proxemics, haptics, and chronemics.

Kinesics

The term *kinesics* refers to the study of body movement, gestures, and posture. Scholars differ whether kinesics represents a formalized "language" code or merely an aid in the complete communication process. The performer of literature soon discovers that carefully chosen body movements enhance the sharing of meaning and emotions in a text. When kinesic behavior is not practiced or planned for, a performer inadvertently sends other messages to an audience.

In chapter one there was a brief discussion of performance anxiety. Every performer has some level of anxiety and learns to control it or, even better, use it. The fledgling oral interpreter may not be aware of how kinesic behavior can send a potent message of nervousness. Notice classmates in any of your classes who are asked to stand and recite or speak. A slumped back, droopy shoulders, head angled down at the floor or shifting head movements from side-to-side, shaking fingers, hand-wringing—these are all kinesic behaviors that scream out, "I am SO nervous!" Some nervous and very insecure performers try to "mask" their feelings, but kinesic codes seem to be foolproof most of the time. The performer who struts to the front of the class, chest held high, head erect, nose slightly elevated, swaggering and cocky with every weight shift may be covering up nervousness by over-doing the confidence poses. Now all of these body movements have an important part in the process of performing if they are linked to personae in a text with these feelings and emotions. Avoid sending messages about your own feelings or how you personally feel during a performance by understanding what a persona in a text experiences—then share that directly and consistently.

Researchers Paul Ekman and Wallace Friesen have divided body movement into five categories that provide oral interpreters with practical areas for performance choices.[5]

EMBLEMS

When you sit down to watch virtually any movie starring Jim Carrey and the obligatory slapstick, intense, but over-the-top tirade is over (be it in on a sidewalk, a party, or merely a humorous venting of emotions), notice that the star frequently turns to his coworkers or girlfriend and raises his thumb in an up position. For an American audience, Jim has told us nonverbally "All right! I won! I got what I wanted!" However, Jim has just told moviegoers in some Mediterranean countries an insulting vulgar commentary, kindly euphemized as "Up yours!"

Catchers signal to their infield and outfield teammates that there are two outs by using the pinky finger and index finger extended upwards. (This gesture also means "Hook 'em Horns" to University of Texas students and alumni.) However, this same gesture in Italy is the ultimate insult and obscenity because it roughly translates to, "Your wife is playing around on you."

What Jim, the University of Texas student body, and American baseball players illustrate here is that some gestures have specific meanings associated with them. These gestures fully substitute for spoken words. Most all of a specific group, class, subculture, or culture know these gestures. The receiver realizes and acknowledges the precise meaning of the gesture. They are called *emblems*.

Performers should learn to collect possible "emblems" for potential use in presentations. A gesture with a specific meaning can reinforce or substitute for a subtextual attitude found in a text. A word of caution is in order, however. Do not follow the example of then Vice President Richard Nixon who on a political visit to Venezuela gave two A-OK digital gestures to a crowd of demonstrators in Caracas. Nixon was told later that the A-OK sign was roughly equivalent to the extension of the middle finger in the United States. Obscene gestures are culturally distinct and are evocatively emblematic. Try not to alienate a sensitive audience by abusing the power of emblems.

You will find additional nonverbal exercises to practice at the end of this chapter, but to assist you in discovering how we use emblems, think of the emblems that represent the following words or phrases and act them out:

I want to vomit!	This guy is nuts!
I don't know.	I need a ride, mister.
Peace, brother!	It is blazing hot!
Hook 'em, 'Horns	I am such a loser!
(When University of Texas students meet)	
I promise . . . and hope to die!	"Live long and prosper!"
	(—Spock from *Star Trek*)
You're dead meat!	"Two Thumbs Up!!!"
	(—Ebert & Roeper)

ILLUSTRATORS

Language is both associated with and augmented by body language. Gestures that are directly tied to or accompany speech are called *illustrators*. Illustrators serve several functions, including emphasis, framing, punctuation, direction, and mental imaging. Illustrators are different from emblems in that they seldom have the capacity to communicate meaning unless accompanying speech.

What happens to your hands and body when you give directions to the nearest bank ATM? You say turn right or left, but your body emphasizes the direction by chopping or flowing or pointing the directions you indicated.

Illustrators have been divided into at least seven categories.[6] *Batons* can be chopping, punching gestures that coincide with the words they accent in a speech. *Ideographs* are gestures that draw or trace an idea or relationship that has been imagined as if on a graph or picture. Raising one hand while lowering the other may show a decline in two variables that are related, such as residence location and car insurance premiums. *Pointers* use fingers or appendages to designate objects, places, or events. *Spatials* depict size and distance relations, such as the closeness of the car that slammed on its brakes near you. *Rhythmic movements* demonstrate pacing, tempo, and timing of events, such as the musical conductor who desires to speed up a portion of the symphony by beating his baton faster and faster. *Kinetographs* attempt to duplicate bodily actions or non-human physical actions, such as a bull heading toward a matador with his head bowed and his fingers analogizing horns. *Pictographs* use gestures to draw imaginary pictures in the air of objects, events, or people. Guys talking to guys may use these gestures to describe a rather attractive and buxom young woman.

Performers rely on illustrators to share nuances of text and create credible, natural personae. Caution should be followed in not practicing certain gestures so often that they become predictable and annoying. But some practice may be helpful at first.

The sample sentences at the end of this chapter are meant to help you feel less inhibited about using illustrator movements when you perform. They are not meant to re-introduce the Elocutionary Movement; they are not meant to imply a "clone-like" gesturing ritual; they are meant to give help in an exercise format. Illustrator gestures may be used to emphasize a word or phrase, point in a direction, or at an object, indicate spatial relationships, demonstrate a bodily action, match the timing or rhythm of a concept, or a myriad of other applications.

It is not recommended that you "practice" gestures immediately before a performance. It appears more natural and credible to let your body move as seems appropriate for the text as you are performing. Timing is crucial also. Your audience will laugh if gestures do not appear simultaneously with the spoken word. (Test it out: Say a line and gesture *after* you finish saying the line. It looks strange and people will laugh.)

REGULATORS

Regulator gestures aid in interaction. They are the body movements that include head nods, hand gestures, and shifts in posture which signal reaction to dialogue. We communicate to others that it is "time" to speak or that it is my "turn" to further a conversation. Regulators are closely associated with verbal cues or sounds that signal the time to speak or respond.

The performer of literature mainly uses regulator gestures in the performing areas of duo drama interpretation (two performer scenes) or Readers Theatre (multiple reader/performer scripts). When the other performer is speaking, the regulator gestures sustain the interactive illusion as the performers react to the others' lines. As a responder, the performer "listens" and reacts with appropriate head nods or signals of response by using the entire body.

AFFECT DISPLAYS

Though our faces are primarily the means to reveal emotional feelings nonverbally, several body movements and posturing can reveal an intensity level of emotions. Such *affect displays* as erect or slumped shoulders reveal attitudes ranging from pride to humiliation. Clenching and unclenching fists may reveal inner turmoil, building to anger. A performer that internalizes a strong, building sense of frustration may find the body shaking as an affect display. More insight into the face as affect monitor will follow in the discussion shortly.

Play the "Body Walks" exercise game. How does the body show emotion? How do different body parts react to different feelings or emotions such as happiness, depression, or fear? Affect displays are an excellent means to share emotional feelings with an audience. In the following selection, consider how you would change your facial features to coincide with the feelings of pain described:

from *Dune*
Frank Herbert

He felt calmness return, said: "Get on with it, old woman."

"Old woman!" she snapped. "You've courage, and that can't be denied. Well, we shall see, sirra." She bent close, lowered her voice almost to a whisper. "You will feel pain in this hand within the box. Pain. But! Withdraw the hand and I'll touch your neck with my gom jabbar—the death so swift it's like the fall of the headsman's axe. Withdraw your hand and the gom jabbar takes you. Understand?"

"What's in the box?"

"Pain."

He felt increased tingling in his hand, pressed his lips tightly together. *How could this be a test?* he wondered. The tingling became an itch. . .

Paul clenched his left hand into a fist as the burning sensation increased in the other hand. It mounted slowly: heat upon heat upon heat. . . upon heat. He felt the fingernails of his free hand biting the palm. He tried to flex the fingers of the burning hand, but couldn't move them.

"It burns," he whispered.

"Silence!"

Pain throbbed up his arm. Sweat stood out on his forehead. Every fiber cried out to withdraw the hand from that burning pit. . . but. . .the gom jabbar. . .

Pain!

Adaptors

Some gestures are merely frequent; they carry no direct communicative message, but they reveal much about a person's internal state. Called *adaptors,* these gestures become a means to create and sustain a persona in the hands of a competent performer. Mike Myers creates two unique personae, Austin Powers and Dr. Evil, with finger-pointing and pinky extending, in the *Austin Powers* series of films. After studying a text, a performer may offer a persona that habitually scratches an arm, plays with a mustache or hair-do, bites a fingernail, pushes up eyeglasses, or folds arms across the chest. These actions seem in some way to satisfy physical or psychological needs. The performer uses them to establish the credibility or true inner attitude of a character.

Kinesic behavior study is essential for the performer of literature. To share the nuances and subtleties as well as the overt and ostentations of a persona, one must let the body communicate consistently and truthfully. The second classification for study may be the most powerful nonverbal performance ally: the face.

Oculesics

The face is the most communicative part of the body and the eyes are the most communicative part of the face. Cliches like "I could see it in his eyes" or "She couldn't hide it; it was all over her face" reveal this communicative power. Physiologists estimate that muscles in your face can be shifted to display 20,000 different expressions and some researchers argue that the face is capable of producing 250,000 expressions.[7]

Oculesics, the study of facial expressions and eye behavior, reveals how humans express interpersonal feelings, serve as regulators, show anxiety, arousal, joy, surprise, tension, and related behaviors. Research is too extensive and vast to summarize all findings on facial expression communication, but a few aspects are essential for the performer of literature to know and master.

Performers learn quickly the power and impact of the *gaze.* This term in simplest form means looking at another person or object. In chapter six, there will be a complete discussion of eye gaze, focus, and the location of scenes, but for now all you need to know is that the performer must learn to simulate eye gaze variables. The performer who addresses the audience as a narrator or monologic persona usually applies *direct eye contact,* a reciprocal eye-to-eye gaze. The performer who represents a persona in interaction with another persona—real or imagined—must simulate "conversational" eye gaze that has the appearance of "seeing" the imagined respondent. Performers make choices to stare, avert glances, squint, open up the eyes, drop the eye gaze, and other variables to share emotional ranges of feelings. It is possible for a gifted performer to make the eyes glaze over, simulating blindness or hypnotic state also.

After you practice the face and eye exercises at the end of this chapter, take a look at yourself in a mirror. You may be self-conscious at first, but test out the flexibility and communicative nature of your face and eyes. What happens to your face and eyes when you show fear, anger, happiness, surprise, disgust, pouting, sadness, or sexual attraction? The practice times and exercises should make you less inhibited and more demonstrative in your presentations.

People who watch performers are attracted not only to the face and eyes, but are influenced by physical appearance variables as well. Clothing choices definitely alter an audience's perspective and appreciation of a performer.

Physical Appearance

The actor is often cast to fit specific physical expectations in a play. Age, gender, body type, and beauty are not hindrances for the performer of literature, however.

Presentational choices allow you to suggest gender differences by variations in voice, posture, and body language. You can suggest age differences by posture and mannerisms, body types by musculature shifts, and attractiveness by attitude and stance. The locus for these transformations is the imagination of the listeners, assisted by subtle but definite changes in nonverbal communication.

A word about clothing choices is important here. You need not wear precise costumes as a performer of literature, but sensitivity to the influential power of clothing choices is frequently helpful. If you are presenting a selection of literature that is Elizabethan, you need not dress in a period costume with ruffled neck piece. However, a colored turtleneck sweater and a "regal" stance suggest the mood and atmosphere to an alert audience.

Academic and popular treatises about physical dress echo the same sentiment: Clothing has a persuasive value that alters perceptions and affects the opinions of others.[8] When you perform literature you may be more persuasive when you choose colors or styles that fit the context of the text. A reader makes more of an impact on a collegiate class audience when the dress is attractive, stylish, and not too casual. It should not surprise you that a student performing a soliloquy from a Shakespeare play in a frayed fraternity athletic shirt, grass-stained tennis shorts, and thong sandals does not overwhelm a college classroom. But be aware that you can over-dress as well. A tuxedo or well-tailored dark business suit may seem to draw too much attention to you and not your text, causing distracting perceptions from your class audience.

While an audience psychologically responds to your physical appearance and clothing choices, they also react subconsciously to your proximity to them in performances.

Proxemics and Haptics

The study of how we use personal space and territory is called *proxemics*. Dogs and lions urinate on bushes and trees to identify a patch of land exclusively as theirs. Humans set up brick walls, barbed-wire fences, signs, and "squatters' rights" to define their territory. Gangs in cities spray-paint territorial symbols, and drive-by shootings catch innocent children in the cross-hairs of spatial disputes.

In what ways would proxemics affect a performer and audience? Generally, the farther away you are from the audience the more likely you are to communicate messages of coldness, aloofness, distance, distrust, and lack of empathy or friendliness. As you step closer to an audience, the performer is seen as more personable and genuine. However, standing too close to an audience signals forwardness, intimidation, lack of sensitivity, and intimacy by force. Find the comfortable distance in space for your performances. Variations in backing up or stepping forward keep an audience interested in your presentation.

When it is possible try to avoid performing directly behind a barrier, such as a podium or desk. When the space between the performer and the audience is free of distraction and comfortably established, maximum interaction in performance occurs. You also need space on each side to move effortlessly as the text dictates or suggests.

Normally, the oral interpreter does not physically *touch* an audience member, but the simulation of this powerful nonverbal behavior (called *haptics* or *tactile communication*) increases audience involvement. By reaching out toward the audience, a performer can mime actual touching behaviors and plant the suggestion of touch in the mind.

A text that shares emotional messages such as greetings or farewells can be augmented in performance by mimed actions and reactions to touch. In a duo drama interpretation or Readers Theatre presentation it is possible to suggest intimate touching behaviors such as kissing. (Left to the mind, this non-touching "touch" simulation of kissing can appear to be very sensuous if the audience has a vivid imagination.) The performer of literature increases that attractive bonding with an audience when sensitivity to personal space and touching behaviors are encouraged. Every performer longs for that moment when they have the listeners "right in the palm of the hand," a feeling of empathy and interrelatedness that is not always achieved, but thrilling when it occurs.

Chronemics

The study of how humans interpret, structure, and make use of time is called *chronemics*. Chronemics is important for the performer of literature for several reasons.

The beginning oral reader naturally tends to read too rapidly, racing past images and set-up lines, all too often missing the subtextual calls for sensitivity to time. Performers can enhance a text's humor, emotionality, sense of time going on by using strategically-placed pauses. More than merely a manipulation of time and silence, the pause can enhance a performer's abilities to create suspense, add impact, or focus the attention of the audience.

In classroom performances you will need to be oriented to a time schedule. Your selection must fall within a time frame. Extreme overtime or brief textual presentations fall outside the parameters of listener expectations. Who has not become frustrated and edgy when the professor continues a lecture past the allotted time for a class meeting? A performer who is not sensitive to time constraints faces the prospect of losing the interest of an otherwise attentive audience.

Occasionally, you must simulate time so that imagination will take over. For example, if you have a persona who is speaking on the telephone you will need to pause ever so slightly after each response to act as if you are listening or receiving a response to your previous comment. Freezing a pose at the end of a sentence and beginning again can simulate or at least suggest that some time has gone by during the pause.

Conclusion

To amplify and reiterate an earlier statement, "A performer of literature cannot *not* communicate." Your nonverbal signals share messages with perceived reliability and accuracy. Researchers interested in the communication of unconscious and conscious deceptions have called this phenomenon "leakage."[9] Although frequently involuntary, "leaking" nonverbal messages of guilt, nervousness, and anxiety about getting caught are not the only deceptions. Some artful con artists attempt to strategically alter their behaviors so as to add a layer onto their lies or deceptions. Still, the point exists that some message is always being communicated whether there is overt intent or not.

As we learn to exist in a "post 9/11" world, one of the adaptations made to counter terrorist threats is the use of training to "profile" and "catch" would be terrorists at airports and other public transportation facilities. Such profiling centers on being able to "read" and "interpret" nonverbal communication and activities. Understanding and interpreting nonverbal communication has become a self-protecting mechanism for our health, safety, and ultimate well-being.

Nonverbal communication variables are effective in communicating obvious as well as subverted feelings, attitudes, and relationships. Although the next chapter focuses primarily on vocal factors such as performance communication, the power and perception of nonverbal messages join with vocal expressions to forge a complete performance discipline.

Assignments

1. Play "Pantomime Exercise." Imagine yourself in one of these situations and nonverbally portray the scene. Mime actions, but also show attitude about the situation facially. Your professor will point to a scene, you will mime it at the front of the classroom, and classmates will try to guess it:

   a. You are captured by terrorists. To intimidate you, they fire off a gun just behind you.

   b. Your child decides to step down off the curb ahead of you without looking both ways and is almost clipped by an oncoming car.

   c. You attempt to be intimate and sexy and the partner slaps your face for being rude and suggestive.

   d. Someone shouts at you in a noisy situation to warn you that a heavy object is falling on the exact spot where you are standing.

   e. You are marooned on a desert island, have been there for months alone, and you spot a ship and try to catch their attention to save you.

   f. You are the local marshal in an Old West town; you stand your ground against a vigilante group of town folk who want to lynch your prisoner before the trial.

   g. You are a traffic policeman at an intersection where the lights have not been working . . . and you have some cars that go out of turn. You are not happy about it.

   h. A waiter comes to a table to pick up his tip, only to find the previous people stiffed him. He is still upset when he takes the order of the new people who sit down.

   i. A person at a baseball game with his/her son watches a foul ball until it almost hits them.

   j. You are in need of a "restroom" stop . . . and are busy asking people where you might find the nearest one. You are desperate.

   k. You are asked to give your first speech in a speech class and you are very, very nervous.

   l. You are watching one of the *Halloween* movies and you didn't know it had so many scary scenes. You react to a sudden unexpected moment while you are eating popcorn.

   m. You are driving along, the weather is very hot, but you blow a tire . . . and have to get out and fix it. You are not happy about it at all.

   n. You are a mother getting dinner and setting the table while trying in vain to keep the two-year old out of mischief.

   o. You are a parent trying to put the new Christmas toy together on Christmas Eve before the kids wake up and see what "Santa" brought. Things are not going well.

p. You are a drunk asking several people for change. You breathe on people and they run away from you.

q. You are a homeless person, trying to make up what little street abode you have for a long and very cold evening. You are not sure if you will live through the night because it is so cold.

r. You are an irate, very angry customer who is coming back for the fourth time to get a suit altered properly. You confront the sales clerk and demand your money back.

s. A rather tired exhausted student, up all night studying for an exam, tries to listen to a professor in another class. The fight to stay awake is not going well. You eventually succumb.

t. You are playing poker with friends and are dealt a royal flush. No one can beat you, but you want to act coy and build up the pot. Occasionally, your "poker face" gives a hint at how excited you are to have a hand like this. You eventually show the hand, "Read 'em and weep, guys!" You win!!

u. A young father has to put a diaper on his little boy for the first time. The little guy "sprays" him while he is attempting to do the diapering.

v. A woman's purse has just been stolen, she runs after him, but can't catch him. She attempts to explain the situation to a local policeman. She is frantic!

w. You are asleep in bed. But you gradually begin to fidget because you are having a nightmare. You bolt up in bed at the worst part of the nightmare . . . and then decide it was only a dream. Go back to sleep.

x. You are a visitor for the first time in Rome. You don't know the local custom is for attractive women to be pinched on the derriere. You are pinched . . . and you don't like it one bit. You retaliate!

y. A carpenter is making a cabinet and hits his thumb with the hammer. Expletives come out of your mouth as you try to soothe your poor aching thumb.

z. It's raining, you forgot your umbrella, you have a business suit on, you are rushing to make an appointment, and you sprain your ankle. It hurts, but you have to keep walking to get there.

aa. You are a beautiful young lady doing her makeup while using a small mirror held in one hand. You really like how you look . . . you'll be a knock-out!!

bb. You are a housewife ironing a dress, only this one is frustrating because it has an endless number of pleats. You seem exhausted when you finish it.

cc. You are a professional baseball coach, situated at third base. You are giving out signs to your batter. The batter bunts the ball and beats out the ball after you've given him the bunt sign.

dd. You are in a doctor's office waiting to be helped. You have a severe stomach cramp.

ee. You are not acting like a good role model for your child because you make faces at people when they walk by your park bench. You and your child are having a great time, until someone turns around and sees you making the funny faces. You are embarrassed.

ff. You are walking along in the park. You are looking up at the sky, enjoying the beautiful day, when you are hit on the shoulder by a "foreign substance" deposited on you by flying seagulls. You are not pleased.

gg. You are in a canoe and you must paddle upstream to avoid a whirlpool you just saw.

hh. You are attempting to hang a picture on the wall and every time you put it up and walk away to stare at it it seems crooked. Finally, you give up and just accept it as it is.

ii. You are a farmer going out at 4:30 AM to milk the cows. You are sleepy, but you know your job and do it well.

jj. A junior high school student brings home a report card. You had 2 Cs and 3 Ds, and an F. Your parents must sign it. How do you get them to do it with out yelling at you? You are pleased you pulled it off.

kk. You are an adolescent picking up your very first date. You are awkward, you hope you don't mess it up . . . and you discover your zipper on your pants is down. You are totally embarrassed.

ll. You are very old and have a "walker." You move very slowly, but you like the opportunity to be mobile. You greet everyone who comes along . . . and are generally happy about your life.

mm. You have just pulled a fresh pizza out of the oven. Since you made it you are responsible for it. You graciously give it to a walk-up customer, but the customer comes back complaining that there is a "hair" on it. You profusely apologize and give them their money back.

nn. Your parents ground you for breaking curfew. You are outraged and begin to pout. You throw a temper tantrum.

oo. You have never been to a Szechwan Chinese restaurant before. You order what appears to be a good meal, but when you begin eating it you cannot believe how hot it is. You try to drink cold water and it only makes the heat on your taste buds worse.

pp. You are a male, taking your girlfriend to the latest "chick flick." It is completely "syrupy" and when she looks in your direction you pretend to be emotionally involved. When she looks away, you get a bored or disgusted look on your face.

2. If you feel inhibited or awkward when you use hand or body gestures, practice alone with these "Gesture Drills". They may seem "elocutionary" and "forced", but they are meant to reduce anxiety and provide you with options to learn how to use your hands. Each section describes a type of hand gesture that could be used. The concluding section is undesignated. Do what seems natural! Say the line and do the gesture simultaneously:

(Pointing)

  a. There's Mr. Smith's desk in the corner.
  b. You'll find the telephone back there on the wall.
  c. Look for the map over there, would you?

(Batons: Accepting or Giving)

  a. Here, this is for you.
  b. Please accept my apologies. I'm sorry.
  c. Tom, I'd like to introduce you to Carol.

(Refusing or Rejecting)

  a. That's completely stupid—it's the dumbest thing I've ever heard of.
  b. No. I'd never do that.
  c. I cannot accept your gift. You are too generous.

(Cautioning)

  a. Now wait just a minute.
  b. Hey, be quiet back there.
  c. I think we need to take a closer look at this problem.

(Dividing)

  a. First, look at this part of the problem. Now, let's look at this.
  b. All the guys over here and all the girls over there.
  c. Half of the grapefruit is yours, the other half is mine.

(Ideographs)

  a. Notice that the car can be seen entering the picture in the lower left corner while the passenger in the cross walk enters in the upper right corner.
  b. As the age increases, notice that the physical stamina lowers.
  c. He was only three feet tall.

(Spatials)

  a. I am not kidding you. He came this close to hitting me with his car.
  b. I went nose to nose with him; you could tell I was very angry.
  c. Come on over here and give your uncle (aunt) a BIG hug!!

(Rhythmic Movements)

    a. Come on, come on, come on. I don't have all day!

    b. We went here and there and everywhere, just as quickly as we could go.

    c. Pick it up, get the lead out, I wanna get outta here now!!

(Kinetographs)

    a. Mime out the category for charades, such as: Hand cranking an old projector for "Movie" or putting your open palms together for the category "Book."

    b. He grabbed her by the throat and began to choke her.

    c. Mime out the various examples of the old game, "Paper, Rock, Scissors."

(Pictographs)

    a. The stick was two feet long.

    b. The mountains seem to tower over the lake.

    c. The park was in the shape of a football.

    d. The particle was really quite tiny.

    e. He is this much taller than I am.

    f. "She's got huge. . .tracts of land."—*Monty Python and the Holy Grail*

(Miscellaneous)

    a. Stay away from me, you hear me!

    b. Please come this way.

    c. Turn to the right at the next corner, please.

    d. Move over one seat, will you please. Thanks.

    e. Put the dishes on the table right there.

    f. What in the world are you doing?

    g. Look, I'm telling you it won't work!

    h. You can't really mean that?

    i. Well, here I am. What do you want me to do now?

    j. Hey, that's a great idea!

    k. I know I can do it!

    l. Well, it doesn't make any difference to me.

    m. Well, one is as good as the other, as far as I'm concerned.

    n. The waves were fifty feet high at the beach.

    o. I don't understand you.

    p. You've had your chance to talk; now you listen to me.

    q. Don't get excited!

    r. Out! Do you hear me . . . out!

    s. That's the funniest thing I've heard in years.

    t. I feel so helpless sometimes.

References

Andersen, Peter A. *Nonverbal Communication: Forms and Functions.* Mountain View, CA: Mayfield Publishing Company, 1999.

Ferrieux, Emmanuelle, "Hidden Messages: A Different Kind of Babel," *World Press Review* 36 (July 1989), 39.

Jones, M. Anway, "The Effect of Attire on Forensic Competitors and Judges: Does Clothing Make a Difference?", *The National Forensic Journal* 5 (Fall 1987), 67-79.

Knapp, Mark L. and Hall, Judith A. *Nonverbal Communication in Human Interactions.* Belmont, CA: Wadsworth Publishing Company, 2001.

Leathers, Dale G. *Successful Nonverbal Communication: Principles And Applications—2nd Edition.* New York: Macmillan Publishing Co., 1992.

Notes

1. D. J. Higginbotham and D.E. Yoder, "Communication Within Natural Conversational Interaction: Implications for Severe Communicatively Impaired Persons," *Topics in Language Disorders* 2 (1982), 4.
2. Peter A. Andersen, *Nonverbal Communication: Forms and Functions.* (Mountain View, CA: Mayfield Publishing Company, 1999), 15-20.
3. Judee K. Burgoon, David B. Buller, and W. Gill Woodall, *Nonverbal Communication: The Unspoken Dialogue.* (New York: Harper and Row, 1989), 155.
4. Burgoon, Buller, and Woodall, 156-161.
5. See Paul Ekman, "Movements With Precise Meanings," *Journal of Communication* 26 (1976): 14-26; Paul Ekman, Wallace Friesen, et al., "The International Language of Gestures," *Psychology Today* 18 (1984): 64-69.
6. Paul Ekman and Wallace Friesen, "Hand Movements," *Journal of Communication* 22 (1972): 353-374.
7. Raymond L. Birdwhistell, *Kinesics and Context.* (Philadelphia: University of Pennsylvania Press, 1970), 8.
8. Loretta A. Malandro, Larry Barker, and Deborah A. Barker, *Nonverbal Communication-2nd Ed.* (New York: Random House, 1989), 86.
9. Andersen, 286-301.

CHAPTER 5

Vocal Factors and Oral Interpretation ——

Overview

As you discovered in chapter four, nonverbal communication provides a wealth of meaning and interpretation, but it cannot be separated from the power of the human voice. With your first words, an image emerges and you either reinforce or counter the nonverbal messages you emit by means of gestures, facial expressions, distance, and other channels.

The bridge that brings nonverbal forms and vocal factors together is called *paralanguage*. Paralanguage is not what you say (content) necessarily, but how you say it (implication). By altering a range of vocal cues you can shade or provide a variety of meanings to virtually any spoken word or phrase.

Verbal language can communicate a cognitive, fairly obvious meaning. Paralinguistic variations, coupled with nonverbal signals, tell the feelings behind the words. For example, the sentence "I'm going out to see the new Disney film tonight" could be uttered as if it were a fun outing with your niece or nephew or a boring concession you made to pacify a friend. The same sentence has a vastly different meaning as determined by vocal variables. G.L. Trager, a pioneer researcher in paralanguage variables, divided the study into three categories: voice qualities, voice set, and vocalizations.[1] Trager's categories provide insights that no performer of literature can ignore.

Voice Qualities

Voice qualities constitute discernible speech characteristics that function within a range. They include pitch, volume, tempo and rhythm control, articulation and pronunciation, and resonance. Each of these qualities is part of the sound of a human voice.

A rudimentary explanation of how the human voice is produced begins with the exhalation of air from the lungs. This exhaled air passes through the *larynx* ("voice box"), where vibrations generate sound. The sound may be amplified and altered as it resonates throughout the throat, mouth, and nasal areas. This resonated sound is shaped to form consonant and vowel sounds by means of the lips, teeth, tongue, and roof of the mouth. The vocal interaction eventually combines to create words and sentences.

As a performer of literature, you will need to know how voice quality variables affect the perceptions of your presentation. In the following subsections, each of these qualities will be discussed.

PITCH

Pitch refers to the highness and lowness of your voice. These high and low variables occur as a result of fast sound wave vibrations (high pitch) sliding down to slower sound wave vibrations (low pitch).

Changes in pitch (called *inflections*) reveal a range of feelings and intent. You can make any sentence become a question by using *rising inflection,* making your pitch go higher, at the end of a sentence. Say this sentence twice, the first time as a simple statement of fact, the second time as a question:

"Major league baseball is boring."

What changes in meaning are effected by these pitch inflections? The statement inflection expresses opinion; the rising inflection suggests that the statement is a question and a question that may be disputed in subsequent commentary.

The pitch inflection you use to make any sentence a statement of fact or conviction usually follows the pattern of having the pitch level go lower or end with finality. This is called *falling pitch.*

If you have a sentence in which rising and falling pitch occur in juxtaposition you have *circumflex pitch.* This unique vocal patterning suggests sarcasm, disbelief, or innuendo. Say this sentence out loud with all the sarcasm you can put into it:

"You know, I've heard he's a whole lot of fun at a party."

Did you notice the pitch inflections you used to share sarcasm?

Most people have a specific, even predictable, pattern of variation in the levels of pitch they use in ordinary conversation. Following the musical metaphor that pitch suggests by being low, medium, and high, the pattern that develops is called the *pitch melody.* Now some people have the reputation for being boring and lifeless. They do not seem to vary their pitch range much at all. Some say they speak in a *monotone.* This is a bit unfair because few people can speak at the same pitch level with no variation. What usually occurs is that a monotonic speaker has a repetitious pitch pattern that varies only a little. They have a restricted pitch melody, in effect.

Oral interpreters need to discover that when they make choices for a persona's pitch range they must be consistent with the text's tone and intent. If you believe a text calls for tension, fear, and anxiety, which aspect (high, medium, or low) of the pitch range would best share those emotions? Usually, when someone is under such stress the pitch level tends to rise.

Performers share gender personae with slight variations in pitch. Female personae have a higher pitch than males, usually. Little children speak at higher pitch levels than do more mature adults. Adolescents experiencing vocal changes "crack," occasionally saying a word at high or low levels in mid-sentence. For some reason, males perceive a "sexy" persona as a temptress with a low or husky pitched voice. (Demi Moore, the actress, should never be out of work as long as males buy movie tickets.)

To make the most effective use of your pitch range in performance, use an unpredictable range of levels. Work to vary the pitch patterns so as to fit the meaning and subtext of the words. Avoid extreme pitch levels that will hurt your voice if sustained over time.

VOLUME

The loudness to softness continuum constitutes volume levels. Volume is best understood in terms of energy, emphasis, and vocal force. The diaphragm, a muscle in the stomach region, generates this energy. Why are opera singers capable of projecting tones at forceful levels without aid of microphone? They sing or speak with air sustained and supported by their diaphragms, not their upper chest or throat muscles.

The average classroom performer will not need to blast their audience with sheer bombast. However, the performer does need to know how far the voice can be heard. *Projection* is that quality of the voice that directs the sound of your voice to a specific target. Ventriloquists speak of "throwing their voice," but what they are really doing is giving the impression of sound coming from a different location by means of projection. When you read a particular passage that suggests distance or a "calling out" to someone far away, you automatically should alter the projection of your volume to suggest that target at a distance. In the opposite mode, if you are reading a passage that needs to sound private or confidential your projection is much more subdued, yet still heard by an attentive audience.

Adjustments always should be made in any performance arena. In most cases, your own voice sounds louder to you than to the audience. If listeners appear uncomfortable and push back in their chairs, adjust the volume downward; if listeners seem to strain and lean in toward you, increase the volume levels. Many performers have the problem of beginning a sentence with a reasonable volume only to have it dissipate to whispers before the end of a line. Project all script lines—even those that are meant to be stage whispers.

Performers soon realize that feelings are shared by varying the volume levels. Pitch is interrelated as well. It seems that as pitch goes higher so too does the loudness factor. Increasing loudness implies such feelings as anger, intimidation, hostility, alarm, and decisiveness. Decreasing levels of soft to quiet volume imply disappointment, shyness, nervousness, and uncertainty. Be careful not to make the mistake that many performers make: Yelling does not mean intensity. As an experiment, say this line out loud in two ways: first, as if you are yelling it; second, as if you are quietly trying to keep the lid on your own internal "steaming, ready-to-burst tea pot":

"You make me so mad, I could just scream!"

If correctly performed, the second use of volume shares more intensity because it seems more internal and genuine. The process of using the opposite volume level to share emotion is called *inverted build.* Anyone can yell; it takes a more gifted performer to be intense without sheer bombastic volume.

Notice how excitement and enthusiasm change the volume level when you read. You make use of volume variations to suggest "calling out" after someone. Imagine that you are a baseball fan attending a game and you are calling out the following advice to a player who is coming up to bat:

> "Base hit! Base hit! That's all we need! Come on, hit it!!!"

It does not matter where you are sitting in a stadium, you will use volume level projection to "assist" the player to hear you and deliver on your request. It is fascinating that so many fans use this type of projected volume, even though in most cases no one outside of your section can hear you at all. The opposite effect can work as well if you are speaking to someone at a distance, but you need to make a confidential and obviously much quieter response to someone nearby. Use the contrasting effect of "throwing" and "contracting" your volume level on this statement:

> "Don't leave yet. I've gotta get my jacket from my room. (pause) Mom, could
> you get my jacket for me. Thanks!"

Understanding how you can use your voice to emphasize meaning as well as distance factors is a product of concentrating on the variables of volume and projection. Lee and Gura accurately summarize that "volume depends largely on adequate breath supply and proper support in exhalation [while] projection combines these physical aspects with the psychological aspect of mental directness."[2]

TEMPO AND RHYTHM CONTROL

The rates at which persons speak comprise the *tempo*. Most beginning oral interpreters read much too rapidly, skipping over images and nuances and textual implications. A rate of more than 185 words per minute is considered too rapid for most listeners and a rate of less than 140 words per minute bores people to tears. A performer soon realizes, though, that it is better to present literary texts at a quicker rate so as not to run the risk of lulling an audience to sleep or inattentiveness.

To help the performer in determining rate choices, a fast tempo suggests feelings of happiness, energy, fear, anger, annoyance, anxiety, and surprise. A slower, more methodical tempo seems necessary when the text has complexities, sadness, uncertainty, aged personae, boredom, or lethargy.

How can you slow down a naturally fast reading tempo? You must concentrate and listen to yourself in contrasting reading or speaking situations. Listen and notice how fast you talk in conversation, then notice how fast you read when offering up a literary selection. If you are prone to speaking or reading too rapidly, then you should consciously try to choose material that tends to be slower paced, perhaps with more moments of hesitation.

As with the other vocal qualities, tempo is most effective when it is varied and not predictable. Tempo variations are enhanced by sensitivity to *pauses*. We discussed pauses in the previous chapter, but pauses have an overlapping "verbal" role. Pausing helps tempo perception by signaling the end of a thought unit, providing time for an idea to sink in, and allowing the audience to know the performer is at the logical end of the selection or performance.

Some literary selections have inherent rhythms that suggest control. When reading poetry aloud, you need to read the rhythms of the poem by thought grouping, not merely by the line composition. Read the following poem, pausing first at the end of each line, then by pausing where the thought or phrase ends, even if it is in the middle of a line:

from "next to of course god america i"

e e cummings

"next to of course god america i
love you land of the pilgrims' and so forth oh
say can you see by the dawn's early my
country 'tis of centuries come and go
and are no more what of it we should worry
in every language even deafanddumb
thy sons acclaim your glorious name by gorry
by jingo by gee by gosh by gum
why talk of beauty what could be more beautiful than these heroic happy dead
who rushed like lions to the roaring slaughter
they did not stop to think they died instead
then shall the voice of liberty be mute?"

He spoke. And drank rapidly a glass of water.

The rhythms and syntax of an e e cummings' poem are not linked to the end of the line. If you sing/chant the patriotic song lyric portions, you abruptly come to the end of one rhythmic pattern, only to begin another, and so on. Rhythm control in line delivery moves along a pattern from smooth to jerky with strategically placed pauses or no pauses.

ARTICULATION AND PRONUNCIATION

Articulation and pronunciation are related, but not identical. *Articulation* is the process of forming sounds, syllables, and words crisply and distinctly with the physical features that produce speech. *Pronunciation*, however, is knowing and speaking a word as it is correctly understood within a culture or subculture. Poor articulation or mispronunciation effects listener perception and any performer of literature must analyze choices to avoid that possibility.

Although serious problems in articulation require speech therapy, most errors in articulation are a result of laziness or sloppy attention to clear and precise speech. Performers need to guard against saying "gonna" for "going to," "wanna" for "want to," "goin'" for "going," and so on. If a performer will identify and eliminate common articulation errors, communication is enhanced and clarity of language usage is improved. Be careful, however, of overdoing a good thing.

Extreme emphasis when articulating sounds gives the impression of prissiness. Sometimes dialogue is written in such a manner that requires sloppy articulation to suggest a persona or an attitude, so you must consciously speak imprecisely as a matter of performer choice.

Everyone mispronounces words occasionally. Some of the most frequently mispronounced words include:

"nuclear"   (new-klee-urr,   not   new-cue-lurr)
(even though President George W. Bush pronounces the word, "new-cue-lurr")
"February"   (Feb-ru-ary,   not   Feb-u-ary)
"recognize" (reck-ugg-nize, not   reck-uh-nize)
"Illinois"   (ill-ih-noy,   not   ill-uh-noise)
"Los Angeles" (loss anj-uh-luss, not   loss ann-uh-luss)

The only way a performer can know if a word is pronounced correctly is to check it in a dictionary, note how television news anchors say it (they are usually correct), or discover how the culture or subculture says it. If you have unrecognizable words or foreign phrases, talk to someone who knows the word and can help you say it correctly.

There are, of course, dialects for regions and sub-cultural groups that will be different, even unusual:

"Lima, Ohio"   (Say: "Lime-uh, Oh-hya")
"Lima, Peru"   (Say: "Leem-uh, Pair-oo")
"Nagodoches, Texas"   (Say: "Nag-uh-dosh-us, Tex-uss")
"Natchitoches, Louisiana (Say: "Nack-ih-tish, Looz-ee-anna")
"praline candy"   (In New Orleans, say: "praw-leen")
                             (In California, say: "Pray-leen")
"Gulf of Mexico"   (In the South, you say "Guff")
                             (In Washington State, say "Gullff")
"strawberry"   (Americans say: "straw-bare-ee")
                             (The English say: "straw-burr-ee")
"aunt"   (In New England, say "ahnt")
                             (In the Southwest, say "ant")
"Cork"   (The Irish pronounce the city as "Kark.")
"about"   (In the United States, you would say "Uh-bow-t.")
                             (In Canada, you would say, "Uh-boot')

If you have a persona in a text that requires a consistent accent or dialect, you may need help to sustain the credible dialect. You will also need to approach the task of duplicating a dialect or accent with the utmost respect for the other culture. Gain an appreciation of the difference between your normal voice and accent and the other's speech. An excellent resource that provides speaking exercises and assistance for learning accents and dialects is David Alan Stern's *Acting With An Accent*, a series of tapes and pamphlets used by Hollywood actors and actresses to assist them in various roles.[3]

To suggest cultural or regional personae, the performer needs to understand two pronunciation variables frequently used: *clipping* and *drawling*. Clipping is a pronunciation device that chops syllables or letters off the end of words. Some black people say "favor" by saying "fav-" and trailing off the last part of the word. Drawling is the elongation of vowel and syllabic portions of words. Southern dialects characteristically have variable drawls. The single syllable word "pen" sounds like "peh-un" or two syllables.

A word of caution is in order for the performer who attempts to duplicate ethnic style and dialect. Too much attention to the dialect may be interpreted by ethnic audience members as stereotyping or ridicule. If you cannot match or sustain a dialect or accent, make the sounds subtler and suggest the accent with attitude, rhythm, and nonverbal communicative body language. The challenge for the performer in a selection such as Alice Walker's *The Color Purple* is to be true to the personae and not demean or stereotype a racial group by exaggerated inflections. Consider how you might perform the following excerpt:

from *The Color Purple*
Alice Walker

Harpo want to know what to do to make Sofia mind . . . He say, I tell her one thing, she do another. Never do what I say. Always backtalk . . .

Well how you spect to make her mind? [Mr._____ say] Wives is like children. You have to let 'em know who got the upper hand. Nothing can do that better than a good sound beating . . .

Next time us see Harpo his face a mess of bruises. His lip cut. One of his eyes shut like a fist. He walk stiff and say his teef ache.

I say, What happen to you, Harpo?

He say, Oh, me and that mule. She fractious, you know. She went crazy in the field the other day. By time I got her to head for home I was all banged up. Then when I got home, I walked smack dab into the crib door. Hit my eye and scratch my chin. Then when that storm come up last night I shet the window down on my hand.

Well, I say, After all that, I don't spect you had a chance to see if you could make Sofia mind.

Nome, he say.

But he keep trying.

RESONANCE

When air from the lungs vibrates the larynx, the resulting interaction causes *resonance*. Vocal quality (also called *vocal timbre*) can be altered by teeth, tongue, nasal cavity, and frequently shades emotional tone to words and thoughts.

Performers of literature frequently decide that a text requires alterations in resonance to suggest subtextual or a persona's attitude. Normally, textbooks suggest ways to recognize and overcome resonance problems, but oral interpreters need to understand the physiology of certain resonance difficulties and "match" them if analysis of a text before performance calls for it. Consider the following resonance variables:

1. *Breathy voice*—The stereotypical "airhead" or "sex goddess" tone is produced by too much air escaping through the larynx. It can also suggest softness, awe, love, passion, and admiration.
2. *Tense voice*—The opposite of the "breathy" voice has very little air crossing the vocal folds. It suggests impatience, anger, rudeness, and insecurity.
3. *Harsh/Raspy voice*—It sounds like the equivalent of rubbing sandpaper sheets together. It comes from constricting your throat. George C. Scott gave Patton a raspy voice in his portrayal on film. It is a vocal variation that can hurt throat muscles if sustained over a considerable length of time.
4. *Nasal voice*—Sounds like a twang and is a result of too much resonance in nasal passages. The voice can sound whiny or suggest laziness, repugnance, complaints, or boredom.
5. *Denasal voice*—The opposite of the nasal voice stops or blocks resonation in nasal passages. The result is the sound of a person with a head cold or the flu. Say "I have a cold in my head" as if it were "I have a code id by head."
6. *Oratorical/Preacher voice*—Caused by too much resonance in the mouth cavity, politicians and preachers use this big full, projected voice. It gives the impressions of haughtiness, patriotism, authority, and frequently pomposity.

Other examples exist as well but these represent ways that vocal quality can be altered for performance choices.

Vocal Set

Trager's second category of paralanguage, *voice set*, uses aspects of voice qualities but links them to physical and psychological characteristics of a persona in a text. Sex differences can be suggested by pitch variables. Age differences can be suggested by pitch contrasts, rate variables, and resonance changes. State of health, body builds, position in society, mood, body condition, and geographic location all bring to mind vocal differentiation.

Famous actors frequently study a character and provide them with a set of vocal distinctions. Jack Nicholson brings to each of his screen characters unique vocal patterning as does Dustin Hoffman. Meryl Streep has been rewarded with numerous Oscars and nominations for a wide range of characterizations. These actors exemplify the wide range of possible vocal usages available for the performer of literature.

Vocalizations

This third category comprises vocal sounds or noises understood as having meaning but separate from language. These include *vocal characterizers* such as crying, laughing, whispering, belching, breaking (as in "breaking character"), yawning, whining, and groaning. Vocal sounds also include *vocal qualifiers* such as intensity (how you emphasize a word with vocal force), pitch height (overhigh to overlow for emphasis), and extent (the application of clipping and drawling to make a point). Finally, there are *vocal segregates* which are vocal "emblems." Can you state the meaning of these vocal segregates?:

"Uh-huh"	"Ah-ah!"
"Uh-uh"	"Hmmm."
"Hunh-uh"	"Whew!"
"Sh—" (for quiet)	"Arrrghhh!!!"

Other vocal segregates serve as *vocalized pauses,* sounds substituted for lack of anything else to say or mental unawareness:

"et cetera, et cetera"	"Duh, duh, duh, duh . . . "
"OK"	"You know"
"Well"	"Uh"
"And uh"	"And . . . "
"Dude! . . . "	"Yada, yada, yada. . ."

Performers do not distort an author's intent by adding such verbalized pauses as long as the text justifies them and they are not detracting because of overuse. (Shakespeare's plays probably require the omission of vocalized pauses since they distort the rhythm and period sound of the language.) The intentional use of stuttering can also be an example of this type of vocalized pause. The rule for performer use is caution and well-timed frequency.

Connotation and Denotation

As every communication text is fond of repeating, "Meanings are in people, not in words." But certain words in a text merely refer to objects, concepts, or referents. These *denotative* words generally reflect an unbiased, descriptive dictionary definition. Other words in a text share an attitude or emotional feeling suggested by a specific word choice.

Dog can mean a denotation of a class of animal. *Mongrel* is a connotative referent to a mixed breed of dog, one that is associated with streets and living at a lower class level. But "dog" can be connotative if used to describe a young lady deemed unattractive by Neanderthal-thinking male gang members. And "mongrel" may be a term of affection attributed to a loving and faithful pet. (Walt Disney's "Old Yeller" was a "mongrel," in the positive sense.)

Literary texts abound with denotative and connotative words. Prior performance analysis of a text provides clues to help an oral reader know how to perform a certain word or passage. Find the denotative and connotative words in these passages and think of how a word or phrase should be presented, given its attitude and tone:

from *The Book of the Dun Cow*
Walter Wangerin, Jr.

In those days, when the animals could both speak and understand speech, the world was round, as it is today. It encountered the four seasons, endured night, rejoiced in the day, offered waking to all of the creatures who dwelt upon it—as it does today. Birth happened, lives were lived out upon the face of it, and then death followed. These things were no different from the way they are today. But yet some things were very different.

For in those days the earth was still fixed in the absolute center of the universe. It had not yet been cracked loose from that holy place, to be sent whirling—wild, helpless, and ignorant—among the blind stars. And the sun still traveled around the moored earth, so that days and nights belonged to the earth and to the creatures thereon, not to a ball of silent fire. The clouds were still considered to flow at a very great height, halfway between the moon and the waters below; and God still chose to walk among the clouds, striding, like a man who strides through his garden in the sweet evening.

from Chapter Forty-Seven *Oliver Twist*
Charles Dickens

It was nearly two hours before daybreak, that time which in the autumn of the year may be truly called the dead of night, when the streets are silent and deserted, when even the sounds appear to slumber, and profligacy and riot have staggered home to dream; it was at this still and silent hour that Fagin sat watching in his old lair, with face so distorted and pale, and eyes so red and bloodshot, that he looked less like a man than like some hideous phantom, moist from the grave and worried by an evil spirit.

He sat crouching over a cold hearth, wrapped in an old torn coverlet, with his face turned towards a wasting candle that stood upon a table by his side. His right hand was raised to his lips, and as, absorbed in thought, he bit his long black nails, he disclosed among his toothless gums a few such fangs as should have been a dog's or rat's. . . .

He sat without changing his attitude in the least, or appearing to take the smallest heed of time, until his quick ear seemed to be attracted by a footstep in the street.

"At last," he muttered, wiping his dry and fevered mouth. "At last!"

The bell rang gently as he spoke. He crept upstairs to the door, and presently returned accompanied by a man muffled to the chin, who carried a bundle under one arm. Sitting down and throwing back his outer coat, the man displayed the burly frame of Sikes.

"There!" he said, laying the bundle on the table. "Take care of that, and do the most you can with it. It's been trouble enough to get; I thought I should have been here three hours ago."

Fagin laid his hand upon the bundle and, locking it in the cupboard, sat down again without speaking. But he did not take his eyes off the robber for an instant during this action; and now that they sat over against each other, face to face, he looked fixedly at him, with his lips quivering so violently, and his face so altered by the emotions which had mastered him, that the housebreaker involuntarily drew back his chair and surveyed him with a look of real affright.

"Wot now?" cried Sikes. "Wot do you look at a man so for?"

Fagin raised his right hand and shook his trembling forefinger in the air, but his passion was so great that the power of speech was for the moment gone.

"Damme!" said Sikes, feeling in his breast with a look of alarm. "He's gone mad. I must look to myself here."

"No, no," rejoined Fagin, finding his voice. "It's not—you're not the person, Bill. I've no—no fault to find with you."

"Oh, you haven't, haven't you?" said Sikes, looking sternly at him, and ostentatiously passing a pistol into a more convenient pocket. "That's lucky—for one of us. Which one that is, don't matter."

"I've got that to tell you, Bill," said Fagin, drawing his chair nearer, "will make you worse than me.". . .

"Speak, will you!" he said; "or if you don't, it shall be for want of breath. Open your mouth and say wot you've got to say in plain words. Out with it, you thundering old cur, out with it!"

"Suppose that lad that's lying there—" Fagin began.

Sikes turned round to where Noah was sleeping, as if he had not previously observed him. "Well!" he said, resuming his former position.

"Suppose that lad," pursued Fagin, "was to peach—to blow upon us all—first seeking out the right folks for the purpose, and then having a meeting with 'em in the street to paint our likenesses, describe every mark that they might know us by, and the crib where we might be most easily taken. Suppose he was to do all this, and besides to blow upon a plant we've all been in, more or less—of his own fancy; not grabbed, trapped, tried, earwigged by the parson, and brought to it on bread and water—but of his own fancy, to please his own taste, stealing out at nights to find those most interested against us, and peaching to them. Do you hear me?" cried the Jew, his eyes flashing with rage. "Suppose he did all this, what then?"

"What then!" replied Sikes; with a tremendous oath. "If he was left alive till I came, I'd grind his skull under the iron heel of my boot into as many grains as there are hairs upon his head."

"What if *I* did it!" cried Fagin almost in a yell. "*I*, that know so much, and could hang so many besides myself!"

"I don't know," replied Sikes, clenching his teeth and turning white at the mere suggestion. "I'd do something in the jail that 'ud get me put in irons; and if I was tried along with you, I'd fall upon you with them in the open court, and beat your brains out afore the people. I should have such strength," muttered the robber, poising his brawny arm, "that I could smash your head as if a loaded wagon had gone over it."

"You would?"

"Would I!" said the housebreaker. "Try me."

"If it was Charley, or the Dodger, or Bet, or—"

"I don't care who," replied Sikes impatiently. "Whoever it was, I'd serve them the same."

Fagin looked hard at the robber; and, motioning him to be silent, stooped over the bed upon the floor, and shook the sleeper to rouse him. Sikes leant forward in his chair, looking on with his hands upon his knees, as if wondering much what all this questioning and preparation was to end in.

"Bolter, Bolter! Poor lad!" said Fagin, looking up with an expression of devilish anticipation, and speaking slowly and with marked emphasis. "He's tired—tired with watching for *her* so long—watching for *her*, Bill."

"Wot d'ye mean?" asked Sikes, drawing back.

Fagin made no answer, but bending over the sleeper again, hauled him into a sitting posture. When his assumed name had been repeated several times, Noah rubbed his eyes and, giving a heavy yawn, looked sleepily about him.

"Tell me that again—once again, just for him to hear," said the Jew, pointing to Sikes as he spoke.

"Tell yer what?" asked the sleepy Noah, shaking himself pettishly.

"That about—NANCY," said Fagin, clutching Sikes by the wrist, as if to prevent his leaving the house before he had heard enough. "You followed her?"

"Yes."

"To London Bridge?"

"Yes."

"Where she met two people?"

"So she did."

" A gentlemen and a lady that she had gone to of her own accord before, who asked her to give up all her pals, and Monks first, which she did—and to describe him, which she did—and to tell her what house it was that we meet at, and go to, which she did—and what time the people went there, which she did. She did all this. She told it all every word without a threat, without a murmur—she did—did she not?" cried Fagin, half mad with fury.

"All right," replied Noah, scratching his head. "That's just what it was!". . . .

"Hell's fire!" cried Sikes, breaking fiercely from the Jew. "Let me go!"

Flinging the old man from him, he rushed from the room and darted, wildly and furiously, up the stairs.

"Bill, Bill!" cried Fagin, following him hastily. "A word. Only a word."

The word would not have been exchanged, but that the housebreaker was unable to open the door, on which he was expending fruitless oaths and violence when the Jew came panting up.

"Let me out," said Sikes. "Don't speak to me; it's not safe. Let me out, I say!"

"Hear me speak a word," rejoined Fagin, laying his hand upon the lock. "You won't be—"

"Well," replied the other.

"You won't be—too—violent, Bill?"

The day was breaking, and there was light enough for the men to see each other's faces. They exchanged one brief glance; there was a fire in the eyes of both, which could not be mistaken.

"I mean," said Fagin, showing that he felt all disguise was now useless, "not too violent for safety. Be crafty, Bill, and not too bold."

Sikes made no reply; but, pulling open the door, of which Fagin had turned the lock, dashed into silent streets.

Conclusion

The word *onomatopoeia* describes words with inherent sounds. The true attitude and tone of such words are shared by an understanding of the paralinguistic devices that best present the nuances of such sounds.

All words, not just the ones linked to specific sounds, have a context and tone that clarifies meaning. The words of a literary text await the sensitive performer who has wisely chosen vocal factors to share the communicative intent. Practicing vocal exercises will not guarantee that a performer has chosen wisely, but when coupled with textual analysis before performance the oral interpreter can justify the presentation as loyal to an author's perceived intent and the independent power of the text to tell its own story.

Assignments

1. Read the following exercises out loud, utilizing various levels of vocal projection to suggest distance, close proximity, confidentiality, or desire to get someone's attention:

   a. Mom, could you leave a house key before you head out? MOM, I need the house key!

   b. OK, first thing is put the table decorations on each table. JACK, could you go over to the theatre and bring us a ladder? THANKS. Cheri, you want to follow Jack over there to be sure he gets that ladder. He may not know where it is.

   c. Can you believe that dress she has on? I wouldn't be caught dead in something that tacky. OH, Jenny, Hi! Cute dress! Where'd you get it?

2. In the following exercise you must know which word to emphasize so as to share the proper message. Give it a try:

   > Ned Nott was shot and Sam Shott was not,
   > So it's better to be Shott than Nott,
   > Some say Nott was not shot, but Shott swears he shot Nott.
   > > Either the shot Shott shot at Nott was not shot or Nott was not shot.
   > If the shot Shott shot shot Nott, Nott was shot,
   > > But if the shot Shott shot shot Shott himself, then Shott would be shot and Nott would not.
   > However, the shot Shott shot shot not Shott but Nott.
   > It's not easy to say who was shot and who was not,
   > But we know who was Shott and who was Nott.[4]

3. For articulation practice, say the following tongue twisters three times each, saying each subsequent one faster than the previous time:

   > Six slim sleek saplings.
   > Old, oily Ollie oils oily autos.
   > The bottom of the butter bucket is the buttered bucket
   > > bottom.
   > Fill the sieve with thistles; then sift the
   > > thistles through the sieve.
   > She sells seashells, sherry and sandals on the seashore.

I'm a critical cricket critic.
Then the thankless theologian thawed thoroughly.
The beasts came to feast, but the geese had
  ceased and were to be released.

4. Make the proper pronunciation distinction between the following words and sentences that are identical yet different:

    a. We polish the Polish furniture.
    b. He could lead if he would get the lead out.
    c. A farm can produce produce.
    d. The dump was so full it had to refuse refuse.
    e. The soldier decided to desert in the desert.
    f. The present is a good time to present the present.
    g. The insurance for the invalid was invalid.
    h. The buck does funny things when the does are present.
    i. After a number of Novocaine injections, my jaw got number.
    j. They sent a sewer down to stitch the tear in the sewer line.

5. Those who live in the Southern portions of the United States enjoy poking fun at themselves in this exercise in regional dialect. Have fun saying these definitions out loud:

    a. *Ah:* The thing you see with, and the personal pronoun used to denote individuality. "Ah, think Ah've got somethin' in mah ah."
    b. *Bleeve:* Expression of intent or faith. "Ah bleeve we ought to go to church this Sunday."
    c. *Far:* A state of combustion that produces heat and light. "Ah reckon it's about time to put out the far and call in the dawgs."
    d. *Ovair:* In that direction. "Where's yo paw, son?" "He's ovair, suh."
    e. *Zat:* Is that. "Zat yo dawg?"

References

Burgoon, Judee K., Buller, David B., and Woodall, W. Gill. *Nonverbal Communication: The Unspoken Dialogue.* New York: HarperCollins Publishers, 1989, 62-71.

Karshner, Roger. *You Said A Mouthful: Tongue Twisters to Tangle, Titillate, Test and Tease.* Toluca Lake, CA: Dramaline Publications, 1991.

Lee, Charlotte and Gura, Timothy. *Oral Interpretation. 10th Edition.* Boston: Houghton Mifflin Company, 2001.

Malandro, Loretta A., Barker, Larry, and Barker, Deborah A. *Nonverbal Communication 2nd Edition.* New York: Random House, 1989, 231-257.

Peterson, Brent D., Stephan Eric G., and White, Noel D. *The Complete Speaker: An Introduction to Public Speaking—3rd Edition.* St. Paul, MN: West Publishing Company, 1992, 148-163.

Rizzo, Raymond. *The Voice As An Instrument. 2nd Edition.* Indianapolis: Bobbs-Merrill Educational Publishing, 1978.

Ross, Raymond S. *Speech Communication: The Speechmaking System. 8th Edition.* Englewood Cliffs, New Jersey: Prentice Hall, 1989, 217-226.

Sprague, Jo and Stuart, Douglas. *The Speaker's Handbook—6th Ed.* Belmont, CA: Wadsworth/Thomson Learning Inc., 2003.

Notes

1. G.L. Trager, "Paralanguage: A First Approximation," *Studies In Linguistics* 13 (1958), 1-12.
2. Charlotte Lee and Timothy Gura, *Oral Interpretation—10th Edition.* Boston: Houghton Mifflin Company, 2001, 83.
3. David Alan Stern, *Acting With An Accent.* Los Angeles: Dialect Accent Specialists, Inc., 1979. Available from: Samuel French, Inc., 7623 Sunset Blvd., Hollywood, CA 90046-2795 (213) 876-0570.
4. Roger Karshner, *You Said A Mouthful: Tongue Twisters to Tangle, Titillate, Test and Tease.* Toluca Lake, CA: Dramaline Publications, 1991, 3.

CHAPTER **6**

Preparation for Oral Interpretation: Analysis

When you decided to sign up for a literature performance course, did you assume that all you would do was read selections aloud for a class audience? The art of literary performance cannot occur with any depth of meaning or insight if the performer has not justified and selected performing choices ahead of time. This prior-to-performance preparation begins with an analysis of the literature to be performed.

There are many methods available to a performer for interpretive analysis. Each method emphasizes a special function or purpose, which ideally fosters decisions for performances that enhance understanding and appreciation. In keeping with the focus of this text, performers should prepare a *rhetorical/argumentative* approach to analysis. Yordon indicates that this approach "is concerned with the persuasive/communicative strategies within the literary work and with the effect the work has on its audience/readers."[1]

This approach does not denigrate other strategies of literary analysis, but seems a proper starting point for a performer in a basic course. John Macksoud agrees, suggesting that a beginning oral interpretation student

> be *linguistic critic of literature,* rather than literary critic . . . [F]rom the reader's first analytic view of the work to the final oral and visual contact between reader and auditor, it is the function of the reader to exploit what is essentially *rhetorical* power to channel listeners' response toward his thesis.[2]

In this chapter, the *rhetorical/argumentative* approach to analysis will emphasize discovery of primary ideas in a text, sequential elements that amplify a message, time aspects, setting, persona point-of-view variables, audience perceptions, and textual language choices.

Primary Ideas in a Text

Just as any effective, well-composed essay or public speech has a thesis statement, so too should a performance text have a central idea or predominant subject. Complex literary texts may have several themes, but one concise premise should be apparent. You will find it easier to compose your introduction for your performance if after several silent readings you write down possible thesis sentences, choosing the one that best seems to describe the primary idea.

Ask yourself, "What does this text say about a topic?" You may begin by isolating the thesis to a common topic of human concern: survival, love, death, esteem, creativity, and war. Next, focus the topic to a narrower aspect addressed in the text (e.g., unrequited love or first love or unconditional love). Finally, write a sentence expressing the summarized tone and position found in the text.

Consider the following poem:

I Sit And Look Out

Walt Whitman

> I sit and look out upon all the sorrows of the world, and upon
> all oppression and shame,
> I hear secret convulsive sobs from young men at anguish with
> themselves, remorseful after deeds done,
> I see in low life the mother misused by her children, dying,
> neglected, gaunt, desperate,
> I see the wife misused by her husband, I see the treacherous
> seducer of young women,
> I mark the ranklings of jealousy and unrequited love attempted to be hid,
> I see these sights on the earth,
> I see the workings of battle, pestilence, tyranny, I see martyrs
> and prisoners,
> I observe a famine at sea, I observe the sailors casting lots who
> shall be kill'd to preserve the lives of the rest,
> I observe the slights and degradations cast by arrogant persons
> upon laborers, the poor, and upon Negroes, and the like;
> All these—all the meanness and agony without end I sitting
> look out upon,
> See, hear, and am silent.

What is this poem about? A persona describes horrible atrocities, pain, and suffering, but the final line reveals that the persona takes no action to correct these evils. Did you think of such topics as: injustice, prejudice, or apathy? This poem reveals that humans are capable of extreme cruelty to each other. If you had to write down a thesis, how would you incorporate these aspects? Write a thesis and discuss it with your classmates and professor.

Sequence Elements and Message

The most captivating and intriguing performance texts, even when edited or cut to a specific time restraint, should reveal series of actions that highlight and expose the primary thesis. Four aspects of sequence should be analyzed and understood: *Build, Crisis, Climax,* and *Denouement.*

The build consists of initial action found in a text before the climax. From the first word, the build should gradually increase in intensity and fervor. Creating or understanding a sense of build does not occur merely because a performer speeds up line delivery or gradually increases volume. Frequently, a build includes expositional introductions of characters, context, and tone. A performer must analyze a text and decide when and how the intensity levels of the build should occur. A build that begins with too much intensity places impossible demands on a performer to surpass each level or "point" toward a climax. Suppose you chose to perform Edgar Allan Poe's classic tale of horror, "The Tell-Tale Heart." The introductory aspects of the story establish that the persona is disturbed and tormented. A subtle use of build would demand that the audience perceive a performer as a persona gradually but clearly revealing examples of madness. If a build is not sensed or planned, the performance seems static and ultimately lulling. Audiences may doze off or lose interest in your presentation.

Complex texts usually have a moment in the build wherein the plot changes direction and the primary idea emerges. Crisis sets up a logical progression of factors that originate with this element. Performers need to emphasize the crisis sensitively but obviously. In the previous Walt Whitman poem, at what stanza do you believe the crisis occurs? Why? What makes that stanza the turning point of the build?

When a crisis hits a peak level of intensity or emotionality, a climax emerges. Characterized by fervor and emotionalism, the climax calls forth a performer's full arsenal of dramatic skills. A climax has minimal impact if the performer fails to build and point to a crisis. Sudden, unmotivated outbursts without logical, progressive performance choices make a climax seem like a surprise or a melodramatic exercise. The serious peak moment can be embarrassing or dismissed by an ill-prepared audience. Sometimes the climax occurs at the end of the selection. But this is not required or true for all texts. Where do you think the climax peaks in the Whitman poem? Why did you choose that stanza or phrase? What alterations in delivery would you adjust as you rehearse the build and crisis to make the climax appear to peak?

The intensity level of a climax usually requires a gradual decreasing before a text concludes. Referred to as the denouement, or falling action, this sequence calls on the performer to decrease intensity gradually and stop. In some cases, the denouement may be as short as a phrase or sentence. More frequently, a text adds paragraphs or stanzas to wrap up action. A performer who chooses to make the final line of a text serve as climax may use silence to impart a sensation of denouement before departing. A performer should not dismiss the power of denouement. You steal an important moment of resolution and completeness for an audience when you rush a climax, hurriedly close a manuscript, and slump down into a classroom chair.

Time Aspects

Not all literary texts follow linear progression. Some events may be relayed in flashbacks, revealing occurrences at an earlier time. Some texts take detours or have intentional digression from a primary idea. Some textual components are best served by performing them as if time has stopped. Pauses or timely silences can suggest this component. A speedy line or stanza may be performed to simulate a jumping forward in time to stop ultimately or slow down for an important moment.

The performer who analyzes the impact of time in a text decides how tempo variations, non-verbal expressions, and pauses can suggest change. Some lines may be tossed out as diversions, but the performance choices emphasize the timely lines.

In the following autobiography, write down comments about how expressions of time past, time present, and time future blend. Though the verb tense varies, the essay does not necessarily follow a linear pattern:

from *My Losing Season*

Pat Conroy

Where did all those games go, the ones I threw myself headlong into as a boy, a rawboned kid who fell in love with the smell and shape of a basketball, who longed for its smooth skin on the nerve endings of my fingers and hands, who lived for the sound of its unmistakable heartbeat, its staccato rhythms, as I bounced it along the pavement throughout the ten thousand days of my boyhood? . . . But the games are fading on me now where once they imprinted themselves, bright as decals, on the whitewashed fences of memory. Once, I could replay them all, almost move for move, from the moment the referee first lofted the ball between the two crouching centers until the losing team launched their desperate, last-second shot, the horn sounded, and the players shook hands and drifted toward locker rooms and the judgment of our coaches . . . Yet I wish to be clear. Basketball provided a legitimate physical outlet for all the violence and rage and sadness I later brought to the writing table. The game kept me from facing the ruined boy who played basketball instead of killing his father. It was also the main language that allowed father and son to talk to each other. If not for sports, I do not think my father ever would have talked to me.

Which lines would you increase in speed to suggest jumping forward in time? Which lines would you slow down, suggesting a nostalgic retreat to a happier time? Which lines need to have an abrupt stop, suggesting time put on hold? Which lines seem detours to a primary idea? Do these performance decisions remain consistent with the rhetorical argument of this autobiography? The answers to these and other questions will generate performance choices for you to consider.

Setting

The environment that a literary text suggests consists of a physical as well as a contextual setting. An audience will be confused if a performer does not offer commentary as well as interpretive insights into the setting of a text. A performer needs to imagine this setting as the text is offered.

If an author provides specific expositional details about setting, do not assume that this description is completely unnecessary and thus open for editing. A text may have been composed to reflect a time-bound political or social climate that may or may not exist currently. In the flux of ever-changing politics the 1986 Tony Award-winning play *A Walk In The Woods* by Lee Blessing cannot be clearly understood apart from its Cold War context. Two arms negotiators— an American and a Soviet—confront, cajole, and commiserate with each other. The performer must imagine a context far different from that that suggests a post-Berlin Wall communism. This context has distrust and meaningless positioning. A performer who analyzes this text also discovers that scenes occur during clearly identifiable seasons of the year. A dialogue scene between the two personae will have different body language if the physical setting is winter or summer. Using this play as an example, the physical setting needs to be analyzed because it may have a direct impact on judgments for performance choices. A persona may shiver, simulating the cold, in the winter scene and wipe his forehead, simulating removal of sweat, in the summer scene. These choices directly and indirectly affect a revealed message in a text.

In the following selection, the physical setting is a large medical center in a suburban American city. The author, Michael Medved, provides a transcript of an actual monologue by the director of oncology at the center. The contextual setting is more complex and multi-layered. As you will see, the persona wrestles with cynicism and the hopelessness of his occupation:

from *Hospital*
Michael Medved

If you look at statistics, nobody does a worse job than me. My patients come to me with cancer. Sooner or later, they all die—almost all of them. In twenty years, I still haven't gotten used to it.

One episode that drove the reality home was a gift I received a few years after I started with oncology. Out of the blue, I get this nice big Christmas gift from one of the local mortuaries. I was never exactly pushing them, you know. I never had any intentions of doing that. But just by sheer statistics, the signatures on the death certificates . . . I can hear them talking it over. "Hey, this guy . . . is all right. He sends us a lot of business. Let's send him a gift, man!"

I kept getting their gifts, and every year they had a kind of macabre quality. Like cutlery. I remember getting the knives in the mail and saying to my wife, "Now . . . [they've] . . . sent me a do-it-yourself autopsy kit!"

Then the ultimate, the absolute gift came about two years ago. Instead of a great big box, I got a little envelope. Sure enough they had given me my own plot, for me and my family. You know, "We do a land office business with that guy . . . Let's line him up with a nice plot, just for him."

In an introduction, the performer would need to tell us that this persona is a medical doctor who treats cancer patients. He has obviously served in his job for a number of years and has developed a cynical outlook to cover his true feelings about the number of patients that he loses each year to the dreaded disease. Without a clear contextual and physical establishing of setting the commentary makes no sense to a listening audience who may or may not have a copy of the text to follow along with you.

Persona Point-of-View

In chapter one you discovered that the author's voice, perspective, and viewpoint are revealed in the persona(e) of a text. Some authors have a persona closely matched with their own character. Autobiographies, public speeches, intimate personal poetry, and nonfiction essays exemplify the author/persona link. However, other authors may choose to create personae whose motivations, moral character, and personality contrast sharply with their own perspectives.

How does a performer discover the author's intent in a text? You should know that the answer to that question might be elusive and completely unknown. That should not deter you from seeking as much information as you can about an author. Look for clues in the title, a preface, interviews with the author, or pointed references within a text. The message implied by context or hidden agenda or tone might be a subtextual one. The analytical critic makes decisions for performance based on an interpretation of what the text appears to be saying, coupled with any additional information or commentary from an author or other critic. A word of caution is needed here: Arbitrary interpretive decisions without analysis of persona or author's perspective may lead to a distorted textual performance.

Read the following poem:

'Out, Out—'

Robert Frost

The buzz saw snarled and rattled in the yard
And made dust and dropped stove-length sticks of wood,
Sweet-scented stuff when the breeze drew across it.
And from there those that lifted eyes could count
Five mountain ranges one behind the other
Under the sunset far into Vermont.
And the saw snarled and rattled, snarled and rattled,
As it ran light, or had to bear a load.
And nothing happened: day was all but done.
Call it a day, I wish they might have said
To please the boy by giving him the half hour
That a boy counts so much when saved from work.
His sister stood beside them in her apron
To tell them 'Supper.' At the word, the saw,
As if to prove saws knew what supper meant,
Leaped out at the boy's hand, or seemed to leap—
He must have given the hand. However it was,
Neither refused the meeting. But the hand!
The boy's first outcry was a rueful laugh,
As he swung toward them holding up the hand
Half in appeal, but half as if to keep
The life from spilling. Then the boy saw all—
Since he was old enough to know, big boy
Doing a man's work, though a child at heart—
He saw all spoiled. 'Don't let him cut my hand off—
The doctor, when he comes. Don't let him, sister!'
So. But the hand was gone already.
The doctor put him in the dark of ether.
He lay and puffed his lips out with his breath.
And then—the watcher at his pulse took fright.
No one believed. They listened at his heart.
Little—less—nothing!—and that ended it.
No more to build on there. And they, since they
Were not the one dead, turned to their affairs.

A student performed this poem in a basic course without researching Frost's motivation for writing it. Her performance choices included a light-hearted lilt and laughing tone, delivering stanzas as if they were part of an elaborate joke. When asked why those choices were made, she responded, "I thought the poem was meant to be funny, so I read it to show how ludicrous the scene was." Had the student done some analytical "homework," she would have discovered that "Frost once said that he never chose this poem for a poetry reading because it was too horrible."[3] Based on a true account found in a newspaper article, Frost writes of a tragedy and the paradox of courage or indifference. Those who did not die must get on with life. No indication suggests that Frost intended the tone of the persona to be frivolous or humorous. This poem demands a serious, dramatic, sober persona to tell the tale.

More often, author's intent is not so clear. Some authors purposely do not reveal their reasons for creating a text. Research into an author's background may provide some clues, but the text itself always remains as a primary source for understanding persona. Suppose that Frost had not made any comment about this poem. Can you find clues in the text itself to justify a somber approach? What intra-textual language choices lead a performer to the poem's argumentative message?

The student who performed the Frost poem with a flippant and humorous approach was not "wrong" in her performance choice. But careful analysis could have given her some better "choices" for performance and that is the essence of any literary analysis. Many postmodern and deconstructionist theorists have downplayed the preeminence of a text's meaning, but the rhetorical/argumentative analytical approach chooses to give each text special attention. Wayne Booth, a rhetorical critic, reminds us that

> when you read three or four books by the same author, you start making inferences that go beyond the individual imaginative act. You can't resist and I don't think you should resist the temptation to start thinking about the qualities of the creature behind all that. I think that because of certain modern dogmas about ruling out the intentions of the author, we have needlessly ruled out some very interesting kinds of criticism by saying that's none of our business.[4]

At best, you as the performer will always be "interpreting" what the author intended and thus, you are performing with choices based on an "implied author" not the "real author."

As you analyze persona, you must also focus upon mental and emotional states. As you learned in chapter one, a performer needs to *match* a tone, an attitude, and a set of feelings with a persona to be consistent with the text's communicative message. If your text's persona seems nervous, your vocal choices will stutter as your nonverbal body language fidgets. If your text's persona is angry, the vocal intensity reveals this in conjunction with facial and physical expressions of rage. Ask yourself questions like: "How would I feel if this happened to me?" and "How do I want my audience to feel as I perform this persona?"

An additional part of persona analysis includes the discovery of point-of-view. Just as a camera lens reveals what a director or cinematographer wishes you to see in a film, so too does the message of a literary text reflect the scope and perspective of a point-of-view. Virtually all literary texts have one or more of these major persona viewpoints: *omniscient, partial omniscient, objective observer, primary participant, minor participant,* and *sympathetic observer.* It is difficult to generate performance options and understand nuances of a text's argument without a study of point-of-view.

The omniscient ("all-knowing") persona provides details of action and knows the thoughts of major characters. A partial omniscient persona shares a specific description of action, but only knows the thoughts of select characters. Objective observers remain aloof and distant; they cannot read minds and thus, only relate actions. From within a text itself, a primary participant describes scenes and activities, but can only share personal expressions of what he/she thinks, using "I" or "we." When a minor participant tells a story, narrated action happens to someone else primarily with occasional references to a minor persona's thoughts. The sympathetic observer has a relationship with the persona(e), but does not use first-person references or reveal thoughts.

While discovering the point-of-view in prose seems relatively easy, evaluating it in poetry or drama may be more of a challenge. Use internal clues from texts to reveal point-of-view.

If you have ever performed in a school play, you may have been required to write out a character analysis. Some rehearsal theater games expect you to extrapolate other actions and characteristics for a persona beyond that which the playwright suggests. The intent of this theater exercise is to provide you with a notion of dimensionality and motivation for a persona. You should not re-write your text to "flesh out" a persona, but study and a few expanded notions may provide you with empathetic understanding. During your own analytical preparation for oral interpretation, "play" a modified version of this persona game yourself.

Test yourself and your ability to recognize differing points-of-view. Re-read the selections sampled in this chapter and indicate the point-of-view. Once you discover this, how does it alter or impact the message of the text? Does intensity level vary if a first-person narrator relates the text? If a persona's thoughts are known, how are performance choices altered? Author Dean Koontz has a reputation for creating personae with terrorizing motivations. Use any series of analytical probes to evaluate performance choices for this persona, a serial killer named Preston Maddoc who has a secret life apart from his academic career as a professor of bioethics:

from *One Door Away From Heaven*

Dean Koontz

As always, Preston forthrightly acknowledged his faults. He made no claim to perfection. *No* human could honestly make such a claim.

In addition to his passion for homicide, he had over the years gradually become aware of a taste for cruelty. Killing mercifully—quickly and in a manner that caused little pain—had at first been immensely satisfying, but less so over time.

He took no pride in this character defect, but neither did it shame him. Like every person on the planet, he was what he was—and had to make the best of it.

All that mattered, however, was that he remained *useful* in a true and profound sense, that what he contributed to this troubled society continued to outweigh the resources he consumed to sustain himself. In the finest spirit of utilitarian ethics, he had put his faults to good use for humanity and had behaved responsibly.

He reserved his cruelty strictly for those who needed to die anyway, and tormented them only immediately before killing them.

Otherwise, he quite admirably controlled every impulse to be vicious. He treated all people—those he had not marked for death—with kindness, respect, and generosity.

In truth, more like him were needed: men—and women!—who acted within a code of ethics to rid an overpopulated world of the takers, of the worthless ones who, if left alive, would drag down not merely civilization with all their endless needs, but nature as well.

Audience Perceptions

Authors may allow their texts to communicate to a wide universe of listeners. Some texts suggest that a persona dialogues with only another individual or group. Still other texts have a persona utter thoughts to no one in particular or merely express inner thoughts in verbalized expression.

In the next chapter you will understand how the analytical decisions you make about different audiences affect where you place eye contact or gaze. Generally, if a persona seems to address or describe scenes with any listeners capable of hearing, then the performer's eye contact will be with the immediate audience for the performance. If two personae dialogue in textual performance, then eye gaze is placed in a non-audience locus, suggesting a limited audience. The most widespread use of this type of eye gaze is above the heads of audience members. If a persona delivers a soliloquy, utters private thoughts, or ventilates frustration or joy to no particular listener, the eye gaze is not precise and fails to have a clear contact point. More will be said about this eye gaze in chapter seven.

Textual Language Choices

As an oral interpreter, you will discover that language usage in a text requires close scrutiny before presentation. An author may write in a *formal* style, using compound/complex sentences, highly sophisticated vocabulary, and rigidly defined parameters of organization and structure. An author may write in an *informal* style, replete with jargon, colloquial expressions, contractions, and crisp short sentences. An author may write in a *casual* style, reflecting an oral quality that introduces familiar epithets, slang, perhaps even profanity and obscenity. An author may use a *freeform* style, a meandering stream-of-consciousness that expresses immediate reactions rather than forethought or structure. Or an author may blur all of these styles in a composite approach to expression.

With all of these possible language styles available in literature, a wide variety of performance choices appear. If a performer "sounds" formal and direct while reading a casual portion of the text, the incongruity may confuse the audience. Make performance choices based on the style of language so that the underlying message is always apparent.

Preliminary analysis can reveal words that are unknown, foreign, or clearly specialized to a subculture. Look up unknown words in a dictionary, paraphrasing them within a text's structure to assist you in a performance decision. Ask someone to help you speak the foreign words by phonetically writing out the syllables. Be sure you understand the definition and tone of these words. Guard against condescension in performing jargon or subcultural slang. Be as accurate as possible in suggesting persona attitude through language choices. If you are not careful you could insult an ethnic minority or cause laughter in an otherwise serious moment due to incorrect pronunciation.

Our language comprises a plethora of associations. Known as *literary allusions,* these referent illustrations assume certain knowledge. Literature may have non-"footnoted" references to stories from the Bible or Shakespeare, mythology, history, and popular culture (notably television, film, and recordings). The text will make no sense to an audience if it does not first create an understanding within you the performer. Re-read the selections of literature in this chapter again, noting allusion to literary and media concerns.

Each genre of literature (prose/drama/poetry) has unique and specialized analytical components. You will find a more detailed description of many of these, including figures of speech, sensory impressions, and rhythm, in later chapters.

Conclusion

Now you may be saying to yourself, "All this analysis seems like I'm dissecting a cat in biology. I have torn apart the literature and I can't possibly see how it all fits back together." To further the analogy, however, a performer cannot truly understand the interactions of structure, persona, audience, and textual language by observing the whole text ("cat"). You must "cut away," label, identify, contemplate, learn—the individual components of a whole. You do this so that as the parts are presented, the message of the whole is clear and consistent and dimensional. The parts "synergize" (our term from chapter one) to enhance the communicated meaning of a text.

Why is analysis necessary? It provides the performer of literature with critical choices useful in "persuading" us by means of a text. "It is the responsibility of the performer to make critical choices to determine the best way to communicate the message. The performance of the literature is the means by which the message is conveyed."[5] In interrelationships with text, performer, and audience a rhetorical situation can occur. Analysis ultimately insures that a performer will remain true to the integrity of a text. A text, thoroughly analyzed, focused, and studied, influences a performer to share important messages to all that will listen. According to John Creagh, "performers do more than embody the printed page; they allow the others in the text to inhabit their physical selves, making performance a rich synthesis of text and performer."[6]

References

Bowen, Elbert R., Aggertt, Otis, J. and Rickert, William E. *Communicative Reading. 4th Edition.* New York: Macmillan Publishing Company, 1978; reprint edition, Salem, WI: Sheffield Publishing Company, 1990.

Ecroyd, Donald H. and Wagner, Hilda Stahl. *Communicate Through Oral Reading.* New York: McGraw-Hill Book Company, 1979.

Pelias, Ronald J. *Performance Studies: The Interpretation of Aesthetic Texts.* New York: St. Martin's Press, 1992.

Sharpham, J.R., Matter, G.A. and Brockriede, W., "The Interpretive Experience As A Rhetorical Transaction," *Central States Speech Journal* 22 (1971), 143-150.

Valentine, K.B. and Valentine, D.E. *Interlocking Pieces: Twenty Questions For Understanding Literature 2nd Edition.* Dubuque, IA: Kendall/Hunt Publishing Company, 1980.

Notes

1. Judy E. Yordon, *Roles in Interpretation. 5th Edition.* Boston: McGraw Hill, 2002, 85.
2. S. John Macksoud, "Anyone's How Town: Interpretation As Rhetorical Discipline," *Speech Monographs* 35 (1968), 70-71.
3. David A. Sohn and Richard H. Tyre, *Frost: The Poet And His Poetry.* New York: Bantam Books, 1969, 65.
4. Mary Frances HopKins, "Interview with Wayne C. Booth," *Literature in Performance* 2 (April 1982), 49.
5. Liana B. Koeppel and Mark T. Morman, "Oral Interpretation Events and Argument: Forensic Discourse or Aesthetic Entertainment?" *National Forensic Journal,* 9, (Fall 1991), 146.
6. John Creagh, "The Interpersonal Metaphor in Literary Criticism: Towards An Attribution-Based Model of Literary Response," *The Carolinas Speech Communication Annual* 2 (1986), 22.

CHAPTER 7

Preparation for Oral Interpretation: Rehearsals and Performance

You have now analyzed your literary selection to the extent that you say, "I could pass a test on this material." You believe you are ready to face a classroom filled with an audience of your peers. But, truthfully, you are not quite ready to perform. You must practice, practice, practice, and practice a few more times. Re-reading a selection is not the practice you need. You must develop your skills by reading *aloud*. Find a private bathroom or force your roommate to be a captive audience. Stand up, fill your lungs with supportive air, and make believe that poster on your wall is an audience member enthralled with every word you utter.

You should not underestimate rehearsal times. A few gifted performers can "wing it" on occasion, but eventually the lack of preparation shows. The analytical choices you made fade into obscurity because you did not practice a means to share the choice. Audiences lose interest because they do not understand the meaning of the performed text or justifications for your reading options. Some interpreters rely on "techniques" that simulate understanding and analysis, but mere theatrics in performance seem forced and artificial. Some gifted performers can read tongue-twisting phrases rapidly and change character voices quickly, but such histrionics cannot sustain a performance. Audience members eventually catch on to the "showy nature" of the performance; techniques can never substitute for substance of text.

You must establish a rehearsal strategy before each performance. It needs systematically to establish criteria for cutting and editing a script and composing an introduction or transitions. The strategy determines script use, focus decisions, and sensory sensitivity. A reasonable rehearsal strategy anticipates responses to audience feedback. Finally, a planned strategy for rehearsal leads to a strong initial impression and a meaningful performance.

Cutting and Editing

You will need to learn how to delete words, phrases, sentences, paragraphs, perhaps even scenes or pages, to bring your performance within a determined time limit. Cutting a script may seem tedious; it may create frustration as you attempt to preserve the primary idea and argument. Prose and drama selections require cutting more often than poetry. To edit a stanza or series of words in a poem may upset the rhythm or the imagery. Whenever possible, perform a poem in its entirety.

To solve the problem of "what to cut," ask yourself, "Do I want to perform the climactic ending or do I reveal scattered portions of the entire text?" If you choose the former approach, you locate the crisis, read through the climax, and end with the denouement. If you choose the latter approach, you will need to highlight early, middle, and final scenes; you will cut out exposition, digressions, and settle for "bare bones" samples. Read and re-read a selection before you begin the editing process.

Cutting a script is no license to rewrite an author's work. It is unethical and a violation of copyright to perform a text that has major paragraphs or dialogue lines paraphrased or given to the personae to speak. It is unethical to alter significantly a text's ending if the new ending changes the tone and the outcome. What is considered unethical and what editing helps in transitions? A general guideline in cutting or editing is: *Add few words or lines to provide transitions, and always maintain the integrity of the tone, intent, and viewpoint of the text.*

To illustrate, each scene in Michael Cristofer's play *The Shadow Box* reveals families, loved ones, and friends coping with terminally ill people. A disembodied voice, portraying the psychiatrist, speaks in some scenes. To cut the psychiatrist's commentary and re-assign it to another persona is tantamount to rewriting the play. The psychiatrist has a tone of sympathy; certain other personae do not. To redivide lines in such a manner alters the playwright's intent, as well as the integrity of the text itself, and should be avoided. However some few additions in a scene between two women eliminate a third, brief unnecessary persona. Consider the original segment and the edited version following:

from *The Importance of Being Earnest*
Oscar Wilde

Cecily: It would distress me more than I can tell you, dear Gwendolen, if it caused you any mental or physical anguish, but I feel bound to point out that since Ernest proposed to you he clearly has changed his mind.

Gwendolen: If the poor fellow has been entrapped into any foolish promise I shall consider it my duty to rescue him at once, and with a firm hand.

Cecily: Whatever unfortunate entanglement my dear boy may have got into, I will never reproach him with it after we are married.

Gwendolen: Do you allude to me, Miss Cardew, as an entanglement? You are presumptuous. On an occasion of this kind it becomes more than a moral duty to speak one's mind. It becomes a pleasure.

Cecily: Do you suggest, Miss Fairfax, that I entrapped Ernest into an engagement? How dare you? This is no time for wearing the shallow mask of manners. When I see a spade I call it a spade.

Gwendolen: I am glad to say that I have never seen a spade. It is obvious that our social spheres have been widely different.

Merriman (the butler): Shall I lay tea here as usual, Miss?

Cecily: Yes as usual. (Merriman begins to clear table and lay cloth. A long pause. Cecily and Gwendolen glare at each other.)

(Edited Version)

Gwendolen: I am glad to say that I have never seen a spade. It is obvious that our social spheres have been widely different.

Cecily: [Ah, Merriman, you may serve tea as usual.]

The added words acknowledge the presence of the butler, maintaining author's intent, but they guard against confusion by maintaining the two primary personae. Other examples of this type of editing include responding to a telephone ring ("The telephone. I'll get it."), summarizing plot developments ("After Bob left, we argued well into the night."), and combining same-persona dialogue lines separated by paragraphs ("I don't care what you think . . . Get out of my house!").

Some further suggestions for cutting may help:

1. In prose, once you have established who the personae are vocally, physically and in character location, you may cut out *tag lines,* the "he said/she said" commentaries. Do not forget to read dialogue lines with the intent indicated by the tag line, however.
2. Passages that provide exposition or details may be excised. Whatever you cut may need explanation in the introduction or transitions.
3. Cut out stage directions in plays, but remember to perform lines with clues provided by the directions within parentheses.
4. Characters who only make brief appearances may be cut and brief references made to them with added lines for transition.
5. Unnecessary subplots or diversions may be cut.
6. Elaborate descriptions can be cut back, reading only that which is essential to establish the setting.

Many examples of literature have profanity and obscenity. These words may be gratuitous and potentially alienate the audience. At the same time, such language may be essential to the essence of the persona and a factor in the emotional or mental state of a scene. Should you edit profanity and obscenity for performance . . . or not edit such language at all?

Some audiences do not want to hear such language, but they need to "hear" the subtext the language suggests. Practice a line with and without the offensive language. Decide if the profanity or obscenity is essential. Make your decision on the basis of sensitivity to the audience and commitment to the integrity of the text. In some texts such use of language must be maintained. Perhaps in other cases the tone can be preserved without excessive use of offending words. Since movies and plays have increased the use of obscene words, some performers may be tempted to enhance a reading with additional profanities. Do not add gratuitous offensive language if the author did not originally include it.

You should not use euphemisms in the place of "dirty words." This apparent substitution draws too much attention to a censorious alteration. "Son of a . . . gun," "go to heck," and "full of . . . crud" turns a serious literary text into a parody. Saying no obscene words at all as a description is preferable to euphemisms if they are deemed necessary.

Editing and cutting should be clear and easy to follow. Editing a larger work to tell an entire story in a few brief moments may do more harm than good. Do not reduce a large text to mere plot lines, devoid of character or tension. Find a method to keep a text focused and tightly structured.

Writing the Introduction

In chapter one you discovered the features of introductions and transitions. Once you have reviewed and noted the essential details, you need to compose a statement with these preliminary remarks.

Some performers prefer to write out an outline of essential background information. They speak the introduction with manuscript closed, forming the sentences in an extemporized fashion. This approach has the advantage of conversationality and naturalness in delivery.

Other performers feel a need to write out the introductions and transitions so they can memorize them. This approach has precision and specific timing to lines, but may sound too rehearsed. You should not attach a formally written introduction to the outside of your script holder and read it; an introduction needs to appear spontaneous and direct, even if it has been specifically composed in written form.

The text you choose to perform has a specific inherent message, but introductions, teasers, and transitions help you and the audience to understand the message. Such composed statements should not be lengthy. Introductions need last only a small fraction of the total performance time. Offer to your audience only that which whets the appetite for what is to come.

Performing with a Script

A three-ring binder notebook can serve a multitude of purposes, not just as a receptacle for a typed rendition of the text. In truth, many performers eventually memorize their scripts and apparently the script seems an encumbrance. The presence of a script symbolically reminds an audience that a text is the focus, not necessarily the performer. A notebook can be transformed into a creative device useful in generating imaginative responses. A script becomes prop when performers use it as a steering wheel, letter, "baby being cradled," or any other suggested object or action.

For the beginning interpreter, the notebook can become a crutch to lean on. In cases of lack of preparation leading to loss of place, looking at the notebook may be awkward and an audience soon realizes the loss of concentration and place. You may or may not be asked to memorize your presentations. The performance of literature remains artistic expression whether you use a script or not. The old maxim that argued that looking at a script made performance oral interpretation and looking up made performance acting is irrelevant. But if you use a notebook some helpful guidelines should be followed:

1. Keep the script up high enough to allow your eyes to lower to pick up the lines without bobbing your head up and down;
2. Do not allow the script to creep up so high that it blocks any portion of your face;
3. Hold the script in the same approximate position; raising and lowering the script without motivation is distracting;
4. Pick up the next line or phrase ahead of where you are reading to maintain longer intervals of eye gaze;
5. Even if the text is memorized, when a script is present pages should be turned;
6. A script present needs to be a script that serves as a referent point; occasionally look down at the pages to suggest the "use" and "presence" of the text.

Some conventional practitioners of oral interpretation suggest highlighting script lines in different colors as personae change. Notations in margins remind you of performance choices you wish to make. Certain people prefer to integrate slash marks ("/") into phrases to assist them in pausing. None of these conventions are necessities, but if they help you, feel free to use them.

Still, the beginning performer may be tied to a notebook script. How much of the time should a performer be looking up away from the notebook? Ideally, a 60/40 ratio communicates most effectively. What this means is that a little more than half the time (60% or more) the performer needs to be looking at an audience member or other location.

How do you reach this goal of eye gaze and presentational format? You practice aloud segments until your eyes remember where a textual line appears on the page. For practical help, you should not merely photocopy the text and paste it on notebook pages. Double-spaced and typed texts are easier to read than textual type. Reduce the number of page turns by putting the text on the front and back of notebook pages. If a larger binder is awkward to hold or cradle in one hand, consider using a smaller binder notebook (e.g., 5" X 7" three-ring binder).

Some performing areas have lecterns available to hold your script. This has the advantage of freeing both hands for gesturing. A disadvantage to using a lectern is that it hides portions of your body useful in suggesting nonverbal tensions. A lectern should normally be avoided, but when it is used feel free to step side to side on occasion to allow audience members a full view of your body.

Choosing Focus

Once you have analyzed your text and decided who the audience is for each portion, you must decide where you will place characters and scene action. Another way of understanding this is to say, "Where will my eye gaze be when I am reading each portion of my text?" Eye gaze tells the listeners how to imagine or understand the text's target audience. *Focus* is the term used to describe the location of characters and scene in a text.

Focus occurs in performance in four distinct ways: *audience focus, offstage focus, onstage focus, and inner-expressed focus.* Audience focus consists of direct eye contact between performer and listeners. It is usually the focus of choice for narrative literature (prose), and occasionally drama (when a performer acknowledges the audience as onlookers) and poetry (when the persona addresses a universal audience). Offstage focus suggests that another persona in a text is present or in dialogue. Eye gaze may "imagine" a focal point slightly above the heads of the audience or in a nondescript portion of the audience, "suggesting" the existence of other personae. Dialogue portions in prose, poetry, or drama require offstage focus. Offstage focus may also be used to point out scene components, inanimate objects, and progress when coupled with a narrative portion of audience focus. Onstage focus is the focus of most proscenium drama. Performers deliver lines directly to another performer adjacent to them. Oral interpretation performances involving duos or multiple person casts use onstage focus to highlight intimate scenes or establish camaraderie in shared introductions. Inner-expressed focus is the focus of the soliloquy, the focus of the outward expression of thoughts. Performers with inner-expressed focus address no particular audience; they express their inner thoughts by looking out, up, to the side, and to nowhere in particular.

Beginning performers usually have a difficult time with all non-audience focal points. Eye gaze in offstage areas looks to the audience like "eye glaze." You cannot appear to be looking at nothing in particular if you are using offstage focus. You must imagine that you "see" the persona or object. You may squint, or avert eye gaze, or any number of other eye behaviors to suggest "seeing." Avoid staring at one offstage focal point for long periods of time. (No one stares at another person constantly without creating uncomfortable relationships.) Once you have established an offstage focal point, let your eyes wander occasionally, returning to that focal point often to convey dialogue.

Angles of focus provide interpreters with the ability to place multiple characters within a scene. Remember to keep each persona in the same locus, though. A solo performance involving interaction in dialogue should place personae in distinct angled locations. Each time a persona speaks, the performer should shift the head to the new placement area. Make these angles of focus distinct, but not so sharp that you must turn your head to profile. Your face is so important that an audience needs to see reactions or at least a three-quarters' view always. Angles of focus may also be on a vertical plane. A young person looks up at an older person and so too should personae in a text. Some texts address God and a performance choice may include an angle of focus that is upward or at least outward.

In small group performances, angles of focus may suggest an intersection, somewhere in the realm of the audience:

Figure 7.1 In small group performances, angles of focus may suggest an intersection, somewhere in the realm of the audience.

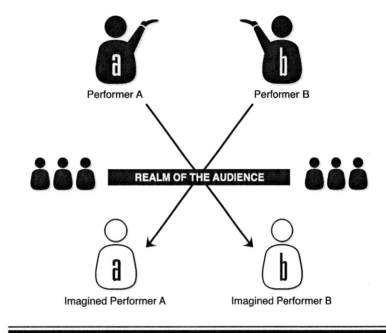

Group performances also use a "wedge," wherein each performer "sees" the other in the apex of the angle offstage:

Figure 7.2 Group performances also use a "wedge," wherein each performer "sees" the other in the apex of the angle offstage.

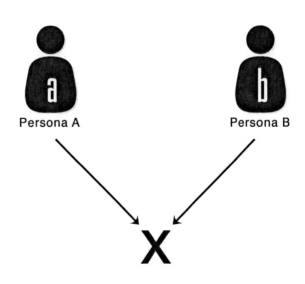

Offstage focus may seem very strange at first, but it has its advantages. The imagined inter-action occurs with full view of the face, and the ramifications of such a focus heighten imagina-tion. If you are "seeing" a persona offstage, you will mime action toward the focal point and receive completed action from out in the realm of the audience back in toward yourself. Imagine the fun of staging an "offstage" fight wherein you punch an opponent out toward the audience and recoil in a timed response. A "kiss" that never touches literally can be suggested and received. (Some audiences do so well at this form of "creating the scene" that they need "cold showers" at once.)

All the actions and location scenes are illusions. They exist only to the extent performers are able to create *psychological closure.* Such closure occurs when a suggested action or substance has a consistency and a completion. If you have a text with a persona who answers and speaks on a telephone, the imagined telephone is picked up, maybe handed to another, or rested on a shoul-der (while you turn a page, for example). The completed action might include a miming action of hanging the phone up on a receiver. If someone "hands" you a drink offstage, you must "receive" it in the completed action. Such closure is destroyed if inconsistent focal use happens. Two personae, dialoguing in offstage focal points, would not "hand" the other a "drink" by touching each other onstage. In much the same way, two performers in dialogue would not sneak glances at each other onstage if the persona clearly responded to the other offstage. Inconsistent focus hurts the illusion of psychological closure.

Mixed focus is not to be confused with inconsistent focus. Some dramatic texts create a per-sona that dialogues with the characters as well as with the watching audience. In Neil Simon's play, *Brighton Beach Memoirs,* the main character, Eugene Jerome, is the only character who talks with direct audience focus and onstage focus. Such a person's eye gaze varies in focal points (mixed focus), but is consistent in how and when each focal point is introduced. A Readers Theatre production with an omniscient narrator may consistently integrate audience focus, onstage focus, and offstage focus. The text of Thornton Wilder's play, *Our Town,* best illustrates this. The primary narrator is omniscient, but occasionally becomes an onstage persona as well.

Remember that choosing and maintaining focus points are not arbitrary. Inconsistency in focus confuses an audience. Rehearse and practice eye gaze so that an audience imagines a scene merely by the power of suggestion and placement.

Sensory Sensitivity

The performer of literature theoretically has spent much time in analysis and preparation for a presentation. A performer must understand the text to a greater extent than a listening audi-ence and does all to recreate the imagery and sensations of a text. Frequently the immediate audi-ence has no text to follow; the text must come alive by means of the oral and physical skills of the interpreter.

A performer brings vitality to a text when sensitivity to imagery and sensory details happen. In literary texts you will discover eight primary sensory details: *auditory, visual, kinetic, kines-thetic, tactile, gustatory, olfactory,* and *thermal.* Auditory imagery emphasizes hearing and the evocative power of sound. Visual descriptions appeal to our ability to see and discern. Kinetic details describe physical action, while kinesthetic imagery suggests the physical action or anxiety levels we sense within our bodies. Tactile data expresses sensations of touching behaviors. Gustatory imagery discloses associations we have with tasting enjoyment as well as repulsion. Olfactory impressions remind us of a variety of smells. Thermal descriptions bring to mind our body reactions to a range of temperatures.

What forms of sensory details can you discover in the following selection?:

from "The City"
Ray Bradbury

"Fire odor, the scent of a fallen meteor, hot metal. A ship has come from another world. The brass smell, the dusty fire smell of burned powder, sulphur, and rocket brimstone.". . .

The great city nostrils dilated again.

The smell of butter. In the city air, from the stalking men, faintly, the aura which wafted to the great Nose broke down into memories of milk, cheese, ice cream, butter, the effluvium of a dairy economy.

Click—click.

"Careful, men!"

"Jones, get your gun out. Don't be a fool!"

"The city's dead; why worry?"

"You can't tell."

Now at the barking talk, the Ears awoke. After centuries of listening to winds that blew small and faint, of hearing leaves trip from trees and grass grow softly in the time of melting snows, now the Ears oiled themselves in a self-lubrication, drew taut, great drums upon which the heartbeat of the invaders might pummel and thud delicately as the tremor of a gnat's wing. The Ears listened and the Nose siphoned up great chambers of odor.

Can you imagine what smells are being described here? What can you actually hear? What does the "tremor of a gnat's wing" sound like to you? How do you feel? The personal associations you have experienced or understood match with an author's sensory sensitivity and the result is a new vicarious experience for the audience. This experience seems to implant the performed text in the arena of the mind. Our minds allow us to encounter hundreds of locales, sensations, feelings, and ultimately new messages.

Audience Feedback

The effective public speaker, sensing a bored or distracted audience, will adapt to such negative responses by consciously altering the speech to induce interest. The speaker may deviate from a pre-planned text to tell a joke or change tactics. The performer of literature must adapt to audience feedback in a different manner.

You cannot cease a performance to tell a joke; to alter the text for the sake of wooing an audience violates the author's copyright. So what can you do as a performer? Perhaps you moved into a predictable vocal pattern that lulls the audience. Change it and consciously expand the pitch range. Your tempo may be too slow and plodding. Vary delivery speeds in a range from rapid tempos to methodical rates of delivery. Use physical actions (hand, body, and facial reactions) to enliven your presentation. Maybe the audience would regain interest if you moved closer to them; maybe you have violated their sense of space and need to back away. If the performing arena requires amplification, you may need to speak more directly into the microphone or increase volume if the amplification system is not present.

If your text has humorous moments, you may have to adjust your delivery patterns. Practicing aloud by yourself cannot prepare you for the audience that laughs at a punch line or humorous description. You must learn to "hold for laughs," waiting a split moment longer before you speak the next line. You may have to repeat a line again after a comic moment if the audience laughs long and heartily, covering up your line. If you do not hold, eventually the audience stifles their response and an opportunity for an empathic relationship is lost.

Performing for an audience is an exhilarating experience. Professional and amateur performers love the relational feeling that emerges in a performance. Euphemistically called "good vibes," this unexplainable feeling of oneness with an audience does not always occur with every audience. It certainly is a goal for which every performer strives. Every audience deserves your best efforts in performance, even if every audience responds differently.

Making a Strong Initial Impression

The day for your performance arrives. You are understandably a little nervous and that is quite natural. All of your nervous energy can be channeled into your physical and vocal choices. You analyzed your text and now you are prepared to walk to the front of the classroom and begin.

The audience watches you from the moment you leave your seat until the time you return to your place. Make a strong initial impression by remembering to:

1. Be well-groomed in clothing and appearance. If your hair is longer, make sure it is pulled back to reveal much of your face, your most important asset in performing literature. Dress appropriately, not too casual or too formal;
2. Although baseball hats and large floppy hats may be your own personal fashion statement, they tend to cover up your face as well. Take hats off and leave them at your seat when performing;

3. Walk confidently, but not in a cocky manner, up to the front of the classroom. Attempt to stand so that half of the audience is on each side of you. Do not stand too close or too far away from the first row of listeners;

4, Distribute your body weight evenly on both feet. Avoid standing cross-legged or leaning on an adjacent table or lectern;

5. Check that your text is right side up. It is embarrassing to create a good impression only to open the binder and have to turn it right side up to read it;

6. Wait for the audience to give you their attention before you begin;

7. Pause at the end of your presentation, letting the last thought linger. Do not rush off-stage; it tells the audience you cannot wait to sit down. (Even if you feel that way, you do not want the audience to know. As a well-known television commercial implored, "Never let them see you sweat!").

Your preparation skills are now ready for action. Each of the subsequent chapters will focus on genres of literature and format options. You will discover that performance skills adapt as genres and formats differ. Enjoy each moment as you explore the communicative world of ideas awaiting you in the performance of literature.

Assignments

1.   Discuss with your professor the limits of cutting or editing performance texts because of copyright laws. Do some authors require that their material be performed uncut, without any alteration? (In the preface to his plays, playwright Neil Simon requires unaltered performances.) Should profanity or obscenity remain intact in all performance texts? Where should ethics be a consideration in editing a script for performance?

2.   Begin to look for literature to perform for your first graded assignment. Review the criteria for evaluation found on the critique sheets at the end of this text. Choose a selection you like and understand; choose a selection easily understood in a single hearing by an audience. Practice, practice, practice!!!

References

Bowen, Elbert R., Aggertt, Otis J., and Rickert, William E. *Communicative Reading. 4th Edition.* New York: Macmillan Publishing Company, 1978; reprint edition, Salem, WI: Sheffield Publishing Company, 1990.

Buck, Steven M. *A Guidebook To Oral Interpretation.* Dubuque, IA: Kendall/Hunt Publishing Company, 1985.

Gamble, Teri and Gamble, Michael. *Literature Alive! 2nd Edition.* Lincolnwood, IL: National Textbook Company, 1994.

Gottlieb, Marvin R. *Oral Interpretation.* New York: McGraw-Hill Book Company, 1980.

Gray, Paul H. and VanOosting, James. *Performance in Life and Literature.* Boston: Allyn and Bacon, 1996.

Lee, Charlotte and Gura, Timothy. *Oral Interpretation—10th Edition.* Boston: Houghton Mifflin Company, 2001.

Long, Beverly W. and HopKins, Mary Frances. *Performing Literature: An Introduction to Oral Interpretation.* Englewood Cliffs, NJ: Prentice-Hall, Inc., 1982.

Sessions, Virgil D. and Holland, Jack B. *Your Role In Oral Interpretation. 2nd Edition.* Boston: Holbrook Press, Inc., 1975.

Yordon, Judy E. *Roles In Interpretation—5th Edition.* Boston: McGraw Hill, 2002.

CHAPTER **8**

Oral Interpretation of Prose

"**W**ell, if it doesn't rhyme and it consists of more than dialogue lines, it must be prose." All too often that is the best definition one can give of what prose literature is. As you will discover, drama and poetry have such specific forms that prose frequently appears to be the only remaining category. Prose is the ordinary composition of spoken or written expression. Prose differs from poetry primarily in form; prose consists of sentences, paragraphs, chapters, and sections. Poetry is normally brief, consisting of lines and stanzas. Prose may consist of descriptive or expositional writing to establish a context; drama communicates these elements in the commentary of character dialogue or proscenium scene directions and spectacle.

Performing prose material is generally easier than poetry or drama. Why? The length and style of prosaic expression are most like our normal speech patterns. Authors have the capacity to create imagery without the restrictions of abbreviated form or dependence on dialogue. The beginning performer needs to experience the power of sharing sensory impressions in an expanded form such as prose before tackling the more complex performance tasks found in communicating drama and poetry.

Categories of Prose

Prose consists of numerous categories of fictional and nonfictional writing. Short stories, novels, fables, and tales exemplify fictional attempts to share ideas, morals, and even persuasive messages. Most people think these fictional types constitute the bulk of prose literature. The performer of literature should realize that prose literature includes numerous nonfiction groupings as well.

Great speeches, transcribed from oral tradition or presentation, become a literary form worthy of renewed performance:

from "First Inaugural Address (1861)"
President Abraham Lincoln

In your hands, my dissatisfied fellow-countrymen, and not in mine, is the momentous issue of civil war. The government will not assail you. You can have no conflict without being yourselves the aggressors. You have no oath registered in heaven to destroy the government while I shall have the most solemn one to "preserve, protect, and defend."

I am loathe to close. We are not enemies, but friends. We must not be enemies. Though passion may have strained, it must not break our bonds of affection. The mystic chords of memory, stretching from every battle-field and patriot grave to every living heart and hearthstone all over this broad land, will yet swell the chorus of the Union, when again touched, as surely they will be, by the better angels of our nature.

Letters provide an unexpected delight as a prose form. They are personal, communicative, confrontational, intimate, and emotional. Some letters, like Martin Luther King, Jr.'s "Letter From The Birmingham Jail," are in the form of rhetorical pamphlets, rallying followers to a social movement. Other letters are intimate, romantic dialogues as seen in the correspondence between nineteenth-century poets Robert and Elizabeth Barrett Browning. And some letters reveal the inner thoughts, anger, and resolve of the writer:

from "A Letter To Robert Dudley, Earl Of Leicester"
Queen Elizabeth I (February 10, 1586)

How contemptuously we conceive ourself to have been used by you, you shall by this bearer understand, whom we have expressly sent unto you to charge you withal. We could never have imagined had we not seen it fall out in experience that a man raised up by ourself and extraordinarily favoured by us above any other subject of this land, would have in so contemptible a sort broken our commandment, in a cause that so greatly toucheth us in honour; whereof, although you have showed yourself to make but little accompt, in most undutiful a sort, you may not therefore think that we have so little care of the reparation thereof as we mind to pass so great a wrong in silence unredressed: and, therefore, our express pleasure and commandment is, that all delays and excuses laid apart, you do presently upon the duty of your allegiance, obey and fulfil whatsoever the bearer hereof shall direct you to do in our name: whereof fail you not, as you will answer to the contrary at your uttermost peril.

Fables frequently emphasize values and morals, though couched in language that sometimes appears juvenile and childlike. Far from being mere "kid's stories," some fables reveal anthropomorphic dialogue with a definite "adult" orientation:

"The Peacelike Mongoose" from *Further Fables for Our Time*
James Thurber

In cobra country a mongoose was born one day who didn't want to fight cobras or anything else. The word spread from mongoose to mongoose that there was a mongoose who didn't want to fight cobras. If he didn't want to fight anything else, it was his own business, but it was the duty of every mongoose to kill cobras or be killed by cobras.

"Why?" asked the peacelike mongoose, and the word went around that the strange new mongoose was not only pro-cobra and anti-mongoose but intellectually curious and against the ideals and traditions of mongoosism.

"He is crazy," cried the young mongoose's father.

"He is sick," said his mother.

"He is a coward," shouted his brothers.

"He is a mongoosexual," whispered his sisters.

Strangers who had never laid eyes on the peacelike mongoose remembered that they had seen him crawling on his stomach, or trying on cobra hoods, or plotting the violent overthrow of Mongoosia.

"I am trying to use reason and intelligence," said the strange new mongoose.

"Reason is six-sevenths of treason," said one of his neighbors.

"Intelligence is what the enemy uses," said another.

Finally, the rumor spread that the mongoose had venom in his sting, like a cobra, and he was tried, convicted by a show of paws, and condemned to banishment.

MORAL: Ashes to ashes, and clay to clay, if the enemy doesn't get you your own folks may.

You should not neglect the wealth of expressions found in essays, newspaper and magazine editorials, diaries, journals, histories, and documentaries. Tom Brokaw, news anchor for NBC, wrote in his best-selling book, *The Greatest Generation,* that the impetus for the book came from work on a televised documentary of the D-Day invasion in 1984. What Brokaw collected in his 1998 written "documentary" and "ethnographic study" is a testament to the heroes of the Second World War and an outlet in print for their stories.[1] Such "documentary-like" prose constitutes a goldmine of possible performance material. A performer could explore public prayers that have been occasionally published as have sermons. These and other prose forms constitute a wide and varied genre for you to study and perform. The following editorial in the *Los Angeles Times* could be a portion of a program on the problem with professional sports:

"Swing at a Bigger Problem"

Baseball forever will be watching out for things like corked bats, but the sport's caretakers should worry more about the win-at-all costs message delivered to scholastic and collegiate athletes by pro sluggers whose chiseled physiques and impressive stamina come from a bottle rather than the weight room. The sport could do more to restore its increasingly tarnished image by immediately banning the supplement ephedra—already illegal for athletes competing in the Olympics, the National Football League and the National Collegiate Athletic Association—and by doing even more to crack down on steroid abuse.

A veteran like Sammy Sosa knows better than to tee off on a ball outside the zone. The X-rays of Sosa's bats and the investigation into the apologetic slugger will fuel endless radio-talk show chatter. But if baseball wants to swing away, why not take aim at something that's killing the sport?

Component Features of Prose

All the aforementioned categories of prose have characteristics that affect performance choices. These features include: *point-of-view, tone, mood, tag lines and dialogue,* and *rhythm.*

You learned the importance of analyzing point-of-view in chapter six. The six viewpoints (omniscient, partial omniscient, objective observer, primary participant, minor participant, and sympathetic observer) translate into first- or third-person perspectives in prose literature. First-

---

[Excerpt from the Editorial Page, *Los Angeles Times* (June 6, 2003): B16.]

person perspectives use personal pronouns such as "I" or "we" to describe action, events, and conflict. First-person approaches occur more frequently in prose; it is the point-of-view for speeches, letters, diaries, and editorials. Many students choose a first-person literary selection because they feel the task of matching emotions and sensitivity is easier with a first-person narrative.

In the following first-person essay notice how much is revealed about a persona by merely allowing him to tell us about his personal belief system:

from *A Prayer for Owen Meany*
John Irving

I am doomed to remember a boy with a wrecked voice—not because of his voice, or because he was the smallest person I ever knew, or even because he was the instrument of my mother's death, but because he is the reason I believe in God; I am a Christian because of Owen Meany. I make no claims to have a life in Christ, or with Christ—and certainly not for Christ, which I've heard some zealots claim. I'm not very sophisticated in my knowledge of the Old Testament, and I've not read the New Testament since my Sunday school days, except for those passages that I hear read aloud to me when I go to church. . .

In Sunday school, we developed a form of entertainment based on abusing Owen Meany, who was so small that not only did his feet not touch the floor when he sat in his chair—his knees did not extend to the edge of his seat. . . Owen was so tiny, we loved to pick him up; in truth, we couldn't resist picking him up. We thought it was a miracle; how little he weighed.

Third-person approaches to a literary text emphasize the point-of-view that exists outside and apart from the primary action. Third-person narrators may be omniscient or not, relaying the action of the text through third-person pronouns such as "he, she, and they." Short stories, novels, or essays with third-person observers have the characteristics of a report. A third-person narrator reveals the story as it unfolds; a third-person narrator can be objective or subjective, but the perspective remains independent of the story line. Great prose selections, written in third-person style, abound for the performer of literature. The performer must work harder to match descriptive scenes with character interaction in these texts, however.

Analyze the objective and subjective "report" style format in this prose narrative:

"Two Monks"

Irmgard Schloegl/The Wisdom of Zen Masters

Two monks on a pilgrimage came to the ford of a river. There they saw a girl dressed in all her finery, obviously not knowing what to do since the river was high and she did not want to spoil her clothes. Without more ado, one of the monks took her on his back, carried her across and put her down on dry ground on the other side.

Then the monks continued on their way. But the other monk after an hour started complaining, "Surely it is not right to touch a woman; it is against the commandments to have close contact with women. How could you go against the rules of monks?"

The monk who had carried the girl walked along silently, but finally he remarked, "I set her down by the river an hour ago, why are you still carrying her?"

In both of the previous prose selections as well as all literary texts, *tone* is present; tone is the inherent attitude of a text or author. Tone includes qualities that suggest a text is serious, spirited, poignant, tragic, pedantic, sympathetic, or many other possibilities. What is the tone in *A Prayer For Owen Meany?* What is the tone in "Two Monks"? How do you know the tone is different? What alterations in performance do you make to project this tone to an audience?

Go back and re-read the letter written by Queen Elizabeth I. The tone she had in writing that letter is inherent in the text itself. She refers to herself in the plural, because she and the Throne of England are inseparable. Her indignant tone evolves into a tone of power and dominance. The performer must match that tone to be true to the text itself.

A related aspect found in prose literature is *mood.* You can sense an author's emotional mental state or the feeling of a text when you read or perform literature. Mood is the atmosphere created by the voices in a text. It pervades the narration, the events as they unfold, and the context of the selection.

What words best describe the mood in this selection from a novel? A devout Irish Catholic mother seeks out the parish priest to confess her "sin":

["Two Monks" by Irmgard Schloegl/The Wisdom of Zen Masters. Excerpted from Jack Canfield and Mark Victor Hansen, *Chicken Soup for the Soul.* Copyright © 1993 by Jack Canfield and Mark Victor Hansen. Published by Health Communications, Inc., Deerfield Beach, FL.]

from Part Three—The Booley House—Chapter Three
Trinity
Leon Uris

Having come to the most awesome decision of her life, Finola was determined to steel herself to go through with it, take all the necessary humiliation, for in her own eyes her sins were enormous. . . .

She twisted her fine linen handkerchief nervously and struggled to keep her composure. "I've a lot on my conscience, Father. What I am about to tell you should have been confessed many times over the years."

Father Lynch grimmed up and braced.

"Father," she whispered, lowering her eyes and voice weakening with shame, "I have been the wife of Tomas Larkin almost twenty years and I have sinned all during the marriage." She squirmed, then blurted out, "I have always enjoyed pleasures of the flesh."

The priest shot to his feet, clasped his hands behind him and thrust his face heavenward. "I see," he sighed. "Would you kindly amplify that remark?"

"I've almost always enjoyed the sexual act," she whispered.

"That's quite unnatural, you know."

"I know."

"Exactly what is it you enjoy?"

"Everything," she whimpered.

Father Lynch pulled his chair up close and poked his face next to hers. "What you have told me is extremely serious. If I am to counsel you properly you must purge yourself here and now. Are you ready?"

"Aye. . . I am ready."

"Look at me, Finola." She did so out of the corners of her eyes and blushed with guilt. "We must go over this, item by item," he commanded.

It was degrading but if the gates of heaven were ever to open to her it had to be done. She confessed to one hedonistic pleasure after another, building a mountain of debauchery and mortal sins the likes of which he had never heard in his thirty-five years as an agent of God. . . .When Finola had drained herself, she sobbed. Father Lynch was ashen.

"These are unnatural acts under the influence of Satan!"

She wailed, he paced.

"I knew something might be wrong, Father, but so long as our purpose was to try to make babies and I couldn't help myself for enjoying it, I thought it really wasn't actual pleasure I was feeling but some kind of holy experience about the possibility of becoming pregnant."

"It's a curse," he said. "I know of many other women who have had these same carnal sensations but nothing as profane as you have spoken about." . . . .

"Oh, Father, help me," she cried, falling to her knees.

He hovered above his victim, then pointed a bony finger. . . . "The reason you have these unnatural and evil desires is because of your neglect of mother church. Instead of yielding to temptation, you should have been confessing for years. You should have fortified your soul and you should fill yourself with the pain, the goodness and the mercy of Jesus and Mary. You have offended, God, grievously."

Finola Larkin howled.

"You are fortunate, woman, in that your Church is all-forgiving. Are you ready to submit to the supernatural redemptive powers of God?"

"I'll do anything!"

She remained on her knees as he considered the alternative. "Your case is extreme. I must meditate for guidance. In due course I will work out a course of penance through prayer and offerings to the Church. When I do, do you swear to adhere to it faithfully?"

"Yes, Father, yes."

"Through this devotion, you will eventually find the strength to continue to live with Tomas in the only way possible. . . as brother and sister. You are never again to submit to him for sexual ravagement, for that sin would be final. Well, I'm waiting for your answer . . . it's that or hell!"

The performer who chooses such a text as this must create a mood indicative of the relationship between nineteenth-century Irish Catholic peasants and the Church hierarchy. In this piece the pervasive mood of guilt and penance overwhelms the woman and she submits to the admonitions of an unfeeling and insensitive priest.

How does such a text make you feel as a performer? If it angers you, you must channel that emotion by letting the tone and mood of the text elicit sympathy from a contemporary audience, appalled that a religious leader would condemn sexual pleasure between a married couple. The scene itself seems so melodramatic at times that to a modern sophisticated audience a possible reaction might be laughter. Stay true to the subtleties and power of the selection and let the audience sense the atmosphere and attitude inherent in the piece. No one will laugh if the tone is intentionally serious and the performance matches that emotional state.

Tag Lines and Dialogue

Tag lines, the "he said/she said" descriptions, provide performers with clues for sensory projection. Many tag lines may be cut once a persona's voice and demeanor are established. Once tag lines are cut dialogue lines gain a continuity that seems smooth and natural. Dialogue is conversation between personae. Each persona is unique in dialogue, and requires a definitive voice and clear focal point. To establish this difference, use varying vocal and nonverbal skills. You should remember to strive to keep dialogue lines credible, smooth, and focused. As a rule, try to avoid looking down at a script text in between interactive dialogues. Pause, then respond as the other persona before glancing down to pick up the next cue. This performance strategy prevents confusion and assists the audience in following the dialogue portions.

A general guideline to use in including tag lines in prose is: Keep tag lines intact long enough to let the audience know who is speaking. Leave tag lines in if they enhance the inherent rhythm of the prose selection.

Rhythm

Rhythm in poetry is more obvious and discernible, but the rhythm of prose creates power and understanding of a text as well. Prose rhythm frequently has an irregular, non-predictable pattern. However, certain linguistic devices create prose rhythm.

Repetition is key to the rhythm intrinsic in performing Martin Luther King, Jr.'s, "I Have a Dream" speech:

from "I Have A Dream"
Martin Luther King, Jr.

I say to you today, my friends, so even though we face the difficulties of today and tomorrow, I still have a dream. It is a dream deeply rooted in the American dream. I have a dream that one day this nation will rise up. . . live out the true meaning of its creed—we hold these truths to be self-evident, that all men are created equal. . . .

I have a dream that my four little children will one day live in a nation where they will not be judged by the color of their skin but by the content of their character. I have a dream today! . . .

I have a dream that one day every valley shall be exalted, and every hill and mountain shall be made low, the rough places shall be made plain, and the crooked places shall be made straight and the glory of the Lord will be revealed and all flesh shall see it together.

This is our hope. This is the faith that I go back to the South with.

The parallel structure of this black preacher sermon builds the sentences toward a rhythm and climax. Other figures of speech, described in more detail in chapter ten, enhance prose rhythm as well as poetry. Tempo variations create rhythm. Sentence structure in prose can pulsate and provide emphasis units useful for the performer of literature.

Types of Prose

Three types of prose cross all boundaries of fiction and nonfiction literature: *description, exposition,* and *narration.* An author's approach and perspective determine which of these types are used. Many prose categories use more than one type in a selection.

Description amplifies the plot or main point of a prose piece. Images, scenes, contexts, and sensations come alive with vivid descriptions. Can you visualize the scene as it is described? Can you sense the character's relation to setting and tensions by a word picture? Work to convey these descriptions so that the audience vicariously experiences them with you.

Exposition established factual data and information necessary to make a judgment or assessment. A performer should not treat expositional passages with benign neglect but seek to maintain vocal and nonverbal energy. Still, some predominantly expositional material may lack literary depth and interest factors. The performer who was so compelling that she could "make the telephone book sound interesting" still faces the challenge that the "telephone book" has little literary merit. (This is true despite a host of fascinating personae!)

Narration consists of story telling; it thrives in prose because humans are innate storytellers. As time-bound creatures, we enjoy chronological narratives, those with a clear beginning, middle, and end. Performers study and analyze narrative portions in prose to find out:

1. who a narrator is;
2. what message is being shared in the narrative;
3. where the narrative is occurring;
4. when (at what time) does the narrative happen; and
5. how (in what manner) does the narrative evolve.

In the following excerpt, determine what type of prose selection it is and how that classification will assist you in making important performance decisions:

"Napoleon and the Furrier"

Steve Andreas

During Napoleon's invasion of Russia, his troops were battling in the middle of yet another small town in that endless wintry land, when he was accidentally

---

[Excerpt from *A 2nd Helping of Chicken Soup for the Soul.* Copyright © 1995 by Jack Canfield and Mark Victor Hansen. Published by Health Communications, Inc., Deerfield Beach, Fl.]

separated from his men. A group of Russian Cossacks spotted him and began chasing him through the twisting streets. Napoleon ran for his life and ducked into a little furrier's shop on a side alley. . . "Save me, save me! Where can I hide?" The furrier said, "Quick, under this big pile of furs in the corner."

No sooner had he hidden than the Russian Cossacks burst in the door, shouting, "Where is he? We saw him come in.". . . They poked in the pile of furs with their swords but didn't find him. Soon, they gave up and left.

After some time, Napoleon crept out from under the furs, unharmed, just as Napoleon's personal guards came in the door. The furrier turned to Napoleon and said timidly, "Excuse me for asking this question of such a great man, but what was it like to be under those furs, knowing that the next moment would surely be your last?"

"How could you ask such a question of me, the Emperor Napoleon! Guards, take this impudent man out, blindfold him and execute him. I, myself, will personally give the command to fire!"

The guards grabbed the poor furrier, dragged him outside, stood him up against a wall and blindfolded him. Then he heard Napoleon clear his throat and call out slowly, "Ready. . . aim. . ." In that moment, a feeling that he couldn't describe welled up in him as tears poured down his cheeks.

After a long period of silence, the furrier heard footsteps approaching him and the blindfold was stripped from his eyes. Still partially blinded by the sudden sunlight, he saw Napoleon's eyes looking deeply and intently into his own— eyes that seemed to see into every dusty corner of his being. Then Napoleon said softly, "Now you know."

Now that you understand the categories of prose, the features of prose, and the types of prose, you must make performance choices for the presentation of prose literature to an audience.

Prose Performance Decisions

If a prose selection is serious or concerns a strong emotional theme, you must decide how much you should intensify imagery and language. Some prose selections (like the scene from Leon Uris' *Trinity*) are worded so powerfully that extended, forced vocal intensity overdramatizes the scene. Such emphasis may elicit the opposite effect you desire from an audience (in this case, nervous laughter). A general rule to follow is: Let the text communicate the depth of tone and seriousness; use subtlety rather than extreme intensity when the material is emotionally charged.

A humorous prose selection requires sensitivity to timing, pauses before punch lines, and "holding for laughs." An audience feels cheated if the performer continues a line while the audience laughs loudly at a punch line. A technique that helps a performer pick up the rhythm of a piece again after an audience interrupts with laughter is to repeat a line again if you must hold for laughs. Trying to be funny, however, can be deadly. A performer who "telegraphs" that a funny line is coming may spoil the moment. Performers of humorous material must understand incongruity, deviation from the norm, word play, literary pratfalls, incompetence masquerading as skill, insults, double entendre lines with "sexual" meanings, and irony. These literary devices are the "stuff" of humorous writing and are funny only if delivery and timing match up directly. Read Dave Barry's essay and plan out how you would set up the humorous lines for maximum effect:

"Garbage Scan"
by Dave Barry

Monday morning. Bad traffic. Let's just turn on the radio here, see if we can get some good tunes, crank it up. Maybe they'll play some early Stones. Yeah. Maybe they. . .

—*Power On*—

". . .just reached the end of 14 classic hits in a row, and we'll be right back after we. . ."

—*Scan*—

". . . send Bill Doberman to Congress. Because Bill Doberman agrees with us. Bill Doberman. It's a name we can trust. Bill Doberman. It's a name we can remember. Let's write it down. Bill. . ."

—*Scan*—

". . . just heard 19 uninterrupted classic hits, and now for this. . ."

—*Scan*—

. . . EVIL that cometh down and DWELLETH amongst them, and it DID CAUSETH their eyeballs to ooze a new substance, and it WAS a greenish color, but they DID not fear, for they kneweth that the. . ."

—*Scan*—

". . . followingisbasedonan800-
yearleaseanddoesnotincludetaxtags-insuranceoranactualcarwegetyour-house-
andyourchildrenandyourkidneys. . ."

—*Scan*—

"NINE THOUSAND DOLLARS!!! BUD LOOTER CHEVROLET OPEL ISUZU FORD RENAULT JEEP CHRYSLER TOYOTA STUDEBAKER TUCKER HONDA WANTS TO GIVE YOU, FOR NO GOOD REASON. . ."

—*SCAN*—

". . . Bill Doberman. He'll work for you. He'll *fight* for you. If people are rude to you, Bill Doberman will *kill* them. Bill Doberman. . ."

—Scan—

". . . enjoyed those 54 classic hits in a row, and now let's pause while. . ."

—Scan—

". . . insects DID swarm upon them and DID eateth their children, but they WERE NOT afraid, for they trustedeth in the. . ."

—Scan—

". . . listening audience. Hello?"

"Hello?"

"Go ahead."

"Steve?"

"This is Steve. Go ahead."

"Am I on?"

"Yes. Go ahead."

"Is this Steve?"

—Scan—

"This is Bill Doberman, and I say convicted rapists have *no business* serving on the Supreme Court. That's why, as your congressman, I'll make sure that. . . "

—Scan—

". . . GIVE YOU SEVENTEEN THOUSAND DOLLARS IN TRADE FOR ANYTHING!!! IT DOESN'T EVEN HAVE TO BE A CAR!!! BRING US A ROAD KILL!!! WE DON'T CARE!!! BRING US A CANTALOUPE-SIZED GOB OF EAR WAX!!! BRING US. . ."

—Scan—

". . . huge creatures that WERE like winged snakes EXCEPT they had great big suckers, which DID cometh and pulleth their limbs FROM their sockets liketh this, 'Pop,' but they WERE not afraid, nay they WERE joyous, for they had. . ."

—Scan—

". . . just heard 317 uninterrupted classic hits, and now. . ."

—Scan—

"Bill Doberman will shrink your swollen membranes. Bill Doberman has. . ."

—Scan—

". . . glowing bodies strewn all over the road, and motorists are going to need. . ."

—Scan—

". . . FORTY THOUSAND DOLLARS!!! WE'LL JUST GIVE IT TO YOU!!! FOR NO REASON!!! WE HAVE A BRAIN DISORDER!!! LATE AT NIGHT, SOMETIMES WE SEE THESE GIANT GRUBS. . . AND WE HEAR THESE VOICES SAYING. . ."

—SCAN—

"Steve?"

"Yes."

"Steve?"

"Yes."

"Steve?"

—Scan—

"Yes, and their eyeballs DID explode like party favors, but they WERE NOT sorrowful, for they kneweth. . ."

—Scan—

Bill Doberman. Him good. Him heap strong. Him your father. Him. . ."

—Scan—

". . . finished playing 3,814 consecutive classic hits with no commercial interruptions dating back to 1978, and now. . ."

—Scan—

". . . the radiation cloud is spreading rapidly, and we have unconfirmed reports that. . ."

—Scan—

". . . getting sleepy. Very sleepy. When you hear the words 'Bill Doberman,' you will. . . "

—Power Off—

OK, never mind. I'll just drive. Listen to people honk. Maybe hum a little bit. Maybe even, if nobody's looking, do a little singing. [Singing quietly]

I can't get nooooooo

Sa-tis-FAC-shun. . .

In order to perform this hilarious Dave Barry essay, you will have to not only exhibit strong comedic timing, you must decide how you will create unique voices for each of the "radio" voices that meld seamlessly after the "Scan" cue. Some lines are read very rapidly, running words together, while other lines can be slowed down and read with emphasis and occasional pausing. But what is it you want the audience to feel about this piece or any other literary selection?

A performer seeks to "feel with" an audience (*empathy*) by transporting them to a created literary context and promoting interest, entertainment, and consciousness-raising. To achieve empathy while performing prose, an interpreter must show a deliberate response to the text in body language, facial expressions, vocal variety, and delivery patterns. You will know when empathy has been achieved as audience members respond with the same tensions, reactions, attitudes, and impressions. You may not be able to describe the feeling that empathy provides, but it is a strong relational feeling that provides a connection between you as the performer and the listening audience.

As you choose a prose selection for in-class performance, begin by choosing a selection you enjoy. Perhaps you read it in an anthology for an English class or during a summer vacation trip.

Next, choose a selection written in such a manner that an audience will understand most of it merely by hearing the text. Many texts read well silently but are too complex for oral presentation. Third, choose a selection with a range. Soliloquies and monologues may have one persona voice, maintaining a static emotional level. Stretch yourself; choose to perform literature with multiple personae or levels of emotionality with a single persona narrative.

Practically, you might use different color underlining to keep personae distinct in your performance copy. In the margins of your text, you may write reminder notes of subtextual choices or tag line suggestions. Type the copy so that page turns come at natural transitions in time or at the end of a subplot or lesser action sequence. Page turns that occur in dramatic moments can momentarily distract audience members. Make the performance copy of the text work in your favor by using the script as a support for holding audience attention.

The time has come to choose a prose selection for performance. The following list is merely a guideline of possible prose selections. These have been used in class and other performance settings. This list is not exhaustive. It primarily suggests twentieth-century options, but you may wish to present literature from another century. You may choose to explore the prose offerings of ethnic cultures or other minority groups. Whatever type of prose selection you choose to perform, practice and strive to bring it alive. Make this first major performance in class seem real!

Choices for Performance of Prose

SHORT STORIES

Conrad Aiken	"Silent Snow, Secret Snow"
Woody Allen	"The Kugelmass Episode," "The Whore of Mensa"
James Baldwin	"Going to Meet the Man," "Sonny's Blues"
Ray Bradbury	"The Veldt," "The Long Rain," "And There Will Come Soft Rains," "Bless Me, Father, For I Have Sinned"
Kate Chopin	"The Story of an Hour"
James Clavell	"The Children's Story"
Harlan Ellison	" 'Repent, Harlequin!' Said the Ticktockman"
William Faulkner	"A Rose For Emily," "Barn Burning"
Charlotte Perkins Gilman	"The Yellow Wallpaper"
Stephen King	"The Last Rung on the Ladder," "The Body," "Children of the Corn"
Jack London	"The Call of the Wild," "To Build a Fire"
Peter Meinke	"Uncle George and Uncle Stefan"
Carson McCullers	"The Ballad of the Sad Cafe," "A Tree, A Rock, A Cloud"
Flannery O'Connor	"A Good Man Is Hard To Find," "Good Country People"
Frank O'Connor	"First Confession"
Kathryn Ann Porter	"He," "Flowering Judas"
Philip Roth	"The Conversion Of the Jews"

James Thurber	"If Grant Had Been Drinking at Appomattox," "The Catbird Seat," "The Secret Life of Walter Mitty"
Kurt Vonnegut, Jr.	"Harrison Bergeron"
Eudora Welty	"Why I Live at the P.O.," "Lily Daw and the Three Ladies"

NOVELS

Peter Benchley	*Jaws*
Ray Bradbury	*Fahrenheit-451, Something Wicked This Way Comes, Dandelion Wine*
James Clavell	*Shogun*
Pat Conroy	*The Water Is Wide, The Great Santini, The Lords of Discipline, The Prince of Tides, Beach Music, My Losing Season*
Dean Koontz	*Dark Rivers of the Heart, Intensity, Sole Survivor, The Face*
John Grisham	*The Firm, A Time to Kill, The Pelican Brief, The Partner, Skipping Christmas, The King of Torts*
Judith Guest	*Ordinary People*
Ernest Hemingway	*For Whom the Bell Tolls, The Old Man and the Sea*
Frank Herbert	*Dune*
Daniel Keyes	*Flowers For Algernon*
Stephen King	*Carrie, Misery, Cujo, The Green Mile*
Carson McCullers	*The Heart Is A Lonely Hunter, The Member of the Wedding*
John Steinbeck	*Of Mice and Men, The Grapes of Wrath, East of Eden*
J.R.R. Tolkien	*The Hobbit, The Ring Trilogy*
John Kennedy Toole	*A Confederacy of Dunces*
Leon Uris	*Exodus, Trinity, QB VII*
Alice Walker	*The Color Purple*
Elie Wiesel	*Night*

HISTORIES, BIOGRAPHIES, AUTOBIOGRAPHIES

Jim Bishop	*The Day Christ Died, The Day Kennedy Died*
Tom Brokaw	*The Greatest Generation*
Frank Deford	*Alex: The Life of a Child*
Joel Engel, ed.	*Addicted: In Their Own Words—Kids Talking About Drugs*
Dick Gregory	*Nigger*
Torey Hayden	*One Child*
Malcolm X	*The Autobiography of Malcolm X*
Merle Miller	*Plain Speaking: An Oral Biography of Harry S. Truman*
Lynda Van Devanter	*Home Before Morning*

Essays, Letters, Prayers, Diaries

Woody Allen	*Getting Even, Without Feathers, Side Effects*
Dave Barry	*Dave Barry's Greatest Hits, Dave Barry Turns 40, Dave Barry Talks Back, Dave Barry's Guide to Guys, Dave Barry Is From Mars And Venus*
Malcolm Boyd	*Are You Running With Me, Jesus? Human Like Me, Jesus*
Canfield, Jack and Mark V. Hansen	Any of the *Chicken Soup for the Soul* books
Anne Frank	*The Diary of Anne Frank*
Garrison Keillor	*Lake Wobegon Days*
Martin Luther King, Jr.	"Letter From the Birmingham Jail"
Stephen Leacock	"My Financial Career"
C.S. Lewis	*The Screwtape Letters*
S.J. Perelman	"Dental or Mental, I Say It's Spinach"
Andy Rooney	*A Few Minutes With Andy Rooney*
James Thurber	*The Thurber Carnival, Further Fables For Our Time*
Judith Viorst	*Necessary Losses*
E.B. White	"The Color of Mice"

Assignments

1. You should prepare a reading of prose literature for an in-class graded presentation. Your professor will indicate the time limitations and the class day for your performance. A critique sheet in this book's appendix is provided to assist you in performance evaluation. Discuss your performance strengths and weaknesses with your professor and classmates.

References

Bacon, Wallace. *The Art of Interpretation. 3rd Edition.* New York: Holt, Rinehart, and Winston, 1979.

Gamble, Teri and Gamble, Michael. *Literature Alive! The Art of Oral Interpretation. 2nd Edition.* Lincolnwood, IL: NTC Publishing Group, 1994.

Lee, Charlotte. *Speaking of . . . Interpretation.* Glenview, IL: Scott, Foresman, and Company, 1975.

Scrivner, Louise M. and Robinette, Dan. *A Guide to Oral Interpretation 2nd Edition.* Indianapolis: Bobbs-Merrill Educational Publishing, 1980.

Notes

1. Tom Brokaw, *The Greatest Generation.* (New York: Random House, 1998).

CHAPTER 9

Oral Interpretation of Drama: Solo and Duo

Before you signed up for this course in performance, you may have enjoyed the exhilarating experience of performing in a play. Drama has a captivating appeal to student performers and observers alike. We go to the theater or sit down to read silently a play because we love the opportunity to be transplanted into a different realm. Since most dramas emerge as self-contained stories, we in the audience take on the role of eavesdroppers. We sit in the dark and become engrossed with the unfolding action and events we see on a stage.

We love to be moved by dramatic literature. A Shakespearean tragedy or a contemporary Neil Simon comedy provides a wide range of emotions for us to feel. We go to the theater to sense vicariously the deep dimensions of the human experience.

Dramatic literature has an inherent appeal to the performer precisely because it was written to be performed. The silent reader must have an active imagination, recreating scenes and the sound of dialogue in the arena of the mind. In a course such as the one you are taking, the performer needs to prepare in a similar manner to the actor, but the actual performance may require deeper concentration to recreate a scene. Without benefit of costume, scenery, proscenium stage, lighting, and other theatrical accouterments the classroom performer must let the text come alive in the imagined space available.

Interpreters in a classroom, thus, rely on their inner strengths to visualize the elements of dramatic literature. *Internalization* is the process of experiencing an emotion, a context, and a motivation for characters inwardly. True internalization leads to credible vocal and nonverbal actions outwardly. This internalization is the prime experience necessary to sustain true and believable performance choices. Internalization can be a factor in the performance of all literature, but it is especially crucial for the performer of drama literature.

In this chapter, you will build a basis for your performance choices by looking at features of drama literature, suggestions for projecting dramatic elements, performance decisions for the solo performer and pairs (duo) performances, and special considerations for those who tackle the reading/performance of any of the works of William Shakespeare.

Features of Drama

Some unique features of drama separate the genre from prose. Most prose literature relies on a narrative voice to describe scene, context, motivations, and progression of events. Such narrative aspects frequently call forth the audience-centered focus. Since drama literature is predominantly character dialogue, interaction among personae must subtly but definitely reveal expositional elements. The focal point for most parts of drama literature is offstage, the focus for imagined character interaction. Drama literature has segments called "scenes," "acts," "prologues," and "epilogues"; these parallel the "chapters" and "sections" of prose literature. A scene in a play has a specific rhythm, akin to but unique from prose. Also, most prose fiction uses past tense, while the majority of drama literature relies on present tense to tell a story.

Just as prose has numerous subcategories, so too does drama. Drama literature may be: tragedy, comedy, melodrama, tragicomedy, farce, or history. Sources for drama literature reflect the mass media in: radio plays, television plays, and screenplays. Skits and routines may be written and performed in dramatic format also.

A feature of most (but not all) drama literature is the suggestion of a "fourth wall." This "wall" is the invisible barrier set up between actors and the eavesdropping audience. Actors sense the presence of an audience, but aim their focal point gaze onstage, ignoring direct eye contact with the observers. This implication for literary performers justifies sole offstage focal points during personae interaction.

Shakespeare frequently would begin and end his plays with a single actor (Chorus) presenting expositional material that was directly aimed and addressed to the audience. Some contemporary playwrights seek to break down the "fourth wall" barrier on occasion. Thornton Wilder's *Our Town* has a narrator who addresses the audience and interacts on stage as a persona. Movie screenplays break down the "fourth wall" too. Consider Matthew Broderick's running dialogue with the camera lens (the audience) in *Ferris Bueller's Day Off.* The dramatic element known as the *soliloquy*, a monologue outwardly expressing inner thoughts, seems to break down the wall, but may in fact sustain the illusion. Read the following selection and determine whether the "fourth wall" exists:

from *As You Like It*
William Shakespeare

Jaques: All the world's a stage,
And all the men and women merely players:
They have their exits and their entrances;
And one man in his time plays many parts,
His acts being seven ages. At first the infant,
Mewling and puking in the nurse's arms.
And then the whining school-boy, with his satchel
And shining morning face, creeping like snail
Unwillingly to school. And then the lover,
Sighing like furnace, with a woeful ballad
Made to his mistress' eyebrow. Then a soldier,
Full of strange oaths, and bearded like the pard,

Jealous in honour, sudden and quick in quarrel,
Seeking the bubble reputation
Even in the cannon's mouth. And then the justice,
In fair round belly with good capon lined,
With eyes severe and beard of formal cut,
Full of wise saws and modern instances
And so he plays his part. The sixth age shifts
Into the lean and slipper'd pantaloon,
With spectacles on nose and pouch on side,
His youthful hose, well saved, a world too wide
For his shrunk shank; and his big manly voice,
Turning again toward childish treble, pipes
And whistles in his sound. Last scene of all,
That ends this strange eventful history,
Is second childishness and mere oblivion,
Sans teeth, sans eyes, sans taste, sans every thing.

Aristotle provides us with a continuing means to analyze drama literature. In his collected lectures entitled *Poetics*, Aristotle describes six elements found in drama: *plot, character, diction* (language), *music, thought* (idea), and *spectacle*. In the next section each of these elements will be introduced with suggestions for the performance of drama literature.

Projecting Dramatic Elements

Plot, the first of Aristotle's elements, is more than what happens in a play; it is also the order in which events occur. A play may be written with a *linear plot,* a cause-effect relationship of events leading to a climax. Linear plots follow a chronology, but may occasionally divert to describe sub-plots. Shakespeare's plays *Macbeth* and *A Midsummer Night's Dream* are linear with sub-plots. A play may be written with *episodic plot,* featuring scenes ordered by exploration of an idea or a persona. Two of Horton Foote's Academy Award-winning screenplays have episodic plot structure (*To Kill a Mockingbird* and *Tender Mercies*).

When a time limit restricts a performer to presenting only a segment of a dramatic work, the performer must still study and analyze the entire plot. Performance choices should be based on how a segment fits into the whole dramatic work. Analysis that fails to acknowledge the complete plot motivations misses the mark in preparation. When a performer knows where the plot is going, performance options should coincide to lead the audience through crisis, climax, and resolution.

Playwrights create *characters* to fulfill a number of dramatic purposes. Plays that emphasize dimensional and complex personae frequently downplay the importance of plot in favor of characterization. Plays that have one-dimensional, flat characters may aim only to entertain or call attention to action alone. David Rintels' one-man show, *Clarence Darrow*, has a linear plot-line, a chronological exploration of the life of the famous trial lawyer, but the character of Darrow is the prime focus, not the events of his life. Michael Stewart's musical-comedy text for *Bye Bye Birdie* has stereotypical personae that act unidimensionally, yet collectively entertain the audience.

The previous discussion of plot is meaningless without characters. In a real sense, character is action. Characters in drama literature serve a function. Here is where the performer of literature steps in to begin pre-performance analysis. Does a character express opinions that reflect the overall theme or "argument" of the text? How does a character carry out the plot? How does a character fit into the schema of the play, its look, its feel, and its spectacle?

The performer seeks answers to these and other questions in several ways:

1. Stage directions or play prefaces frequently provide clues. Robert Harling provides a note to performers in his play, *Steel Magnolias,* concerning the portrayal of characters:

    The women in this play are witty, intelligent, and above all, real characters. They in no way, shape, or form are meant to be portrayed as cartoons or caricatures.[1]

    Thus, the performer will prepare these characters to respond genuinely and not in a broad or farcical manner;

2. Characters reveal much information about themselves in their own spoken words. The performer will need to interpret what the self-descriptions mean, but they do help in analytical preparation. Elwood P. Dowd, the lovable lunatic in Mary Chase's delightful play, *Harvey,* reveals much about himself and his imaginary rabbit friend, Harvey;

3. Other characters comment and flesh out descriptions and motivations for personae in a play. You will need to filter these comments as they reveal others' attitudes and may not be accurate. We learn much about Felix and Oscar from hearing others talk about them in the Neil Simon comedy *The Odd Couple;*

4. When you notice the actions of a character, you gain clues to justify their motivations. Our behaviors frequently (but not exclusively) reflect inner feelings. Characters in a play perform actions that suggest a psychological profile. The character of Beth (played so marvelously well by Mary Tyler Moore) in Alvin Sargent's screenplay, *Ordinary People,* hides her feelings of intimacy and demonstrates her inability to respond to love by inaction. As her son, Conrad, hugs her she is incapable of returning his sign of affection. Analysis might suggest that Beth does not love her son or has a myriad of competing stresses that diminish her capacity to reciprocate physically.

Some types of characters appear in many examples of drama literature. The *protagonist* is the primary figure in the prevailing plot. A *confidant(e)* is a trustworthy friend to the protagonist. Frequently, there exists an *antagonist,* a villain who conflicts with and is opposed to the protagonist. Authors may create a *raisonneur,* a persona who gives opinions reflecting the author's viewpoint. A *foil* is the character who contrasts another character; a foil may be comical, serious, intelligent, or naive. Characters may be *sympathetic* or *unsympathetic,* created to establish audience interest or dislike.

The performer must never forget that while dramatic characters are not identical to human beings, dramatic personae must be credible and truthful. Preparation to perform a dramatic character includes an understanding of motivations, a consistency in portrayal, and a commitment to accuracy.

Diction, or the language of a play, offers the meaning in a play. It reveals features of character (social/economic state, dialect, level of intelligence, and emotional/mental state). Key words used repetitively suggest meaning. Figures of speech (such as metaphors or analogies) serve as a subconscious source of meaning. In the following selection, a purported Nazi war criminal retells his chilling devotion to Adolf Hitler. (Note how the diction of the play creates and sustains a mood of horror and disgust):

from *The Man In The Glass Booth*
Robert Shaw

Goldman: People of the word, let me speak to you of my Fuehrer with love. (*He pauses. Very quietly.*) He who answered our German need. He who rescued us from the depths. His family background was not distinguished, his education negligible. At the end of that First World War not even a German citizen. To whom did he appeal? To the people. His power lay in the love he won from the people. When he spoke at first he was shy, he would hesitate, he would stammer, his body stiff, he felt for his love like a blind man, the voice hushed, the voice was flat, then the words came stronger, came steadier, his body grew free, he would bang out his right arm like a hammer, louder and louder and louder he spoke, a torrent, a waterfall, the climax was shouted and shouted, out and up and beyond, and the end was absolute. Silence. Utter silence. A great wide sweep of the right arm and so to the tremendous cry, the vast overwhelming cry, the call of love from the people.

Deutschland Erwache. Heil Hitler. Sieg Heil. Sieg Heil. Do I see you begin to raise your hands? Do I hear you stamp your feet? He gave us our history. He gave us our news, he gave us our art. He gave us our holidays, he gave us our leisure, and he gave our newly marrieds a copy of *Mein Kampf.*

At the end we loved him. In *Gotterdammerung* we loved him. With the killers of the world at our throats, the hordes from the East and West, the capitalists and the communists, the bombers of cities, the murderers of our children, with bullets in our guts we loved him. Starving, we loved him. With his head wobbling, his left arm slack, his hands a-tremble, we loved him. His generals lost him the war. His subordinates were unworthy. There was no successor. There was only him. Hess was mad. Goering reviled, Himmler rejected. He? He was loved.

"Great King. Brave King. Wait yet a little while and the days of your suffering will be over. Already the sun of your good fortune stands behind the clouds and soon, beloved Fuehrer, soon this sun will rise upon you." He never deserted us. All but he! He, only, loved to the end. While he lived, Germany lived. And the people demanded it. We never denied him. People of Israel, we never denied him. And those who tell you different. . . lie. Those who tell you anything else lie in their hearts. And if, if he were able to rise from the dead, he would prove it to you now. All over again. If only . . . if only we had someone to rise to. . . throw out our arms to. . . love. . . and stamp our feet for.

Someone . . .someone to lead. *(Pause. Then calculatedly.)* People of Israel . . . people of Israel, if he had chosen you . . . if he had chosen *you* . . .*you* also would have followed where he led.

Performers must recreate the diction of a play truthfully. If an accent or dialect is essential to share the text's meaning, then you must attempt the language choice. If the text is universal, consider concentrating on projecting the tone and attitude of the text. Study figures of speech, allusions, and repetition to bring deeper understanding and impact to your performance of drama.

Aristotle's term *music* has a wider application than mere lyrical melodies. Drama has rhythm that is "musical" in the sense that some passages demand rapid, staccato delivery while other passages are slower, more melodic, and less accentuated.

The performer of drama literature may actually sing some passages, chant the rhythm, or suggest the "music" of a text. In Stephen Sondheim and James Lapine's Tony Award-winning musical, *Into the Woods,* five fabled personae meet and argue in a complex, chant-like musical number entitled "Your Fault." A performer of such a text faces the gargantuan task of keeping the personae voices distinct and of sustaining the musical rhythms and pitch. A solo performer of drama may choose to sing or recite musical lyrics from a dramatic context. For example, a selection from the Andrew Lloyd Webber/Charles Hart/Richard Stilgoe libretto of *The Phantom of the Opera* may include spoken as well as singing phrases in the segment "The Music of the Night."

Thought shares the ideas of a dramatic text. Plays vary in the sophistication of thought and message. Since this text has a theoretical commitment to the rhetorical weight of a literary message, a performer should therefore seek drama literature with clear and provocative intent. The thought of a play can be entertaining or serious or contain elements of both extremes.

Plays offer many meanings with performance options to consider. A performer should compare these possibilities and choose the best message segment to perform. Look at character speeches and interactions to discover a predominant thought. Perform so that this thought and message are apparent and consistently emphasized.

Finally, drama literature has inherent *spectacle.* You will initially have to imagine the scene, the costumes, and the design of the production to project the flavor to an audience who must imagine as well. Spectacle is all the accouterments of the stage plus the imagination. Audiences for an oral interpretation performance know that they must allow their imaginations to create the spectacle. Through suggestion and symbolization the imagination can envision reality and fiction. The earliest professional Readers Theatre production of "Don Juan in Hell" (1951) came into existence because of the difficulty in staging the George Bernard Shaw act from *Man and Superman.* Four superior actors, using only lecterns and manuscripts, recreated the realms of Heaven and Hell in the greatest theatrical arena we know: the human mind. Spectacle is, thus, nonexistent without benefit of the imagination.

Drama Performance Decisions: The Solo Artist

The single performer who chooses to present a dramatic text must strive to be natural. Artificiality can be easily spotted and noted by an audience. The performer who analyzes a text and prepares extensively can become too "technical" if not careful. The "technique" of performing drama draws too much attention to the conscious use of voice and body movements. It is as if you are so rehearsed the presentation seems too perfect, too mechanical, lacking in spontaneity or restraint. The opposite extreme is similarly to be avoided. The performer who waits to be "inspired" so he can perform fails to grasp the basis for a performance. Seek to make a dramatic persona credible as a genuine, believable representation in your arena of performance.

Solo performers need to choose a dramatic text with a range commensurate with abilities. Avoid a play with too many characters unless you can recreate all voices distinctly. Establish clear focal points for the object of your interaction as a persona. When rapidly delivering an interaction between personae, minimize the movement of your head and move your eyes to the focal points. As you learned with prose performances, try to smooth out the eye contact with your script as you carry forth dialogue lines.

When presenting a drama monologue, avoid static, predictable vocal patterning. Seek out monologues that reveal layers of a character and practice so that those layers are apparent to the audience.

In multi-personae dramatic texts, provide each persona with individualized character, features, and attitude. Do not settle for a mere external projection of a dramatic personality, but delve deeper. Decide what goes on *inside* your persona: the thoughts, fears, joys, guilt, regrets, and values.

Be careful! In seeking a voice or mannerisms for a persona, do not go to extremes, creating a cartoony or caricatured personality. Subtlety and economy are two standards to help you in your performance choices.

Some plays are more physical than literary. Do not choose texts that require excessive physical action without accompanying commentary. The scene of recognition in William Gibson's *The Miracle Worker* consists of a gripping physical ordeal between Annie Sullivan and Helen Keller. However, eight minutes of mime actions, followed by the triumphant cry, "Wah-, wah-!"

does not work in a solo format. The best solo performance texts have a preponderance of dialogue over physical action.

Drama Performance Decisions: Duo Sharing

Traditional texts in oral interpretation omit references to duo dramatic interpretation in sections on drama performances. This omission fails to recognize that classroom assignments typically offer such a paired sharing of drama.

Duo Drama Interpretation emerged as a separate event category in the early 1970s in regional and national collegiate forensics contests and festivals. Coaches and faculty members assigned to teach sections of oral interpretation provided their students with opportunities to explore dialogic drama.

Duo Drama Interpretation has some unique values that solo drama interpretation cannot offer as well. As Frank Trimble notes:

> Duo interpretation encourages the audiences to view a play in terms of its filmic qualities. A duo performance offers two "camera angles" simultaneously, much like a director who shoots footage from multiple perspectives, and in turn passes it to an editor. The advantage in duo is that *we,* the audience, serve as editor, selecting the individual on whom we focus. True, a skilled duo team might force upon us a particular perspective at any given moment (for example, a performer turns his back), but the audience still "edits" the scene. Concomitantly, the performer is encouraged to polish subtle performance skills and highlight character thought processes, for he or she is no longer just on stage but also under the careful scrutiny of the "camera" (audience).[2]

Conventions for this duo performance variable have evolved over the years. Aspects of these conventions include: shared introductory remarks, focus points, choreographed posing, and physical action/reaction.

Since two people stand side-by-side in front of an audience, it seems natural to bifurcate introductory remarks between the performers. During this preparatory time, some performers glance at their partners onstage sharing in their own personal voice the essentials of theme, literary message, and author/title of the text. This time period should appear to be separate from textual performance. As in all introductions, the manuscript should be closed and eye contact directed primarily to the audience.

Duo partners should stand close enough side-by-side that the audience can view both faces without moving their heads. If the play is predominantly character dialogue, the duo partners need to "see" the other persona in an offstage focal point. (The wedge-shaped focus is most typically used in duo drama interpretation.) For beginners, the greatest temptation is to sneak a side-glance at the partner. Keep the illusion alive you establish with offstage focus and only "see" the other persona in that spot. You should occasionally avert eye gaze since no normal human interaction sustains long staring segments. To understand and remember what facial reactions the partner provides, practice your duo script several times with onstage focus, looking at each other. Practice in front of a mirror will help you as well.

Different poses can suggest time elapsed, scene changes, or editing in the play. You may begin standing back-to-back, looking offstage over the shoulder. A scene shift to a three-quarter front view suggests a new day, place, or location. Another shift to full-face forward signals a scene change or script edits. Too many of these physical shifts confuse an audience so use them sparingly.

Choreograph all physical action so that there is initiation as well as completion of the action. Direct touching confuses audiences because of the offstage locus; action is out front and back to yourself in the offstage focal mode. You can simulate some physical action but duo partners must time and respond to these actions. Kissing, handshakes, passing and receiving objects, fighting, and other physical elements in drama should be choreographed onstage first, than transferred to the offstage mode.

Performing Shakespeare

Many beginning oral interpretation classes embark on the difficult challenge of having a unit or performance venue for the works of William Shakespeare. Shakespeare's work makes an excellent transition that encompasses the dramatic presentation of dialogue as well as the sensitivity to poetic line delivery so characteristic of his plays (and clearly his poetry, as we will see in the next chapter).

John Barton, author of *Playing Shakespeare,*[3] reminds all performers that the key to presenting the works of Shakespeare can be found in the words of the Bard himself:

Speak the speech, I pray you, as I pronounced it to you, trippingly on the tongue. But if you mouth it as many of our players do, I had as lief the town crier spoke my lines. Nor do not saw the air too much with your hand, thus. But use all gently. For in the very torrent, tempest, and, as I may say, whirlwind of your passion, you must acquire and beget a temperance that may give it smoothness. . . Be not too tame either. But let your discretion be your tutor. Suit the action to the word, the word to the action, with this special observance, that you o'erstep not the modesty of nature. . .For anything so o'erdone is from the purpose of playing, whose end, both at the first and now, was and is to hold, as t'were, the mirror up to nature. [Hamlet: III:2]

Thus, overdoing a standard British accent or using excessive hand and body gestures merely create a "poor" performance, not one that "mirrors nature." Subtlety and gentleness seem higher virtues to emulate than "over-the-top" caricatures of dramatic personae.

You must begin the preparation of a Shakespeare segment as you would any other literary selection, with some specific attention to details. As Printer and Colaianni remind us, "Shakespeare's words are four hundred years old, and they often don't have the same meaning as they did back then."[4] You should look at key words in your dramatic selection and compare them with a dictionary that will give you several meanings, including one that could reflect the meaning of the word in Shakespeare's time. The Oxford English Dictionary is a key resource to prepare to present Shakespeare's lines to an audience. Once you have determined a meaning, looking at the context and editorial comments made by scholars, *paraphrase* (i.e., say it in your own words) the segment in lines that you understand. Use words that would be consistent with the meaning, yet reflect your understanding of the line in a contemporary setting.

Next you must find the *rhythm* of the Shakespearean line since most of his lines are written in poetic form, even if following a "dramatic" dialogue line sequence. Most of Shakespeare's lines are written in *iambic pentameter* (more about this in the next chapter on poetry). Basically, his lines are in groups of ten syllables with accents on the first and every other syllable. These five groupings of accent/non-accent words and portions make up five groups of two words/syllables each, hence the term *penta* (five)-*meter* (rhythm). Should you prepare to read Shakespeare by accenting every other syllable? Absolutely not! But to begin with this approach allows you to consider the next level of presentation: *syncopation*.

Syncopation in music accents beats that are not normally or even regularly stressed. This "interpretative" means to performance adds levels of nuance and distinction to musical renderings. The same can be said for the performance of Shakespeare's works. You already know from previous chapters that vocal emphasis can make a word in a context stand out. If this emphasis occurs when an unpredictable beat or rhythm is due, the emphasized word may be "heard" differently or a meaning shared that otherwise might be lost by "predictability" in rhythm and stress. You can use syncopation for meaning by emphasizing verbs and nouns in a phrase. Notice in this line from the opening Chorus' monologue in *Romeo and Juliet* that regular iambic pentameter stress could give a proper interpretation:

Doth *WITH* their *DEATH* bur*IE* their *PArents STRIFE.*

However, the mind-numbing "sing-song" type of approach wears thin for an audience that may artificially nod in rhythm with your stress and emphasis marks. Instead, a syncopation approach changes the stress to pick out key verbs and nouns for emphasis, still retaining a semblance of rhythm:

Doth with their *DEATH BUR*ie their *PA*rents *STRIFE.*

Read both of these lines aloud to notice how regular and syncopated rhythms vary in reading Shakespeare's lines. You must ask yourself also, "Which of these versions makes more sense to me?" The answer should be the syncopated version and the truth is, it will also make more sense to your audience as well.

As with any "rule" in English, it seems that there are always opportunities to "break the rules" and Shakespeare is no exception. Some contexts may have key prepositions or adverbs or adjectives that may need the stress because the meaning of the line rests with an understanding of the descriptive portions rather than merely action or character found in verbs or nouns.

Prior preparation for the presentation of a Shakespearean passage must also take note of the rich aspects of language used. You will find that there is a connection that is not accidental between sound and meaning of words. Shakespeare liked to use repeated words in a single sentence as adjectives or modifiers for different concepts. Shakespeare also liked to use *alliteration* (repeating consonant sounds) and *assonance* (repeating vowel sounds) and some of his plays are "verse plays" incorporating rhyming sequences at the end of lines or thought groups. Pritner and Colaianni recommend that you avoid overemphasizing rhymed words in Shakespeare's verse plays because it tends to diminish meaning and draw undue notice to words that may or may not carry the ultimate meaning of the thought group.[5] A commitment to improvisational syncopation will not obscure the rhyming portions at all; they are frequently heard even when de-emphasized.

Punctuation can have inherent "stage directions" to help the performer know how to deliver a line. While commas separate ideas, a performer would not necessarily pause at every comma in a line. Semicolons (;) and colons (:) may imply slight pauses as they suggest that portions of a sentence have a relationship with the other. Periods (.) tend to signal an end to the thought as they do in modern English. You can suggest parentheses by altering your vocal pattern and vocal register to suggest an *aside* (information said "secretively" to the audience).

All of this pre-preparation work may seem daunting, but it is necessary in order to be faithful to Shakespeare's rich presentation of language and thought. Another hurdle to cross is the accent itself. If you choose to attempt to duplicate a standard British accent, there are tapes available with exercises to assist you in your quest for precise English performance.[6] Many Shakespearean scholars prefer to suggest to American performers that they choose to offer the words so that they are understood in the cultural context. Pritner and Colaianni state emphatically that "it is our conviction that ordinary American pronunciation is the most appropriate way for American actors to speak Shakespeare."[7] That being said, there are always words found in Shakespeare that require additional syllables (designated frequently with accents over the –ed ending of a word; e.g. betrothéd) or alterations so that the word links with another (e.g., the word *war* frequently rhymed with the word *far* in Elizabethan English). Barton notes that Shakespeare frequently capitalized the word "Time" and in its initial context was pronounced not as one syllable, but as two vowel sounds (e.g., "tay-eme").[8] A good rule to follow is: Make the choice that seems the least distracting to an American audience, helping them attend the "play" not your "pronunciation."

Brine and York suggest that a first step for any student desiring to present the dramatic soliloquies, monologues, and dialogues from a Shakespeare play is to begin with the sonnets. (More about this poetic form will be discussed in the next chapter.) "Students can be encouraged to recite a sonnet before the class, and the listeners (who have their books shut) are then asked, " 'Did you understand it?'. . .[And] the sonnets are wonderfully corrective for those students who like showing off—who want to rush into 'feeling' things, or pretending to be someone they are not."[9]

Louis Fantasia summarizes the process for preparing and presenting a passage from the works of Shakespeare:

1. Know what the original words really mean (dialogue),
2. Know where the play is going (structure),
3. Know the rhythm and sense of the line (character), and
4. Know what the play is about (the central event).[10]

Your task now as a performer of Shakespeare is to find out how to bring credibility, authenticity, and a general sense of "presence" to your performance. But keep in mind that "presence will not be commanded. It comes with hard work and faith—faith that what you say and how you say it are significant; that even in failure you have done your best. . .Technique in the absence of presence is the province of the performing seal or prostitute."[11] Convicting words, but words to help us as we attempt to share our own beliefs about Shakespeare's timeless phrases and circumstances.

Now it is time to perform a drama selection for your class. If you choose to perform a duo drama interpretation, choose a text with segments that are fairly and equally balanced in lines and attention, so that neither performer appears to dominate the reading. You may have to edit long sections of uninterrupted commentary to keep the pacing energetic and interactive. The following lists provide suggested plays with scenes for solo and duo performers. You may know of other plays equally productive for performance.

Choices for Drama Performance: The Solo Interpreter

MONOLOGUES

Jerome Alden   *Bully*
   (A one-man show about Theodore Roosevelt)
Jane Martin   *Talking With. . .*
   (A series of female monologues, each approximately 3-5 minutes in length)
William Mastrosimone   *The Woolgatherer*
   (A serious play for male and female personae; several monologues occur in this play)
David Rintels   *Clarence Darrow*
   (A one-man show focusing on the trial lawyer's life and philosophy on crime)
Willy Russell   *Shirley Valentine*
   (A one-woman show about an English housewife and her adventures)

COMEDIES

Woody Allen	*Play It Again Sam, Death Knocks*
Philip Barry	*The Philadelphia Story*
Leonard Gershe	*Butterflies Are Free*
Garson Kanin	*Born Yesterday*
Peter Shaffer	*Lettice and Lovage*
Larry Shue	*The Foreigner, The Nerd*
Neil Simon	Most all of his plays have comedic elements.

SERIOUS PERIOD DRAMA:

Maxwell Anderson	*Mary of Scotland, Elizabeth the Queen*
Jean Anouilh	*Becket*
Robert Bolt	*A Man for All Seasons*
Peter Shaffer	*Amadeus*

CLASSICS

Anton Chekhov	*The Three Sisters, The Cherry Orchard, The Sea Gull*
Lorraine Hansberry	*A Raisin in the Sun*
Lillian Helman	*The Children's Hour, The Little Foxes, Another Part of the Forest*
Henrik Ibsen	*A Doll's House, An Enemy of the People, Hedda Gabler*
Eugene Ionesco	*The Bald Soprano, The Chairs*
Arthur Miller	*Death of a Salesman, The Crucible, All My Sons*
Moliere	*Tartuffe, The Misanthrope*
Eugene O'Neill	*Ah, Wilderness!, The Hairy Ape*
Elmer Rice	*The Adding Machine*
Shakespeare	All of his plays
George Bernard Shaw	*Pygmalion, Major Barbara, Arms and The Man*
Ntozake Shange	*For Colored Girls Who Have Considered Suicide/When the Rainbow Is Enuf*
Sophocles	*Antigone*
Oscar Wilde	*The Importance of Being Earnest, Lady Windermere's Fan*
Tennessee Williams	*The Glass Menagerie, A Streetcar Named Desire*

CHOICES FOR DRAMA PERFORMANCE: DUO PERFORMERS

(m/f=male and female;m/m=male and male;f/f=female and female)

Edward Albee	*The Zoo Story* (m/m)
Robert Anderson	*I Never Sang for My Father* (m/m)
Lee Blessing	*A Walk in the Woods* (m/m)
D.L. Coburn	*The Gin Game* (m/f)
Noel Coward	*Blithe Spirit* (f/f and m/f)
	Private Lives (m/f)
Christopher Durang	*Beyond Therapy* (m/f)
	Sister Mary Ignatius Explains It All For You (m/f)
Horton Foote	*A Trip to Bountiful* (f/f)
Herb Gardner	*I'm Not Rappaport* (m/m)
James Goldman	*The Lion in Winter* (m/f)
A.R. Gurney	*Love Letters* (m/f)
Jan de Hartog	*The Fourposter* (m/f)
Ira Levin	*Deathtrap* (m/m)
	Veronica's Room (f/f)

R. E. Lee and Jerome Lawrence	*Inherit the Wind* (m/m)
Clare Booth Luce	*The Women* (f/f)
Marcelle Maurette	*Anastasia* (f/f)
Patrick Myers	*K-2* (m/m)
N. Richard Nash	*Echoes* (m/f)
	The Rainmaker (m/f)
Marsha Norman	*'Night Mother* (f/f)
James Prideaux	*Lemonade* (f/f)
Peter Shaffer	*Equus* (m/m)
Neil Simon	*The Good Doctor* (several scenes: m/m & m/f)
Ted Talley	*Terra Nova* (m/m)
	Little Footsteps (m/f)
Ernest Thompson	*On Golden Pond* (m/f)
Alfred Uhry	*Driving Miss Daisy* (m/f)
Jaston Williams, Joe Sears, Ed Howard	*Greater Tuna* (m/m or m/f or f/f), *Red, White and Tuna* (m/m or m/f or f/f)
August Wilson	*Fences* (m/m)

Assignments

1. Prepare a reading for class as a solo performer or with a duo partner, choosing a drama literature text. Cut the selection down to a prescribed time limit, being careful to keep intact scenes and lines that clearly establish character motivations and meaning. Write an introduction that allows both members of a duo team to participate. Look for a text that demonstrates a range of vocal and nonverbal skills.

References

Aykroyd, J.W. *Performing Shakespeare.* London: Samuel French, Ltd., 1979.

Aristotle. *Rhetoric and Poetics* Tr. by W. Rhys Roberts and Ingram Bywater. New York: The Modern Library, 1954.

Brubaker, E.S. *Shakespeare Aloud: A Guide to his Verse on Stage.* Lancaster, PA: E.S. Brubaker, 1976.

Cameron, Kenneth M. and Gillespie, Patti P. *The Enjoyment of Theatre. 2nd Edition.* New York: Macmillan Publishing Company, 1989.

Earley, Michael and Keil, Philippa, eds. *Soliloquy: The Shakespeare Monologues—The Women.* New York: Applause Theatre Book Publishers, 1988.

Gamble, Teri and Gamble, Michael. *Literature Alive! The Art of Oral Interpretation. 2nd Edition.* Lincolnwood, IL: NTC Publishing Group, 1994.

Gura, Timothy J., "The Solo Performer and Drama," *Speech Teacher* 24 (September 1975): 278-81.

Klope, David C., "Toward A Conceptual Justification for Duo Interpretation," *National Forensic Journal* 4 (Spring 1986): 1-11.

Lee, Charlotte and Gura, Timothy. *Oral Interpretation—10th Edition.* Boston: Houghton Mifflin Company, 2001.

Newell, Douglas, ed. *Shakespeare for One: Men—The Complete Monologues and Audition Pieces.* Portsmouth, NH: Heinemann, 2002.

Notes

1. Robert Harling, *Steel Magnolias* (New York: Dramatists Play Service Inc., 1986), xiii.
2. Frank P. Trimble, "Duo Interpretation: A Double Dilemma," *The Carolinas Speech Communication Annual,* 2 (1986), 33.
3. John Barton, *Playing Shakespeare: An Actor's Guide.* (New York: Anchor Books, 1984), 3-4.
4. Cal Pritner and Louis Colaianni, *How to Speak Shakespeare.* (Santa Monica, CA: Santa Monica Press LLC, 2001), 13.
5. Ibid, 51.
6. You can acquire cassette tapes and manuals of exercises of Standard British dialect from Samuel French, Inc. featuring tapes by: Gillian Lane-Plescia *Standard British for Actors—2nd Edition.* 1997 or David Alan Stern, *Standard British Acting With an Accent.* Dialect Specialists, Inc., 1987.
7. Pritner and Colaianni, 132. See also: Dale Coye, *Pronouncing Shakespeare's Word: A Guide from A to Zounds.* (New York: Routledge, 2002).

8. Barton, 59, 63.

9. Adrian Brine and Michael York, *A Shakespearean Actor Prepares.* (Lyme, NH: Smith and Kraus, 2000), 132-133.

10. Louis Fantasia, *Instant Shakespeare: A Proven Technique for Actors, Directors, and Teachers.* (Chicago: Ivan R. Dee, 2002), 18.

11. Ibid, 185-186.

CHAPTER 10

Oral Interpretation of Poetry —————

Purposely, this chapter on the performance of poetry follows the other chapters on prose and drama performance. Poetry is difficult to share at times. Its inherent nature as a literary form requires a double-effort in analysis and practice. It can be powerfully pointed as well as obtusely obscure. Poetry has the power to move our passions or lull us into inertia. With your previous performance experiences as an introduction, you are now ready to tackle the complex and compelling realm of poetry interpretation.

Characteristics of Poetry

Trying to define poetry is akin to describing the color yellow to a blind person. Saying "Well, if it isn't prose or drama, it has to be poetry" fails to express poetry's unique form or style. Webster's dictionary is certainly little help: "The productions of a poet." Perhaps the best way to describe poetry is to delineate many of its constituent parts.

Poetry is usually a concentrated, compressed formulation of words, rhythms, and sounds that lead to imaginative awareness. This awareness is frequently emotional, but relies on cognitive leaps to draw parallels to other events and concepts. Here are some concepts that may be found in most poetry:

1. *Figurative Language*—The language of poetry may describe more than a denoted object, event, or feeling. Poetry makes use of *illusion* as well as *allusion,* asking a reader or performer to think beyond the obvious meaning of poetic choices. Poetry is occasionally symbolic;
2. *Ambiguity*—Poetry may have layers of meaning. To say a poem "means" is to ignore the more important acknowledgment that a poem "is." From a list of possible meanings, the performer makes a worthy "choice" to offer a viewpoint to poetry's intent;
3. *Stanzas*—The stanza approximates the parallel notions of prose's sentence/paragraph format. Unlike a sentence that contains a complete thought, a stanza in a poem may carry over the thought to the next stanza. A stanza is much more arbitrary in its completeness. A stanza may be composed or divided by a rhyme scheme or clear rhythmical pattern;

4. *Unlimited in Form*—Poetry may be as brief as a *couplet* (a two-line stanza) or as lengthy as epic poems that approximate the novel's scope. Poetry may have a predictable rhyme scheme and rhythm or be less predictable and restricted.

Poetry can be divided into genres. One can best understand poetry by studying its component features: figures of speech, repetition and parallelism, rhyme scheme, and rhythmic meter.

Genres of Poetry

The four genres or types of poetry are: lyric, dramatic, narrative, and song lyrics. Many of these types blend features of the others. In the case of song lyrics, the musical accompaniment is removed or downplayed to accentuate the literary merit of the lyrics.

Lyric poetry is the intimate and personal expressions of the poet or a poet's persona. One notices in this type of poetry an emotional outpouring or transparency that demands responsiveness from performers who strive for matching. Such poetry is usually brief but potent in its revelation of the poet's mood and achings of the soul. Here are some of the most common examples of lyric poetry:

1. *The Sonnet*—A sonnet features fourteen lines, an evident rhyme pattern and beat predictability (called iambic pentameter, which will be described later in the chapter). The sonnet was a favorite artform for classical poets, especially. Note the highly personal and emotional nature of this sonnet:

"Death, Be Not Proud"
John Donne

Death, be not proud, though some have called thee
Mighty and dreadful, for thou art not so;
For, those whom thou think'st thou dost overthrow,
Die not, poor Death, nor yet canst thou kill me.
From rest and sleep, which but thy pictures be,
Much pleasure; then from thee much more must flow;
And soonest our best men with thee do go,
Rest of their bones, and soul's delivery.
Thou art slave to Fate, Chance, kings, and desperate men,
And dost with poison, war, and sickness dwell,
And poppy or charms can make us sleep as well
And better than thy stroke. Why swell'st thou then?
One short sleep past, we wake eternally,
And death shall be no more: Death, thou shalt die!

2. *The Elegy*—This example of lyric poetry reminds listeners of the memory of someone who has died. It is a poetic form of the eulogy. Examples include: Ben Jonson's "On My First Son," Theodore Roethke's "Elegy for Jane," Reed Whittemore's "On the Suicide of a Friend" and this example:

"To An Athlete Dying Young"

A.E. Housman

The time you won your town the race
We chaired you through the market-place;
Man and boy stood cheering by,
And home we brought you shoulder-high.

To-day, the road all runners come,
Shoulder-high we bring you home,
And set you at your threshold down,
Townsman of a stiller town.

Smart lad, to slip betimes away
From fields where glory does not stay
And early though the laurel grows
It withers quicker than the rose.

Eyes the shady night has shut
Cannot see the record cut,
And silence sounds no worse than cheers
After earth has stopped the ears:

Now you will not swell the rout
Of lads that wore their honours out,
Runners whom renown outran
And the name died before the man.

So set, before its echoes fade,
The fleet foot on the sill of shade,
And hold to the low lintel up
The still-defended challenge-cup.

And round the early-laurelled head
Will flock to gaze the strengthless dead,
And find unwithered on its curls
The garland briefer than a girl's.

From The Complete Poems by A.E. Housman by A.E. Housman.

3. *The Ode*—Odes express a celebratory feeling toward a person, object, or occasion. The language chosen for the ode is usually complex, sophisticated, and heavily mythic or metaphoric. Examples include: John Keats' "Ode On a Grecian Urn," Allen Tate's "Ode to the Confederate Dead," and Edward Field's "Ode to Fidel Castro." Here is a contemporary example of an ode (with a sense of elegy also):

"For Grandma (& You)"
Charles Kerns

Someone gently whispered, "goodnight. . ."
And slowly shut the door,
Where my imagination spoke to me
Of snuggle-up dreams and dancing hopes

Which reminded me of my grandma, who
When it was late at night,
Would let me know,
As she tucked me into bed,
That she loved me-
With a story and a hug,
And let me build sandcastles
Of dreams
With friends
Like Pooh and Oliver Twist,
For in that room
Of mothballs
And flannel P.J.'s
I knew that I could do anything—
Because she was there.

And on the day she passed away
I couldn't, I didn't cry
Because
I couldn't, I didn't
Remember.
You see, my long awaited friend
TIME
Met me at the door of the church
And together we had no use
For an old woman and her stories.

Reprinted by permission of Jane Kerns.

But as his fickle nature, is,
Off he ran with another,
And I was left standing with you—
Who opened-up my goodnight door
And said "hello" in no so special a way
But in a way that reminded me of a tiny room
And flannel P.J.'s
And mothballs.

And once again I Danced
And built sandcastles
And finally cried.

4. *Other Lyric Poetry*—Lyric poetry may be predominantly descriptive or reflective or purgative. Such poetry may not have a clearly defined form. "Mountain Lion" is a descriptive lyric poem in the present tense by D.H. Lawrence that relates a South American adventure stalking a wild beast . A past tense recollection is reflective, and a prime example is John Tobias' "Reflections On a Gift of Watermelon Pickle Received from a Friend Called Felicity." Purgative or confessional lyric poetry is brutally honest and personal. Such is the case in Sylvia Plath's scathing attack on her father in "Daddy." Find the lyric elements in this contemporary poem:

"Bit Part"
Charles Kerns

It was a perfect night for love,
And under the moonlight
As I wooed you with Shakespeare
His immortal words struck at my heart—
"All Life is a stage. . ."
Well, I dropped the book right there,
For suddenly I could see that he was right—
All of life IS a stage. . .
And I think that I'm the one who got stuck with a bit part.

You know,
The brother
Of the cousin

Of the step-sister
(twice removed)
Of the ex-girlfriend
Of the Hero.
The one who walks on stage and says,
"Hi Mom, I'm home!"
And then walks off again.

Let me tell you,
It's no fun to sit your life out in the wings—
Especially since you've bragged to everyone about
". . .how great my part is. . ."
And they never see you,
Because,
At the moment you delivered your great oratory
They were searching the program to find your name
(which they never did because it was misspelled)

But I guess I was never meant to play
That big role.
So the curtain comes down,
Everyone goes home
And I'm left reading Shakespeare to you.
To which you reply,
"Oh, I'm sorry, I didn't mean to fall asleep. . .please, keep reading."
And I do, wiping the last bit of make-up from my nose.

Dramatic poetry features a persona independent of the poet. The first-person perspective for a created persona characterizes such poems. Such poems place personae in conflict situations. Dramatic poetry may consist of a *monologue* (addressing a silent character), a *soliloquy* (speaking inner thoughts aloud to no one in particular), or a *narrative* (a personally told story or reminiscence). How would you classify this example of dramatic poetry? Is it truly a soliloquy or is it a monologue or narrative?:

"Soliloquy of the Spanish Cloister"

Robert Browning

Gr-r-r—there go, my heart's abhorrence!
    Water your damned flower-pots, do!
If hate killed men, Brother Lawrence,
    God's blood, would not mine kill you!

What? your myrtle-bush wants trimming
    Oh, that rose has prior claims—
Needs its leaden vase filled brimming?
    Hell dry you up with its flames!

At the meal we sit together:

Salve tibi! I must hear
Wise talk of the kind of weather,
    Sort of season, time of year:
Not a plenteous cork-crop: scarcely
    Dare we hope oak-galls, I doubt:
What's the Latin name for "parsley"?
    What's the Greek name for Swine's Snout?

Whew! We'll have our platter burnished,
    Laid with care on our own shelf!
With a fire-new spoon we're furnished,
    And a goblet for ourself,
Rinsed like something sacrificial
    Ere 'tis fit to touch our chaps—
Marked with L for our initial!

    (He-he! There his lily snaps!)

Saint, forsooth! While brown Dolores
    Squats outside the Convent bank
With Sanchicha, telling stories,
    Steeping tresses in the tank,
Blue-black, lustrous, thick like horsehairs
    —Can't I see his dead eye glow,
Bright as 'twere a Barbary corsair's?
    (That is, if he'd let it show!)

When he finished refection,
    Knife and fork he never lays
Cross-wise, to my recollection,
    As do I, in Jesu's praise.
I the Trinity illustrate,
    Drinking watered orange-pulp—
In three sips the Arian frustrate;
    While he drains his at one gulp.

Oh, those melons! If he's able
    We're to have a feast! so nice!
One goes to the Abbot's table,

All of us get each a slice.
How go on your flowers? None double?
    Not one fruit-sort can you spy?
Strange!—And I, too, at such trouble
    Keep them close-nipped on the sly!

There's a great text in Galatians,
    Once you trip on it, entails
Twenty-nine distinct damnations,
    One sure, if another fails:
If I trip him just a-dying,
    Sure of heaven as sure can be,
Spin him round and send him flying
    Off to hell, a Manichee?

Or, my scrofulous French novel
    On grey paper with blunt type!
Simply glance at it, you grovel
    Hand and foot in Belial's gripe:
If I double down its pages
    At the woeful sixteenth print,
When he gathers his greengages,
    Ope a sieve and slip it in't?

Or, there's Satan!—one might venture
    Pledge one's soul to him, yet leave
Such a flaw in the indenture
    As he'd miss till, past retrieve,
Blasted lay that rose-acacia
    We're so proud of! *Hy, Zy, Hine. . .*
'St, there's Vespers! *Plena gratia,*
    Ave, Virgo! Gr-r-r—you swine!

Narrative poetry has a story to tell and does so with both narrator and character commentary. Audience and offstage focal points combine to establish the locus of interaction and events. The briefest example of narrative poetry is the *ballad*. Ballads have a distinct rhythmic pattern, owing much to a heritage once linked to musical accompaniment. Ballads frequently have a repetitive refrain as many songs do. The language is simple, direct, and repetitive. Examples of ballads include: "Barbara Allan," "Lord Randall," and "The Demon Lover."

The other two prime examples of narrative poetry are long story-poems: the *metrical tale* and the *epic poem*. The primary difference between the two lies in the development of a story. Metrical tales vary in length, but purport to tell a full story in detail. Poems as diverse as Robert

Frost's "Home Burial" or Chaucer's *The Canterbury Tales* represent this type. Epic poems are generally long narratives that convey real and fictional, yet specific, accomplishments of a hero. Such poems frequently represent the mythic aspects of a culture or ethnic group. Classical examples include such epics as the Greeks' *The Illiad* and *The Odyssey*, Milton's *Paradise Lost*, and a contemporary re-telling of the Civil War myth, *John Brown's Body* by Stephen Vincent Benet.

Contemporary performers realize that a powerful new genre of poetry has emerged in recent years: *song lyrics*. Not all musical lyrics warrant performance apart from a melody, orchestrations, and context. Occasionally, a song lyric will stand apart as a compelling rhetorical poetic statement. Lyrics can generate controversy (e.g., 2 Live Crew's rap music), galvanize people together in social protest movements (e.g., "We Shall Overcome"), or speak to personal and private pains:

"I Dreamed A Dream"
from *Les Misérables—The Musical*

Alain Boublil, Claude-Michel Schönberg, Herbert Kretzmer, and Jean-Marc Natel.

Fantine:

There was a time when men were kind,
When their voices were soft
And their words inviting,
There was a time when love was blind
And the world was a song
And the song was exciting.
There was a time.
Then it all went wrong.

I dreamed a dream in days gone by
When hope was high and life worth living.
I dreamed that love would never die,
I dreamed that God would be forgiving.

Then I was young and unafraid
And dreams were made and used and wasted.
There was no ransom to be paid,
No song unsung, no wine untasted.

But the tigers come at night
With their voices soft as thunder.
As they tear your hope apart,
As they turn your dream to shame.

He slept a summer by my side,
He filled my days with endless wonder.
He took my childhood in his stride,
But he was gone when autumn came.
And still I dream he'll come to me,
That we will live the years together,
But there are dreams that cannot be,
And there are storms we cannot weather. . .

I had a dream my life would be
So different from this hell I'm living,
So different now from what it seemed.
Now life has killed the dream I dreamed.

Song lyrics have long served a persuasive function.[1] The challenge for the performer of literature is to let the lyrics function independent of a discernible melody with its own unique rhythms and emphases. The poetry of Bob Dylan, Simon and Garfunkel, Sting, Billy Joel, The Cure, Dire Straits, Smashing Pumpkins, Mike and the Mechanics, and scores of other popular culture performers provide influential commentary and images for this generation. Musicals by Stephen Sondheim and Andrew Lloyd Webber include songs with a social consciousness as well. And the intricate rhythmic banter of rap music holds keen insights into ethnic cultural norms. A performer of literature should not ignore the genre of song lyrics for poetic performance choices.

Component Features of Poetry

As was mentioned in chapter seven, sensory imagery is a necessity for the performer of literature. All of the senses are addressed in poetic literature. During the pre-performance analysis stage, sensory imagery connects a performer to the poem's persona and the audience as well. Appealing to the senses in a poem accentuates the emotional component of poetry.

But poetry has an emotional/cognitive function as well and various figures of speech clarify, rejuvenate, and energize the language of poetry. Many figures of speech appear in and enhance poetic literature.

FIGURES OF SPEECH

Literary figures are forms of expression used to share meaning or alter given assumptions by comparing or identifying one object or concept with another. Twelve of the most common figures of speech used in poetry are: Simile, Metaphor, Allusion, Allegory, Personification, Paradox, Oxymoron, Hyperbole, Litotes, Apostrophe, Synecdoche, and Metonymy.

Simile and *metaphor* are related, but different. A simile correlates two items by the words *like, as,* or *as if.* A metaphor does more than correlate; a metaphor claims that when compared two items are said to be the same. In two popular song lyrics, Bob Dylan uses a simile to link life to being "like a rolling stone" while Bette Midler proclaims in metaphor that "you are the wind beneath my wings." Consider how Shakespeare uses metaphor in this sonnet:

"Sonnet 129"

William Shakespeare

The expense of spirit in a waste of shame
Is lust in action; and till action, lust
Is perjured, murderous, bloody, full of blame,
Savage, extreme, rude, cruel, not to trust;
Enjoyed no sooner but despisèd straight;
Past reason hunted, and no sooner had,
Past reason hated, as a swallowed bait,
On purpose laid to make the taker mad.
Mad in pursuit, and in possession so;
Had, having, and in quest to have, extreme;
A bliss in proof; and proved, a very woe;
Before, a joy proposed; behind, a dream.
All this the world well knows, yet none knows well
To shun the heaven that leads men to this hell.

Allusions are references to other literary works, events, and cultural icons. Frequent allusions to classic myths, references in the Bible, and recent or historical events occur in poetry. "He robbed Peter to pay Paul" is an allusion to the two New Testament apostles.

Allegory and *personification* also share a common theme. Personification consists of attributing human nature to animals, abstract concepts, objects, people, or other observable phenomena. Allegory carries forth the attribution and systematically sustains the imagery. John Donne's poem, "Death, Be Not Proud" uses personification in attributing cessation of life to an entity called "Death." Walt Whitman sustains the imagery of a sea captain and a precarious voyage as a direct allegorical referent to Abraham Lincoln in the poem, "O Captain! My Captain!"

Paradox and *oxymoron* focus on similar images. Both concern apparent contradictions. A paradox states that two contradictory statements can be true and not true simultaneously. An oxymoron is an unresolved contradiction. Solomon used poetic paradox in Song of Solomon 5:2 as he stated to his lover, "I was asleep, but my heart was awake." Comedian and political pundit Mark Russell gave his explanation of an oxymoron when he referred to "The Ronald Reagan Memoirs." A less politically motivated example of an oxymoron occurs in the poetic line, "The soft, smooth surface was jagged and rough hewn."

A statement of exaggeration uses *hyperbole*. Overstatement, when combined with other figures, emphasizes imagery to the extreme. In Alfred Lord Tennyson's poem, "The Eagle," hyperbole is used to describe the eagle's descent: "And like a thunderbolt he falls."

A *litotes* is the opposite of hyperbole. Understatement hides true feelings and that which affirms is suggested by denying the opposite. "He was in no way stupid" is an example of a litotes.

When one addresses an inanimate object, God, or an absent persona, *apostrophe* is the figure. Apostrophes imply pleading and a desire to communicate. David uses apostrophe in the poetry of the biblical Psalms. In Psalm 55:1, David pleads, "Give ear to my prayer, O God; And do not hide thyself from my supplication."

Synecdoche and *metonymy* are closely related. Synecdoche substitutes a part for the whole. Metonymy substitutes one word or abstraction for another closely associated referent. Referring to your automobile as your "wheels" is using synecdoche. "The White House" uses metonymy to imply the President of the United States and his opinions.

Knowing these figures of speech is useless unless you understand their role in the imagery sharing process. Poetry uses such devices to create a beauty and excitement in language and expression. Such figures allow poetry to say in few brief stanzas what novelists and playwrights speak in pages and scenes. Study, analyze, and prepare to share poetic figures of speech when you perform literature.

REPETITION AND PARALLELISM

Poetry frequently shares a variety of repeated sounds and words. As a pattern develops, the performer of poetry needs to be sensitive to accentuating the repetition and at the same time controlling it.

Alliteration is the repetition of similarly pronounced consonant sounds. These consonant sounds are usually at the beginning of words. The key words in a stanza that receive emphasis when performed frequently retain this rather repetitive sound. Note in the following line how alliteration uses /f/ and /s/ sounds:

<u>F</u>ear led them into a <u>f</u>eeding <u>f</u>renzy of <u>s</u>eared con<u>sc</u>ien<u>c</u>es.

Consonance is akin to alliteration, but the repeated consonants are usually internal and end sounds. Hard sounding consonants like /d/ or /t/ exemplify this poetic device:

The <u>t</u>au<u>t</u> <u>t</u>ether stretch<u>ed</u> in<u>t</u>o the pla<u>t</u>inum vaul<u>t</u>.

Assonance consists of repeated vowel sounds within a stanza, phrase, or poetic segment. You should hear the /ool/ sounds in this example:

The gh<u>oul</u> came quietly, nervously, brandishing his t<u>ool</u> to attack the f<u>ool</u>.

Some poetry repeats lines or refrains in a parallel fashion. Parallelism may also be the repeated initial wording with new additions. Ancient Hebrew poetry, as evidenced in the Psalms of the

Bible, integrated parallel form frequently. Contemporary poetry may exemplify the use of refrain or chorus in song lyrics or merely a recurring phrase, repeated to make a point in the literature. Notice the use of parallelism and refrain in this contemporary poem:

"Rain, Rain, . . ."

Todd V. Lewis

I was born in the rain—
      The glistening, translucent droplets
Covered my body.
      Tingling the rain
Coating my soul with a dewy film.
      "Rain, rain, go away, come again some other day."
          Just "singing in the rain" I went through life—
Looking at the beads of sweat in people's eyes.
Seeing the concentration
Of Perspiration on their faces—
"Into everyone's life a little rain must fall," I told myself.

But the rain never stopped!
"Rain, rain, go away, come again some other day!"
Rain had wrinkled my hands
      Had stung my face with its poisonous coldness
      Had made me wet and numb and senseless.
Rain had ruined my chances of basking and tanning
      In the warmth and tenderness of the Sun.

The Sun—The Sun—
      Some said it was above the clouds
      Sending out beams that somehow never penetrated
      The clouds of precipitation.
Existence predicted,
      reality a notion of faith.

"Rain, rain, go away, come again some other day!"
One night as I was about to fall asleep
      From an eternity of being awake
          I had a dream.

I dreamed of a yellow house
      Round and bright
      Glistening with the rays of the Sun.
I touched the handle to the front door,
"Ow! So warm, so hot, so absent of wetness!"
But it would not open at first.

Was it only a dream?
> No, I have found the yellow house—
> Or. . .did the yellow house find me?

Was it only a dream?
> No, I could feel the heat
> Or. . .was I merely deluded by rain?

"Rain, rain—"
> You cannot touch me, caress me, embrace me
> When I am in the door to the Sun.

"Rain, rain—"
> The back door—
>> the door back—
>> is locked forever.

RHYME SCHEME

Most people think poetry must rhyme to be poetry. This is not necessarily always true, but a poem with rhyming features seems cohesive and centered. Rhyme links words with the same vowel and succeeding sounds. The corny "moon/June" rhyme from trite love songs illustrates how rhyming unifies words and expressions, even in weak or simple verse. Dr. Seuss discovered many years ago that preschoolers and imaginative adults responded to rhyme links in stories and fables. Rhymes may be at the end of sentences, in the middle of phrases, perfect in sound matching, or merely similar in spelling.

Rhyming shares a relationship with *onomatopoeia,* the use of words with inherent sounds. Remember the vocal exercises in chapter four expressing sounds and attitudes. Certain sounds help a poet underscore, even "verbally underline," key elements. Be sensitive to bringing out the tone color of literature by analyzing and performing the sound words you discover.

METER

All poetry has rhythm, but only *conventional poetry* has a strict regular rhythm. *Free verse* has rhythm but it is irregular, unpredictable, and not always easy to chart or study. When you study the rhythm of poetry, you naturally focus on where vocal stress and emphasis fall. Not every word is stressed in poetry. Some words are important because they come after stressed words or syllables. The study of emphasis patterns in poetry is the study of *meter.*

In poems that are considered "free verse" a pattern of rhythm can exist without a predictable rhyming feature. Consider the poetic aspects of this "free verse" poem that does not rely on rhyming to create its imagery:

"The Swimming Pool"

Thomas Lux

All around the apt. swimming pool
the boys stare at the girls
and the girls look everywhere but the opposite
or down or up. It is
as it was a thousand years ago: the fat
boy has it hardest, he
takes the sneers,
prefers the winter so he can wear
his heavy pants and sweater.
Today, he's here with the others.
Better they are cruel to him in his presence
than out. Of the five here now (three boys,
two girls) one is fat, three cruel,
and one, a girl, wavers to the side,
all the world tearing at her.
As yet she has no breasts
(her friend does) and were it not
for the forlorn fat boy whom she joins
in taunting, she could not bear her terror,
which is the terror
of being him. Does it make her happy
that she has no need, right now, of ingratiation,
of acting fool to salve
her loneliness? She doesn't seem
so happy. She is like
the lower middle class, that fatal group
handed crumbs so they can drop a few
down lower, to the poor, so they won't kill
the rich. All around
the apt. swimming pool
there is what's everywhere: forsakenness
and fear, a disdain for those beneath us
rather than a rage
against the ones above: the exploiters,
the oblivious and unabashedly cruel.

[from *Thomas Lux: New and Collected Poems, 1975-1995*. New York: Houghton Mifflin Company, 1997.
Used by permission.]

Studying meter can be very complicated and too much detail falls outside the scope of this course or this textbook. But here is some basic information. Dividing a poetic line in a conventional poem into rhythmic units focuses on each *poetic foot.* Trimeter (three feet), tetrameter (four feet), and pentameter (five feet) are the most common line lengths in most poetry you would read.

Varying the stress on syllables or words creates descriptive patterns. *Iambic pentameter,* a very popular poetic rhythm pattern (used by Shakespeare in his verse plays as we discovered in chapter nine), has five feet wherein each foot has an unstressed syllable followed by a stressed syllable. This line is an example of iambic pentameter:

$$\cup \; / \quad \cup \; / \quad \cup \quad / \quad \cup \quad / \quad \cup \quad /$$
Get up/, get up/ for shame/, the bloom/ing morn.

The cupped symbols represent unstressed syllables and the accent marks indicate where stress falls in the sentence.

Other stress patterns include: *Trochaic* (a foot of two syllables with stress on the first syllables followed by an unstressed syllable); *Anapestic* (a foot of three syllables, two of which are unstressed followed by a stressed syllable); and *Dactylic* (a foot of three syllables with a stressed syllable followed by two unstressed syllables).

Are you lost? Are you completely confused yet? Do not be discouraged or overwhelmed by this microscopic view of poetry. If you study the component features of poetry prior to performance, you will make stronger performance choices. Now it is time to prepare a poetry program for a class performance.

Prior Preparation for Poetry Interpretation

Edward Hirsch has seven suggestions for the preparation that goes into reading a poem:

1. Turn off the television
2. Carry a book of poetry with you or have one near at hand for some chance or unexpected moment you have to read.
3. Find a comfortable chair in a place that's quiet, inside or outdoors.
4. Relax.
5. Read the poem silently; then read the poem slowly again out loud to yourself.
6. Pay attention to the sounds of the words and the rhythm of each line.
7. Remember what Wallace Stevens once said: "In poetry, you must love the words, the ideas and images and rhythms, with all your capacity to love anything at all."[2]

As you have learned, poetry has layers of possible meanings. The compact nature of poetry means each line or stanza may be more important in terms of performance than a line in prose or drama. You must not slide over ambiguous or unclear phrases in poetry; stop and know what each section suggests before you move on in rehearsal.

Rhyme and rhythm "should not be stressed to such an extent that they become so noticeable to an audience so as to detract from the meaning and feeling."[3] To illustrate his potential problem, read a segment from Edgar Allan Poe's highly rhythmic poem, "The Bells":

> To the tintinnabulation that so musically wells
> From the bells, bells, bells, bells, bells, bells, bells—
> For the jingling and the tinkling of the bells.

If you were to read Poe's entire poem, performing rhythm patterns exclusively and downplaying thought groups, you would have your audience bouncing their heads to the beat, but failing to understand Poe's content or meaning.

A general maxim to follow may help you when you read poetry aloud in performance: *Perform thought groups, not merely lines.* Some thought groups culminate or have natural pauses at the end of a poetic line; other thoughts carry over to the middle of the next line. Avoid predictability in rhythms unless such parallel rhythm builds to a climax. Keep yourself from a "singsong" pattern that could lull or distract an audience.

When performing contemporary song lyrics as poetry, do not seek to duplicate melodic patterns necessarily. Do not listen to a recording and try to duplicate the rhythms in spoken language. View song lyrics as poetry; view them as an artistic expression distinct from music or melody. Speak the song as a poem, not merely as a truncated tune.

Some performers benefit from marking up a conventional poetry program with stressed and unstressed symbols. The cups and accent marks help them understand the nuances of meter and other poetic features. Prior to your final performance use an unmarked script, however. A marked script may be difficult to read and may force a strict adherence to rhythms you might naturally vary.

In a class performance, poetic selections may be too brief to meet a time limit. Consider a thematic poetry program, linking several poems by the same or different authors. After each poem performance close your manuscript cover and provide an original transition, which connects the poems to each other as well as to the over-all theme.

Poetry is generally brief enough so that editing or cutting is not required. If you must edit, edit stanzas in toto. As a rule, do not cut any part of a short poem.

"Whenever a poem enacts what it is about, it creates a way for itself to live dramatically inside the reader. It becomes an experience unto itself. The great individual poem is the message salvaged from a shipwreck and sealed in the bottle. . .This haunted and haunting message was meant for you."[4]

You can find truly wonderful examples of great poetry in literature anthologies and the poetry section of your library. Choose poetry that has limited ambiguity and sounds clear orally for your class performances. To help you with suggestions here is a sample of possible sources.

Suggestions for Poetry Performance

CLASSICAL POETRY (CONVENTIONAL AND FREE VERSE)

The Bible	*Psalms, Proverbs, Ecclesiastes, Song of Solomon*
William Blake	"Song," "The Tyger"
Robert Browning	"My Last Duchess"
George Gordon, Lord Byron	"The Destruction of Sennacherib"
Lewis Carroll	"Jabberwocky"
Samuel Taylor Coleridge	"The Rime of the Ancient Mariner"
Stephen Crane	"War Is Kind"
Thomas Gray	"Elegy Written in a Country Churchyard"
Henry W. Longfellow	"Evangeline," "Hiawatha"
Andrew Marvell	"To His Coy Mistress"
Edgar Allan Poe	"The Raven," "Annabel Lee"
William Shakespeare	Any of his sonnets
Percy Bysshe Shelley	"Ozymandias," "Ode to the West Wind"
Alfred Lord Tennyson	"The Charge of the Light Brigade"
Walt Whitman	Any poem from Leaves of Grass
William Wordsworth	"The World Is Too Much with Us"

MODERN POETRY

Maya Angelou	"On the Pulse of Morning" (1993 Presidential Inaugural Poem)
W.H. Auden	"The Unknown Citizen"
Stephen Vincent Benet	*John Brown's Body,* "Nightmare at Noon"
Ray Bradbury	"Why Didn't Someone Tell Me About Crying in the Showers?"
Gwendolyn Brooks	"We Real Cool"
Gregory Corso	"Marriage"
e e cummings	"anyone lived in a pretty how town" "somewhere i have never traveled"
Emily Dickinson	"I Heard a Fly Buzz—When I Died"
Paul Lawrence Dunbar	"We Wear The Mask"
T.S. Eliot	"The Love Song of J. Alfred Prufrock" "The Waste Land"
Edward Field	"Unwanted," "A Note to My Father," "Mae West"
Robert Frost	Any poem
Allen Ginsberg	"Death to Van Gogh's Ear"
Nikki Giovanni	"Knoxville, Tennessee"
Gerard Manley Hopkins	"God's Grandeur"
Langston Hughes	"Mother to Son," "Dream Deferred"
Keillor, Garrison	"The Old Shower Stall"

Amy Lowell	"Patterns"
Claude McKay	"Outcast," "If We Must Die"
Mall, Taylor	"Voice of America Voiceover," "Totally Like Whatever, You Know," "Like Lilly, Like Wilson"
Mason, Dave	"Song of the Powers"
Ogden Nash	*Good Intentions*
Wilfred Owen	"Arms and the Boy," "Dulce et Decorum Est"
Sylvia Plath	"Lady Lazarus," "Daddy," "Ariel"
Edwin Arlington Robinson	*Spoon River Anthology*
Carl Sandburg	Any poem
Robert Service	"The Cremation of Sam McGee"
Karl Shapiro	"Auto Wreck"
Dylan Thomas	"Fern Hill," "Do Not Go Gentle Into That Good Night"
Judith Viorst	*People and Other Aggravations* *Forever Fifty and Other Negotiations*
Diane Wakoski	"Dancing on the Grave of a Son-of-a-Bitch"
William Butler Yeats	"The Second Coming," "Byzantium"

SONG LYRICS

Aerosmith	"What It Takes," "Nobody's Fault" (Steven Tyler, Joe Perry, Desmond Child, Brad Whitford)
Pat Benatar	"Hell Is for Children"
Blink 182	"Stay Together for the Kids"
Counting Crows	"Mr. Jones"
The Cure	"A Letter to Elise"
Dave Mathews Band	"Seek Up"
Dire Straits	"Industrial Disease," "It Never Rains"
Larry Gatlin	"The Big Time Again"
Amy Grant	"Love of Another Kind," "I Will Remember You"
Billy Joel	"Pressure," "We Didn't Start the Fire"
Kansas	"Dust in the Wind"
Mike and the Mechanics	"In the Living Years"
Paul Simon	"The Sounds of Silence"
Smashing Pumpkins	"Disarm"
Stephen Sondheim (James Lapine)	"Send In the Clowns," "No One Is Alone"
Sting	"I'm So Happy I Can't Stop Crying"
Pearl Jam (Eddie Vedder)	"Jeremy"
Andrew Lloyd Webber, Charles Hart, Robert Stilgoe	"The Music of the Night," "All I Ask of You"

Assignments

1. Prepare a poetry program for class presentation. Make sure that multiple poem programs have poetry linked thematically and by the communicative premises shared in the literature. Write out transitions that further the theme as well as connect the individual pieces.

2. Discuss with your classmates the meanings of contemporary song lyrics. Choose a current popular song and ask small groups to describe the theme, the context, and the intent of this poetic form. Can you perform song lyrics without having heard the original tune or rhythm? How does one practice saying or doing the rhythm of a rap song?

References

Athanases, Steven Z. "When Print Alone Fails Poetry: Performance as a Contingency of Literary Value." *Text and Performance Quarterly* 2 (April 1991): 116-127.

Ciardi, John. *How Does A Poem Mean?* Boston: Houghton Mifflin Company, 1975.

Haas, Richard and Williams, David A. *The Study of Oral Interpretation: Theory and Comment.* Indianapolis: The Bobbs-Merrill Company, Inc., 1975.

Keefe, Carolyn. "Verbal Interactions in Coaching the Oral Interpretation of Poetry," *National Forensic Journal* 3 (Spring 1985): 55-69.

Keillor, Garrison, ed. *Good Poems.* New York: Viking, 2002.

Koppell, Kathleen S., ed. *Live Poetry.* New York: Holt, Rinehart, and Winston, Inc., 1971.

Lee, Charlotte and Gura, Timothy. *Oral Interpretation—10th Edition.* Boston: Houghton Mifflin Company, 2001.

Williams, David A. *Poetry As Communication.* Lanham, MD: University Press of America, Inc., 1992.

Yordon, Judy. *Roles In Interpretation-5th Edition.* Boston: McGraw Hill, 2002.

Notes

1. See Chapter 13, "The Persuasive Functions of Songs," in Charles J. Stewart, Craig Allen Smith, and Robert E. Denton, Jr., *Persuasion and Social Movements. 2nd Edition.* (Prospect Heights, IL: Waveland Press, Inc., 1989).
2. Edward Hirsch, "Let It Flow," *Los Angeles Times* (April 28, 1998): E2.
3. Paul Hunsinger, *Communicative Interpretation.* (Dubuque, IA: William C. Brown Publishers, 1967), p. 86.
4. Hirsch, E2.

CHAPTER **11**

Readers Theatre and Other Group Forms of Interpretation

One of the most exciting variables in the performance of literature occurs when you form a group to present a text. Multiple performers join forces to transfer literary texts to the playing arena of the human mind. Group performances of literary texts share commonality with play productions and media offerings, but are not limited to dramatic literature, proscenium or thrust stages, costumes, lighting, or theatrical trappings. At the same time, the group performance of literature is not bound by rigid rules that require manuscripts or scaled down production elements. The emphasis for the group performance of literature centers on fostering the imagination and critical thinking processes of the audience.

One of the oldest forms of group performance is *choral reading.* Choral reading, the unison recitation or chanting of literary phrases, stanzas, or refrains by multiple performers, was a feature in ancient Greek drama. Frequently this chorus of voices would summarize plot developments or relay a moral and philosophical message. A parallel use of choral recitation occurred in the religious services of the ancient Hebrews. The legacy of this religious tradition passed to Christian worship practices and the emerging Catholic Mass. Even to this day, Catholic and some Protestant liturgical services include choral reading/recitation of scripture and service formats. In recent times, Reform Jewish synagogue services have developed a choral reading liturgy as well.[1] Today choral reading occurs in schools (used by teachers to teach reading and performance skills), dramatic productions, prisons, psychological therapy sessions, religious centers, or as an incorporated group performance option in *Readers Theatre.*

What is "Readers Theatre"? In this chapter, Readers Theatre (or RT) will be the generic term used to describe a highly flexible and innovative performance form. No longer a "poor" theatrical substitute, Readers Theatre has no limitations in genres of literature or production aspects. It does have definitive features, however.

Definitive Features of Readers Theatre

Readers Theatre is a hybrid theatrical form. Two or more performers perform literary texts composed of prose, drama, or poetry so that a communicative message emerges and fosters imaginative responses in the minds of an audience. One should not argue that RT and conventional drama are distinct merely because RT calls for audiences to use their minds. Conventional drama is clearly imaginative. RT has been called "Theatre of the Mind" because it asks audiences to use psychological closure to imagine scene contexts, historical ambiance, multiple character portrayals, and message elements. Some RT productions approximate fully produced stage plays while other productions are stark, using only stools and lecterns and minimal theatrical accouterments.

The "hybrid" nature of RT comes from what Coger and White call "a fusion of acting, interpretation, and rhetoric."[2] In practice, Readers Theatre tends to be even less restrictive theatrically than solo or duo literary performances. In content, a Readers Theatre presentation needs to have a clearly developed theme, argument, message, or communicative intent.

In a RT production manuscripts may or may not be present and used. The term *Readers* should not imply reliance on a manuscript, but refers to the more generic universal *readers* who hear and participate as performers and audience members. Still, when a notebook manuscript is present it suggests a symbolic commitment to a text as well as a commitment to the use of script as imaginative prop or device. Most RT productions today place more emphasis on the term *Theatre,* preferring to generate audience interest and imagination by the devices of the theatre. Thus, performers can be expected to move locations in a playing area, join in performing multimedia augmentations (e.g., music, slides, video, film), or wear clothing corresponding to the actual costume or mood necessary for a scene.

RT makes use of such focal points as audience focus, offstage focus, inner-expressed focus and a fourth focal point: onstage focus. Onstage focus, the focus of conventional drama, calls forth direct eye contact and interaction with fellow performers. Using onstage focus does not necessarily transform Readers Theatre into a play. However, when used to highlight intimate aspects of a scene in RT, onstage focus serves to draw attention.

As in solo or duo performances eye gaze determines scene location. Offstage focal points may be wedged (seeing the "other" character at the apex), cross-focused, or directly onstage. Focus in RT can be *mixed,* but it should never be *inconsistent.* It makes sense to stage an omniscient narrator so that onstage focus occurs. It is inconsistent to have one per-

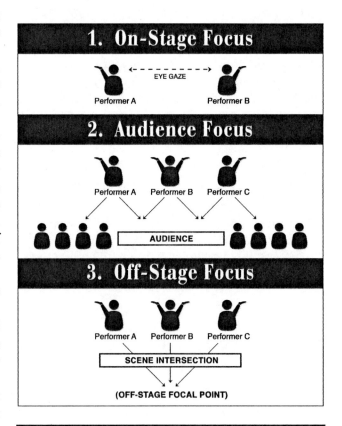

Figure 11.1 Three Focal Points in Readers Theatre

former address a persona offstage while the other performer responds by looking directly at the colleague onstage.

A word is necessary here about the communicative dimension of RT. The performance of literature in any group format should be more than mere entertainment. RT needs to provide opportunities for audiences to think, ponder, and perhaps even alter behavior or attitudes. Michelle Miller-Rassulo believes that such an emphasis in scripting can be used to "trigger" persuasion and

> link public speakers with interpreters in an effort to make informed choices and decisions about their lives and influence the world around them through the sensitive communication of literature.[3]

Readers Theatre has no restrictions in terms of literature or space. While conventional drama requires scripting into dramatic mode, all genres may be "dramatized" in RT. Novels, short stories, essays, poems, chants, songs, oral histories—all these and more can be divided into lines and offered in a group performance format. Generally, conventional drama requires *pictorial space* (the limited performance arena); RT uses *found or acoustic space* (the whole environment, including the audience's minds).

RT has now invaded Broadway. For years certain plays and musicals have had elements of RT concepts. The epic production from the Royal Shakespeare Company of *Nicholas Nickleby* included multiple casting, cast as narrators, minimal sets, and audience focus. Director and compiler Frank Galati, an oral interpretation and Readers Theatre text author, won the 1990 Tony Award for Best Direction of a Play for *John Steinbeck's The Grapes of Wrath.* Galati's adaptation makes use of many RT features but more closely approximates a specialized group performance format called *Chamber Theatre.*

Chamber Theatre is a specific term used to describe the staging of prose fiction. The format was described and developed by Robert S. Breen of Northwestern University. In Chamber Theatre the narrative point-of-view is paramount. While personae are frequently fully costumed and a text memorized with full production elements, narrators gain equal stature with the characters of the literature. Narrators move in and out of scenes, serving as observers, commentators, or interpreters. Some Chamber Theatre productions leave prosaic tag lines in a script to reveal narrative functions and rhythmic elements as well. The 1993 London production of Graham Greene's novel, *Travels With My Aunt,* transformed the novel into a Chamber Theatre. Four men, dressed alike, performed all character roles and each played the same character in different scenes. Tag lines were frequently left stated in asides to the audience. No scripts were apparent, but narrative portions were addressed directly to the audience while dialogue lines were delivered directly onstage.

Chamber Theatre and most Readers Theatre productions utilize principles of theatrical *alienation.* Experimental playwright/director Bertolt Brecht introduced alienation principles into his plays so that audiences would not forget that his plays were predominantly persuasive (frequently politically motivated). Alienation, from Brecht's perspective, is not a negative factor.

Here is a list of alienation devices that break down the imagined "fourth wall" of a play and bring the audience to a place of cognitive involvement:

1. *Scripts may be present.* Narrators may use them exclusively or all performers may have them;
2. *Offstage or Audience Focus is used.* This clearly places the location of the scene and interaction in the realm of the audience;
3. *Narrators and performers may portray more than one persona.* By moving location, altering vocal patterns, or adding or subtracting costume features, performers present multiple characters;
4. *Narrators and performers may collectively portray one persona.* Called *bifurcation,* two performers may represent inner or outward expressions or complexity of personality. *Trifurcation* uses three performers to portray one persona;
5. *Physical action may be mimed or suggested.* Scripts may be used as props. Set pieces may become imagined properties. Pantomime frequently replaces actual activities;
6. *Performance space may include the realm of the audience.* Personae may walk, exit, or enter to a scene from a seat or location in the audience. Some interaction may occur from playing area to the audience seating space;
7. *Live action performance may be juxtaposed with multi-media presentation.* Performers may act out a scene while slides, video, film, or musical presentations occur onstage with them.

The actual scripted format of a Readers Theatre presentation features many different variables. Whether presenting a single source or multiple source program, some of the primary adaptive mechanisms in scripting include:

1. *Choral Line:* More than one performer reads simultaneously with another, matching pitch, volume, tone, and rhythm so that a single sound is suggested;
2. *Antiphonal Line:* A performer begins a phrase, and without pause, another performer responds or completes the sentence;
3. *Repeating Line:* To emphasize a word or phrase of text, one performer will repeat the portion as an interjection between lines;
4. *Character Lines:* Each time a persona has dialogue have a performer say it. Bifurcate the lines or narration to show contrast between actual dialogue and inner thoughts;
5. *Fade In/Fade Out Line:* Two performers playing the same person can segue one to another in the middle of a line by gradually decreasing and increasing volume. Only a small portion is overlapped and choral;
6. *Split Word Line:* This device is very difficult to accomplish without rehearsing. Each reader states one word of a line with tone and timing making it sound like one person reading one line. Speech and tempo are at a normal speed and performers must learn timing and rhythm of speech to make it sound like one person speaking without halting or breaking.

Line division features are a part of the script preparation process. In the next section, you will discover how to adapt a single or a compiled script selection for use in group performance.

Script Preparation

A script for Readers Theatre needs to be prepared in such a manner that all cast members have an equal and fair opportunity to perform. When possible, all cast members should have moments to "star" or be the focus of attention. Scripts with three to six performers tend to be the norm, due mainly to the logistics of using few performers in the limited confines of found space. Generally, line divisions in a performance script should not exceed two minutes in length without interruption (with the possible exception of lengthier monologues). This prevents audience boredom and helps generate energy in smaller, quicker presentational units.

It is easier to read and perform from a script with clearly designated line divisions and parts. Since performers may play more than one character role, indicate what lines will be presented by numbers (e.g., Reader 1, Reader 2, etc.). Indentations from the left margins allow for notebook holes without cutting out lines. If you wish to reduce the number of page turns, type even numbered pages with a greater right hand margin and adhere odd and even pages back to back. This should allow even pages to be spread out on the left side of your script and odd pages on the right.

Even though virtually any literary text can be presented in a Readers Theatre format, remember to choose literature that is stimulating, dimensional, credible, and not too complex. You may mime physical action in RT, but it should not dominate a scene. Choose literature that expresses points-of-view by means of enriched language.

You must consider the length of your production. Class assignments may range from fifteen to twenty-five minutes in length. Some audiences may have shorter or longer attention spans. If you must edit a larger work, seek wholeness and consistency. Present episodes that have completion and a sense of finality. Cut out nonessential scenes; summarize events with transitional narrative material if you must.

How do you make decisions about dividing lines as you prepare a script? There is no one way or right way to divide the lines. Adding additional voices in juxtaposition or in choral variations give variety to a literary text. To show you an example of adapting a script through line division, consider the following poem in its original form and in its group performance adapted form:

"Atonement"
Todd Lewis

The politicians lied to us.
"Vote for me and I will be responsible."
We voted for them
And they blamed events for their own shortcomings.
"The Buck Stops Here!"

Is a despair-filled lie!!—
A monumental deception
With a magnitude that blares forth
The inescapable excuse.

We read their lips
And they sounded like trust.
But the chant is hollow
And empty
And without substance.
Denial,
After denial,
After denial
Only postpone
The inescapable excuse.

The time has come, my friends,
To deny the politicians
And do what they are too proud to do.
When no politician claims fault,
We must be responsible.
We have the answer to
The inescapable excuse.

The forest fire does not implode
Because we deny setting the spark.
The fire of hatred and injustice
Will not abate when we look another direction.
The fire that consumes us,
Like a St. Elmo's Fire from the pits of Hell,
Knows the answer to
The inescapable excuse!

The answer is a simple, yet humbling act.
Not exclusively the rite of the pious,
It serves heretic and saint alike.
The answer to
The inescapable excuse
Is—

Atonement.

What does it mean?
Why does it heal?
Why must it be personal?

Because
It and it alone
Transforms Blame into Shame
And the inescapable excuse. . .
Into Hope.

Reader 5:	The politicians lied to us.
Reader 1:	"Vote for me and I will be responsible."
Readers 2,3,4:	We voted for them and they blamed events for their own short-comings.
Readers 1,5:	"The Buck Stops Here!"
All:	Is a despair-filled lie!!——
Reader 2:	A monumental deception with a magnitude that blares forth the inescapable excuse.
Readers 2,3,4:	We read their lips
Reader 5:	And they sounded like trust.
Reader 3:	But the chant is hollow
Reader 2:	And empty
Reader 4:	And without substance.
Reader 1:	Denial,
Readers 1,2:	After denial,
Readers 1,2,5:	After denial
Reader 3:	Only postpone the inescapable excuse.
All:	The time has come, my friends, to deny the politicians and do what they are too proud to do.
Reader 4:	When no politician claims fault,
Readers 4,5:	We must be responsible.
All:	We have the answer to the inescapable excuse!
Reader 1:	The forest fire does not implode because we deny setting the spark.
Reader 3:	The fire of hatred and injustice will not abate when we look another direction.
Reader 2:	The fire that consumes us, like a St. Elmo's Fire from the pits of Hell,
Readers 4,5:	Knows the answer to the inescapable excuse!
Reader 3:	The answer is a simple yet humbling act.
Reader 1:	Not exclusively the rite of the pious, it serves heretic and saint alike.
Reader 2:	The answer
Readers 1,2:	To the inescapable excuse is—

All:	Atonement.
Reader 4:	What does it mean?
Reader 5:	Why does it heal?
Readers 3,4,5:	Why must it be personal? (Pause)
Reader 2:	Because it and it alone transforms
Readers 1,2:	Blame into Shame
All:	And the inescapable excuse. . . into Hope!

Script preparation varies depending on the type of group performance text you present. Readers Theatre texts may be *single* or *compiled formats.* In single format texts one literary selection comprises the performances. Plays are the easiest single format text to convert to Readers Theatre. The best plays for Readers Theatre presentation feature message-oriented dialogue and interaction, superseding spectacle and physical action. Epic novels or poems adapt well to this single selection approach to scripting also.

Compiled texts may use a wide variety of literary genres and authors. The compiled script gathers many sources and finds unity in a common theme or rhetorical message.[4] If you have a strong desire to communicate an argument or thesis, than you will arrange your pieces as you would arrange a persuasive speech: Introduction/Thesis/Examples of the Extent of the Problem/Examples of Solutions/Ending Statement. Another possible structure may emerge from the topic of the performance. A Readers Theatre compiled script entitled "The Stress Mess" linked various literary selections together as examples of low level to high level stress moments as indicated on a psychological test. The performance text evolved from the simple stress of changing eating habits to the devastation resulting from the death of a child or spouse. An author's works may be the connection in a compiled script (e.g., *The World According to Carl Sandburg*, a 1950s Broadway adaptation). Other formats may strive to follow a musical structure, with a literary selection or song lyric recurring as a bridge or transition device. Compiled scripts need to achieve a rhythm and balance between serious drama and humorous release as well.

A second approach to the compiled script turns a program into a *collage.* A collage has recognizable component parts but they are juxtaposed seamlessly into a program. Fragments may be used of newspaper headlines or stanzas of poems or paragraphs from short stories or novels. While the director and the cast must attempt to keep the personae distinct to honor the authors of each text, the juxtaposition, in effect allows the compiler, the director, and the cast to make their own performative statement or persuasive intent.[5]

The number of persons you decide to cast should be determined by the literary selections you use. Multiple casting for a variety of personae makes smaller casts possible. Sometimes you must have the precise number of textual readers indicated or implied. For example, a Readers Theatre program that features "Your Fault," a semi-rap chant from Stephen Sondheim and James Lapine's *Into the Woods* requires five performers since five distinct personae interact in this rhythmical "tour-de-force" musical number.

Once you have determined to perform a specific text, you must audition, cast, and rehearse the performers. Rehearsal times will vary in length and the preparatory process should take from three to five weeks, depending on the sophistication of the text and the experience of the performers.

Casting and Rehearsing

Your instructor may provide you with sample Readers Theatre scripts or ask you to compile your own for an in-class activity. You should be able to choose a script you prefer to perform. Once your performance group has been formed, you will need to determine who should read individual lines.

The first rehearsal should consist of random part distribution and "cold readings." If a director is involved, have several participants read scenes or segments until the best match emerges in various parts. Ratliff suggests that at the first reading one should "indicate the literary character's emotional or intellectual condition and reveal the chronological or sequential events revealed in the story line."[6] A script should be divided into segments or scenes so that subsequent rehearsals can focus on polishing smaller increments of the entire text.

Early rehearsals in group performance need to allow time for discussion of the production concept and theme. Analysis of the literary texts is necessary for all performers. The compiler or director may need to share the broader context if some selections are obtuse or edited or unknown. Without dictating a "clone-like" replication, a director may have to read a line to help performers catch the vision of the show. Hugh Morrison addresses the controversy of "demonstration" in rehearsal directly when he states that wise directors give very clear advice and frequently show a performer what is expected. When "demonstration" is ignored, "the result has been a woefully large amount of undirected rubbish in all areas from the fringe to theatres of repute."[7] Directors and cast members should be mutually supportive and encouraging as a production begins. Performers seem more willing to work and spend tedious moments going over sections if a director or cast members offer constructive criticism and helpful commentary.

Middle rehearsals may focus on individual line interpretations. These rehearsals need to stress energetic cue pickups, consistent phrasing rhythm, matching voices in pitch harmonies for ensemble portions, consistent focal points, timing, and credible personae choices.

Eventually, staging and blocking arrangements need to be rehearsed. (We will develop this topic in the next section.) Bring a pencil to rehearsals, marking stage directions and movements in the margins of the performance scripts. Later rehearsals need to emphasize off-the-script focal point clarity, smooth movements in transitions, and continued growth and maturity in line interpretations.

Whenever possible, have two "dress" rehearsals. Invite a small select audience of friends to come to both rehearsals. Remember that when an audience laughs, you must hold the next line delivery until the laughter subsides. Be ready for something to go wrong. The unexpected usually happens in RT. Learn to keep going, covering for another's mistakes or omissions, and not breaking the mood or the rhythm. At the conclusion of the final dress rehearsal, evaluate the presentation and invite the select audience to comment. If any minor adjustments need to be made before a performance, schedule a brief scene-refinement rehearsal.

Before you reach the final performance stage, you must decide on staging and movement choices. These decisions will make the aural text visually appealing.

Staging and Blocking

Since RT techniques call for an audience to use imagination, set pieces, movements, and physical arrangements can be subtle or suggestive. Know how much found space you have in which to perform. Compose a schematic with drawings indicating set pieces used and playing area. Readers Theatre does not demand elaborate sets, scrims, thrust stages, furniture, or flats. Nondescript, multi-functional boxes and blocks aid perceptual imagination. Many RT productions use ladders, stairs, stools, and other platform variables to set the scene.

Any found space can be diagrammed as if it were a theatrical playing area. The diagram below indicates nine segment divisions used for staging:

Upstage R	Upstage Center	Upstage L
Center Stage R	Center Stage	Center Stage L
Downstage R	Downstage Center	Downstage L

Figure 11.2 Performance Areas in Found Space

The areas that draw the most attention are "strong" areas. Center stage is the most powerful area; you should place important characters and scenes at center stage. Downstage areas (those closest to the audience) are also influential. Designations of right or left are from the perspective of the reader who faces the audience. Upstage positioning should be used for supportive personae, background narrators, observers, or as a retreat for those who are momentarily out of the scene.

Textual clues or transitions should generate decisions on when and how to move. As a rule, move to new locations or formations while someone is delivering a line. "Dead air" silence as you move is annoying and causes distraction and a disruption in the flow of the production.

To best understand movement variables consider three axis planes or dimensions: *x, y,* and *z.* The "x" axis consists of the stage right to center to left positions. Readers A, B, C, and D can be juxtaposed along an imaginary line like this:

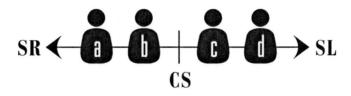

Figure 11.3 "X" Axis

The "y" axis dimension moves performers upstage to downstage, along this continuum:

Figure 11.4 "Y" Axis

The "z" axis plane uses vertical space. By using height variations of blocks, sets, stools, and ladders, performers move along this path:

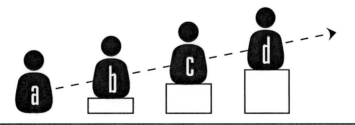

Figure 11.5 "Z" Axis

Effective blocking and staging attempt to use combinations and variations of these formats. Angles of bodies, cluster groupings, curving formations, and various geometric shapes create interesting stage pictures. Try to avoid straight lines; they lack dynamic perception. Keep taller performers in back of shorter performers or compensate with height variables from set pieces. No one should intentionally be blocked out of view if an ensemble portion is offered.

Movement for the sake of movement sends a distracting message. People in the audience will watch the movements and not pay attention to the language of the text. Avoid walking in front of any other performer delivering lines with offstage focus. You may or may not wish precision page turns together if scripts are used. Your movement decisions are ideal if the audience is unaware of the magnitude of the changes. Smooth and subtle movement furthers the aesthetic beauty in this artistic production format.

Unlike conventional dramatic productions, RT performers seldom walk off the playing area. Entrance and exit techniques suggest your presence or absence from a scene:

1. *Bowed Heads.* Dropping your chin to your chest communicates that you are out of the scene. Raising your head brings you back into the scene;
2. *Turn Around.* Turning your back to an audience removes you from view and the scene. Turning to full or half front stances serves as an entrance;
3. *Moving to a New Scene Location.* This device signals that you are reading a different persona, or a new location now exists for the next episode;
4. *Stand or Sit.* When you do either of these actions, coupled with others indicated above, you signal an exit or an entrance;
5. *Lighting.* Spotlight or flashlight or candlelight can bring you in or out of a scene too.

When a director needs to simulate the passage of time or the sensation that time has stopped, certain movements help relay information about time:

1. *Freeze.* Remaining motionless tells an audience that time has momentarily stopped. When you resume action or break the freeze, time begins again;
2. *Slow Motion.* It can comedically appear to portray rapid movement slowed down to highlight physical activity. The musical *Les Misérables* uses this device to link the beginning of Act Two to the end of Act One after the Intermission as the crowd mimes the riotous actions of a mob in slow motion;
3. *In-Place Movement.* It gives the impression of walking or running without leaving the spot. Such motions are suggested and understood as connected to time passage by the audience;
4. *Accelerated Movement.* Fast movements, similar to an old silent movie, speed up time in a comical manner.

RT productions have in recent days integrated live music or a cappella singing into the production. Such use of music should be on pitch or in harmonies; music should not be used merely as a gimmick, but be connected thematically and attitudinally to the production concept. Clothing choices may be ensemble dress, in actual costumes, or color-symbolic variations. Consider what apparel looks best in the playing area. Darker colors show up better against lighter backdrops. Whatever "special effects" you choose to use should enhance the presentation, not draw attention away from the language and message of the text.

Conclusion

The time has come to perform your Readers Theatre script. Hopefully, the hard work and hours of rehearsal time have prepared you for an outstanding performance. Many students who have taken a beginning level oral interpretation course indicate that this assignment is their favorite. Enjoy the moment and bring all of your previous solo and duo experiences together into superior performance choices as a group.

Assignments

1. If your campus has a Readers Theatre class or troupes, watch a videotape of a rehearsal or performance. Notice the use of movement and line divisions for cast members. How do focus lines differ? Do all cast members share equally in importance and line readings? Do you notice group cohesiveness in ensemble work (e.g., choral reading)? Discuss the presentations with constructive criticism and commentary in your class.
2. Your instructor may assign you to a pre-written RT script or ask you to compose your own. Set aside class time for rehearsals, establish two out of class dress rehearsals, and perform your group project in class. Receive constructive criticism from your professor and classmates after the presentation. Grades for this assignment may be given individually or to the entire group.
3. Now that you have a production completed and performed, seek other outlets for performance. Take it to other college classes or elementary schools or churches or hospitals. RT has creative possibilities in a wide variety of settings.

References

Adams, William. *Institute Book of Readers Theatre: A Practical Guide for School, Theater, & Community.* San Diego, CA: Institute for Readers Theatre, 2003.

Breen, Robert S. *Chamber Theatre.* Evanston, IL: William Caxton Ltd., 1978.

Coger, Leslie Irene and White, Melvin R. *Readers Theatre Handbook. 3rd Edition.* Glenview, IL: Scott, Foresman, and Company, 1982.

Kaye, Marvin. *From Page to Stage.* Garden City, NY: The Fireside Theatre, 1996.

Kaye, Marvin. *Reader's Theatre.* Newark, NJ: Wildside Press, 1995.

Kleinau, Marion L. and McHughes, Janet Larsen. *Theatres for Literature.* Sherman Oaks, CA: Alfred Publishing Company, 1980.

Lee, Charlotte and Gura, Timothy. *Oral Interpretation-10th Edition.* Boston: Houghton Mifflin Company, 2001.

Lewis, Todd V. *RT: A Readers Theater Ministry.* Kansas City, MO: Lillenas Publishing Company, 1988.

Lewis, Todd V., Thomas, Jerry and Anthony, Elizabeth Ryrie. *RT For Christmas.* Kansas City, MO: Lillenas Publishing Company, 1998.

Long, Beverly Whitaker; Hudson, Lee; and Jeffrey, Phillis Rienstra. *Group Performance of Literature.* Englewood Cliffs, NJ: Prentice-Hall, Inc., 1977.

Maclay, Joanna Hawkins. *Readers Theatre: Toward A Grammar of Practice.* New York: Random House, Inc., 1971.

Ratliff, Gerald Lee. *Introduction to Readers Theatre: A Guide to Classroom Performance.* Colorado Springs, CO: Meriwether Publishing Ltd., 1999.

Tanner, Fran A. *Readers Theatre Fundamentals.* Caldwell, Idaho: Clark Publishing Company, 1987.

Yordon, Judy. E. *Experimental Theatre: Creating and Staging Texts.* Prospect Heights, IL: Waveland Press, Inc., 1997.

Notes

1. See a sample group performance liturgical service liturgy at Temple Beth Tikvah, Columbus, Ohio in Todd V. Lewis, "Traditions of Group Reading," unpublished master's thesis, The Ohio State University, 1974, 79-82.

2. Leslie Irene Coger and Melvin R. White, *Readers Theatre Handbook. 3rd Edition.* Glenview, IL: Scott, Foresman, and Company, 1982, 3.

3. Michelle Miller-Rassulo, " 'Trigger' Your Audience: Trigger Scripting as a Contemporary, Integrative Event," *National Forensic Journal* 6 (Spring 1988): 22.

4. See: Michael Leigh, "Composite RT: Strategies, Structures and Tactics"; Gertrude Breen, "Making a Composite Script"; and Janet Brehe, "Script Compilation: Steps in Becoming a Connoisseur", *Readers Theatre News* 10 (Fall/Winter 1982), 3-8.

5. Judy E. Yordon, *Experimental Theatre: Creating and Staging Texts.* Prospect Heights, IL: Waveland Press, Inc., 1997, 15-16.

6. Gerald Lee Ratliff, *Introduction to Readers Theatre: A Guide to Classroom Performance.* (Colorado Springs, CO: Meriwether Publishing Ltd., 1999), 20.

7. Hugh Morrison, *Acting Skills.* New York: Theatre Arts Books, Routledge, 1992, 157-158.

CHAPTER **12**

Evaluating Oral Interpretation Performances

Your professor in this oral interpretation course is not the only person who evaluates a performance. When you are not performing you need to be learning about performance by observing and evaluating others. If being an audience member was insignificant you could make an appointment, read your selection, and depart. The truth is you improve as a performer with each experience, and you develop a style and a wider selection of presentational options when you respond as an audience member.

In this chapter you should learn techniques to become a fair and objective listener as well as a helpful evaluator and critic. Exposure to lay and professional performances enhances your presentational maturity by expanding your choices. You can also learn practical and theoretical aspects of performance by means of journal articles and academic treatises.

Listening to a Performance

Communication research reveals that we spend most of our time listening; we spend an average 45 to 55 percent of our time listening. We frequently develop poor listening habits, though, because we live in a world where natural and technological stimulations compete for our attention always. The radio constantly blares in our cars. The headsets drum out our favorite music. The sounds of shrill birds, a pounding rain, an alarm clock, a professor's lecture—all these sounds and more bombard us with distractions. We "hear" these sounds but we do not attach meaning to them until we "listen" to them. *Listening* is an active decisive process of receiving aural stimuli and of organizing the results into cognitive patterns. Listening gives meaning to sound. Listening is a crucial skill for any audience member in a performance setting.

There are three general types of listening: *enjoyment, information,* and *help.* You listen for enjoyment to the CD player as it reproduces your favorite music. You listen for enjoyment to a radio broadcast of a basketball game or the comedic happenings on a television show. You listen for enjoyment to a dramatic production on a stage. This type of listening is relaxing and relatively passive. Listening for information is more active. You concentrate to obtain data or learn a new skill or pass a test. We listen to gain knowledge we do not have. Listening to help requires empathy and receptivity. We assess the data and respond with advice or reactions.

The audience member for an oral interpretation context should listen with each of these purposes in mind. To facilitate such listening we need to be physically and mentally alert. Such simple reactions as upright posture, heads leaned toward a performer, and a stance that is quiet and still assists active listening. An effective listener must come to a context awake and capable of concentration. Few things upset a performer as much as an audience member who falls asleep, snores, or nods continually in quick catnaps.

Audience members need to listen to performers in a nonjudgmental manner. Prejudgment is an especially unfair attribute. The critic who sits in an audience and mentally tunes out a performer, saying, "I really hate material from this author. I refuse to listen," is discourteous. We need to delay judgment until a performance is complete, than assess the result of the performance.

Although performers need to choose presentational material adapted to particular audiences, do not terminate listening because the literature is difficult to understand. You may need to listen more intently when the literature is complex. Perhaps the most difficult listening task is to confront unpleasant or uncomfortable topics. Attempt to assess the validity or credibility of persona choices even if the content of a literary selection is deemed by you to be profane, obscene, or inappropriate. For example, as difficult as it may be for you to listen to a program on the theme of suicide when your best friend took his own life, the performer deserves a fair hearing and you can indicate your discomfort and still provide helpful commentary about the textual performance.

Audiences should allow themselves the freedom to empathize with a performer. To feel as a character feels may elicit tears or understandable anger. To nod in agreement or smile or react emotionally is to experience the listening opportunity fully. The audience member who can participate at this level of empathy knows the thrill of careful listening and responsiveness.

Distractions abound in any performance situation, but the sensitive audience member will attempt to filter out other stimuli to give undivided attention to a performer. Unexpected noises or interruptions will upset a performer only if the interruptions disturb the audience's attention. You cannot stay attuned to a performance continually, but you can will your mind back to concentration by volition.

A courteous audience will strive to respond to each performance with kindness as well as critical assessment. An empathetic audience gives clear feedback in verbal and nonverbal reactions to performance elements. An audience that refuses to prejudge will evaluate a performance by its consistency to a text, even if the text itself is distasteful or unappreciated. A fair audience exercises effective listening habits.

Evaluating a Performance

In the appendix of this text you will find several perforated sheets that are available to you. You will need to submit these to your professor for evaluative purposes. Each time you perform in class a written assessment of your performance is made and returned to you. For at least one of your class presentations your peers may evaluate you in a group-graded format. You should improve your performance with each subsequent presentation, especially when you adjust and correct critical areas indicated on these written evaluation sheets.

Just as management and leadership strategies emphasize the need for positive reinforcement in business, so also should evaluations of performance support positive results. The performer needs to know when he or she does something well so that success can motivate. Look for examples in performance that represent excellence and encourage a performer by indicating them. A positive evaluator might say, "You did an excellent job of projecting volume. I was sitting here in the back corner and could hear every word."

To be balanced, however, we do student performers very little service if we exude all positive comments, say how great the performance was, and give a "C" grade. Evaluations need to answer the question: "Why?" Offer constructive criticism that suggests alternatives or weaknesses in communicative effectiveness. Indicate specific areas where improvement is needed. Such criticism should never be malicious or become a personal attack on a performer. It is completely unacceptable to criticize a performance by saying that the performer is stupid or mentally inferior. Make sure you do not make a fool of yourself as an evaluator as did the critic who commented to the British foreign exchange student, "The British accent is really phony. Lose it." An evaluator helps a performer improve when criticism is direct, operational, and caring.

It is not that unusual for two or more students to choose the same literary text to perform. This can be a source of embarrassment to some readers who may feel inferior or may feel like the audience is bored because they are hearing the same piece again. As a critic, you have a unique opportunity to comment on how two or more individuals, working independently, make choices for performance. You should comment and encourage the "choice" selection while at the same time commenting on "choices" that worked and "choices" that were not as compelling.

To elicit evaluative commentary, you will need to ask probing questions of yourself. The answers to these questions will generate constructive commentary that you will write on evaluation forms. Break down your commentary into segments of preparation and performance. The following categories will help you make comments other than "Good job. I liked it!":

COMMENTS ON INTRODUCTIONS AND TRANSITIONS:

1. Is a clear *theme/argument/communicative intent* indicated?
2. Does the introduction establish a *context* (e.g., time, setting, necessary background details, etc.)?
3. Is there enough information given about *characters* to understand what is happening? Do we know who is talking to whom?
4. Are the introduction and transitions too wordy? Are they too brief to be helpful?

COMMENTS ON LITERARY CHOICE:

1. Does this literary text connect to the *theme/argument/communicative intent* mentioned in the introduction and transitions?
2. Has editing been done in a manner that makes the text easy to follow and understand?
3. Does the text have a sense of "quality" and "literary merit"?

4. If asked to compare performance texts and performance matching, which performer accomplished the performance task with more difficult or complex material?
5. Does the performer understand the language of the text?
6. Is the text appropriate or suitable for the specific audience?

COMMENTS ON PORTRAYAL OF PERSONAE:

1. Does each "new" selection or text have a unique persona in multi-text programs?
2. Are the personae distinct in a single text?
3. Are the personae credible and genuine?
4. Does a monologic persona *grow* or *change* or *evolve* in a text?
5. What kinds of verbal and nonverbal character tags does a performer give to each persona? (Can you recognize actions or expressions that seem to be identified with a character's motivations?)

COMMENTS ON DELIVERY TECHNIQUES:

1. Is volume varied and projected?
2. Has the pitch range been widely and credibly used?
3. Do tempo and rate variations occur consistently with intent of the text? Is the reading too fast or too slow in segments?
4. Does the performer offer any subtextual clues to explain tone or motivations?
5. Is emotionality credible and sustained in performance?
6. Are words pronounced correctly? Do words sound clearly articulated?
7. Are focus and location of scene clearly represented? Is focus consistent?
8. Does the performer know the text well or is the performer dependent on the script? (Is eye contact minimal because a performer is reading the script too much and not looking up and out?)
9. Is phrasing smooth and fluid rather than choppy and unclear?
10. Does this performance lead in pacing toward a sense of finality and conclusion?
11. Is rhythm emphasized naturally and not excessively, leading to a sing-song pattern?

COMMENTS ON NONVERBAL COMMUNICATION:

1. Does the performer exhibit poise, confidence, and self control?
2. Are gestures motivated, well-timed, and natural in appearance?
3. Do postural changes and movement enhance the performance?
4. Do facial expressions seem consistent with the tone and attitude of the text?

CONCLUDING COMMENTS:

1. If a time limit is in force, was it within the time range?
2. Where is improvement primarily needed?
3. What aspects of performance require special commendation?
4. What "overall impressions" remain?

Listening Reports

Another means to improve your performance skill is to compare your choices with those lay and professional performers who have recorded some of their presentations. "Books on Tape" and other audio literature formats are a growing phenomenon, allowing busy commuters as well as home consumers to "hear" novels and other literary texts on audiotape or recording. Mystery and suspense is the most popular genre in the audiobooks format.[1]

Many college and university media centers have collections of performance tapes available for your use. You may check them out also from local libraries. Perhaps there is a special campus area that makes these tapes available for listening. Some campuses videotape theatrical and Readers Theatre performances and these tapes may be available for viewing.

Although the history of oral interpretation indicates the performance prowess of such literary giants as Mark Twain and Charles Dickens, not all authors who read aloud their own works are effective performers. Evaluating a taped presentation by an author who struggles with performance can be helpful to the novice performer. You may learn that certain performances could be improved with evaluative criticism.

At the end of this chapter you will find a sample listing of performance recordings and recording companies. Take the time and effort to listen to some of these recordings. Incorporate effective stylistic choices into your own performances. You can learn to avoid presentational choices that annoy or are weak after listening to these tapes.

Journal Articles

Oral Interpretation has a rich heritage, but new advances and applications to performance occur yearly. Textbooks cannot stay current with all trends and theories, but professional journal articles can. Seek out several key academic journals that include articles about the performance of literature.

Your professor or library may have back issues of these and other performance journals:

Text and Performance Quarterly
Readers Theatre News
National Forensic Journal
Issues in Interpretation
Educational Theatre Journal
Literature in Performance

Occasionally, performance-oriented journal articles appear in these journals as well:

Quarterly Journal of Speech
Communication Monographs
Communication Education

Critical Studies in Mass Communication
Journal of Media and Religion
Journal of Religion and Communication

Though frequently theory-oriented, these journal articles assist in the understanding of the performance of literature. Your library may also have access to theses and dissertations based on performance pedagogy, theory or history. They also provide penetrating analysis of performance options. You have the task of translating theory into practice after reading and studying these research articles and print resources.

During this term you will be asked by your professor to contribute to the class by offering peer evaluations. Do not be afraid or inhibited. The comments you make should not offend your friends. You offer criticism to help them improve. They, in turn, offer you help. Learning to be a thoughtful and caring critic usually serves you in your performances and you should be able to notice definite progress because you have served as an evaluator of others.

Sample Suggested Recordings and Publishers

The Poetry of Dylan Thomas (Read by Richard Burton)
Carl Sandburg Reads His Poetry
e e cummings Reads His Poetry
Edith Sitwell Poetry (Read by John Gielgud and Irene Worth)
The Lost World by Sir Arthur Conan Doyle (Read by James Mason)
Nicholas Nickleby by Charles Dickens (Read by Roger Rees)
Old Possum's Book of Practical Cats by T.S. Eliot (Read by John Gielgud and Irene Worth)
The Diary of Anne Frank (Read by Claire Bloom)
The Belle of Amherst—Emily Dickinson (Read by Julie Harris)
"The Green Hills of Earth" by Robert C. Heinlein (Read by Leonard Nimoy)
"Petrified Man"—(Written and Read by Eudora Welty)
The Hobbitt—(Written and Read by J.R.R. Tolkien)
The Little Prince by Antoine de St. Exupery (Read by Peter Ustinov)
The Screwtape Letters by C.S. Lewis (Read by John Cleese)

Audio Literature, Inc., 3800 Palos Verdes Way, So. San Francisco, CA 94080
Audio-Text, 8110 Webb Ave., No. Hollywood, CA 91605
Caedmon, 1995 Broadway, New York, NY 10023
Folkway Records, 43 W. 61st Street, New York, NY 10023
The Library of Congress, Recorded Sound Section, Washington, DC 20540
Spoken Arts, 310 North Avenue, New Rochelle, NY 10801

Assignments

1. For one of the class performance assignments, your professor will choose several students (who are not performing that day) to participate in a group-graded activity. Using the evaluative sheets available in the appendix, comment on a classmate's performance, offering constructive criticism and an assigned grade. Do not sign the evaluation sheet. Return it to the professor anonymously so that the grades of the group may be averaged with the professor's grade. All evaluation sheets will be collected and returned to each performer, multiplying the responses and evaluation commentaries normally received in class. Do not panic about peer grading; the average usually works out to the same grade you would have received originally from the professor. In some cases, the grade may be better than what you would have received.

2. Twenty to twenty-five percent of your course grade will be determined by "contract." Your professor will establish the contractual requirements for grades of "A, B, C, D, and F." You may be asked to fill out one or more "Listening Report" forms (found in the appendix). These reports should evaluate the performance skills of an audiotape performance, a videotape theatrical performance, or a dramatic radio play. Your contract may also include collateral reading of performance-oriented journal articles. Use the Journal Article Reading Report Forms found in the appendix. Finally, the contract may ask you to observe or participate in an intercollegiate performance festival or forensics tournament. Summarize your reactions on the form found in the appendix. Your professor will indicate to you when they are due during the course's term.

References

DeVito, Joseph A. *Human Communication 4th Edition.* New York: HarperCollins Publishers, 1988.

Lewis, Todd V. "Evaluation Criteria For Oral Interpretation and Readers Theatre Events at Collegiate Forensics Tournament." Unpublished paper presented at the Western Speech Communication Association Convention, Albuquerque, New Mexico, February 22, 1983.

Lewis, Todd V. "Toward a Dialogue: Oral Interpretation of Literature-Classroom Performance in Relation to Forensic Activity." Unpublished paper presented at the Speech Communication Association Convention, San Francisco, CA, November 19, 1989.

Wolff, Florence I., Marsnik, Nadine C., Tacey, William S., and Nichols, Ralph G. *Perceptive Listening.* New York: Holt, Rinehart and Winston, 1983.

Notes

1. Patricia Ward Biederman, "Readers Find Voice With Audiobooks," *Los Angeles Times* (June 11, 2001), B3.

CHAPTER 13

Specialized Forms and Outlets for Oral Interpretation

Special forms of oral interpretation narrow the focus of performance to the interests of particular audiences and topics. The strategies for analysis and preparation are identical, but the applications are unique and intriguing. You may wish to present literature that falls into one or more of these categories: program oral interpretation, original material interpretation, children's literature interpretation, multicultural interpretation, and religious scripture interpretation.

Program Oral Interpretation

Whether it is called "program reading" or "lecture-recital reading" or "reading on a theme" or "mixed interpretation," *program oral interpretation* (POI) intertwines distinct literary selections from diverse genres that are connected by a central theme. The performer seeks to compile a program of texts that gradually reveals a communicative perspective about values, issues, or themes. You may choose this format to comment on the life and interests of a particular author. You must do more than merely link the selections by author; you should indicate "theses" or "themes" that an author explores.

The "mix" of texts compels you as a compiler and performer to see the communicative center of a variety of literary texts. You may choose to create programs of literature with such themes as love, pain, war, guilt, death, blame, or loneliness. You may need to refine or narrow such general themes to unrequited love, emotional pain, war's effect on children, and so on. You are, in a true sense, an additional "creator" in this format. You decide the order and progression of the thematic texts as well as the communicative focus. An example of a mixed interpretation program with a theme centered on "the voyeurism of violence" might include such selections as: "I Sit and Look Out"—a poem by Walt Whitman; "The Congressman Came Out to See Bull Run"—an excerpt from the epic poem, *John Brown's Body* by Stephen Vincent Benet; "Out, Out—"—a poem by Robert Frost; and "Going To Meet The Man"—a short story by James Baldwin. Each of these selections focuses attention on people who watch violent acts and respond with apathy, voyeuristic fascination, unconcern, or distasteful bigotry.

The creative process of compiling a mixed interpretation program begins with one text that you enjoy and wish to perform. Careful analysis convinces you that a central message is apparent. Now you begin the search for other texts to go with this piece. Find and save more text options than you think you might need, because it is always easier to edit and cut than it is to add or "stretch" time and content. After your search you may discover that the original text is not the central part of the program. The initial piece may serve a stronger function as a transition piece to another. Within your prescribed time limit for performance, you cut, edit, and juxtapose your selections. You may want a humorous text to be included to contrast serious texts. You may wish a quick teaser to set the tone for the rest of the program. Choose the option and format that best highlights the texts and your chosen theme.

One formula for POI follows the pattern of: Introduction or Teaser/Selection/ Transition/Selection, etc. This approach requires audience focus and closed manuscripts to sep- arate text and commentary. A second formula follows a compiled or collage Readers Theatre for- mat. You present an Introduction that includes source listings of all textual references and the performance merges portions of each text into a seamless effect.

The primary danger of POI is the danger discussed in chapter three: forcing a text to say a message it does not intend. Any programming choices should maintain a commitment to each text's integrity and to the overall theme. Extreme care must be taken when performing using the second formula or collage effect. Since texts are "blurred" in the actual performance the distinc- tions in personae and integrity of individual texts require special attention. Observers should be able to delineate textual changes by your performance choices and not confuse texts. Remind yourself as a performer to keep the textual personae separated and vocally unique.

This should not hamper your creative abilities as a compiler to become a co-creator with the original authors or texts. Explore the creativity of a multi-text program and let literature share great ideas and perspectives.

Original Material Interpretation

Few oral interpretation textbooks mention the performance of *original material interpreta- tion*. Controversy surrounds this topic. The debate rages on and the arguments against such stu- dent performances may be summarized as:

1. Analysis of literature prior to performance is preempted when original material is per- formed;
2. Students write for "performance" not for "literary" expression;
3. Using "pen names" to protect personal identity is deceptive and unethical;
4. Evaluative commentary about author intent by a critic is made irrelevant.[1]

To be fair, these arguments specifically indict the use of original material in contest situa- tions. But for many of the critics of original material the concerns remain the same in any per- formance context.

Arguments in favor of the use of original material by student performers consist of:

1. Analysis of literature is *not* preempted by the use of original material;
2. Evaluative commentary should be text-centered, rather than author-centered. Author-intent is arbitrary and possibly difficult to assess, but textual commentary has a basis in hermeneutic analysis;
3. "Pen names" do not suggest unethical or deceptive behavior. Famous authors, such as Mark Twain and Stephen King, used pseudonyms during their careers and unethical behavior was never an issue over the names used for authorship;
4. Performing original material brings together two creative outlets: composition and performance. Performance studies scholars need to encourage this creativity.[2]

By allowing an opportunity to perform original material in performance classes we foster creative outlets. Integrity and ethics are not violated when original material is performed. Performers feel a surge of pride and accomplishment when they perform their own work.

Such outlets to present original material should be encouraged in the classroom and in other contexts also. Mary Frances HopKins, professor-emeritus of performance studies at Louisiana State University, echoes the sentiments of many scholars who believe that the use of original material can be an integral part of the study of literary performance as long as the text itself is available to evaluators and a text-centered analysis occurs.[3]

Ask your professor if it is permissible for you to perform original material. Indicate to the professor the genre of literature (prose/poetry/drama) and provide an advance copy. Learn from class evaluations and dialogue about your own performance skills and connection to your own text. See this situation as an occasion to improve your own writing as well as performance skills. You should discover that an "author" of literature has opportunities to become an excellent "performer" of original material.

Performing Children's Literature

Long after you have finished this course and this textbook, the principles of performing literature will still be useful to you. You will possibly be a parent one day and you will have the wonderful chance to read to your kids. Perhaps you might be a favorite aunt or uncle who comes over to babysit and you must read to the kids before they go to sleep. Children are a marvelous audience, but they have a limited attention span and they are so uninhibited that they will provide you with a clear indication of what they think of your performance skills. Take the challenge and be an effective reader or storyteller for children. What is it about this classic children's novel that continues to captivate children?:

from *The Lion, The Witch, and the Wardrobe*
C. S. Lewis

They looked around. There, shining in the sunrise, larger than they had seen him before, shaking his mane (for it had apparently grown again) stood Aslan himself.

"Oh, Aslan!" cried both the children, staring up at him, almost as much frightened as they were glad.

"Aren't you dead then, dear Aslan?" said Lucy.

"Not now," said Aslan.

"You're not— not a—?" asked Susan in a shaky voice. She couldn't bring herself to say the word *ghost* .

Aslan stooped his golden head and licked her forehead. The warmth of his breath and a rich sort of smell that seemed to hang about his hair came all over her.

"Do I look it?" he said.

"Oh, you're real, you're real! Oh, Aslan!" cried Lucy and both girls flung themselves upon him and covered him with kisses.

"But what does it all mean?" asked Susan when they were somewhat calmer.

"It means," said Aslan, "that though the Witch knew the Deep Magic, there is a magic deeper still which she did not know. . . ."

Children respond to strong rhythms, repetition, broadly caricatured personae, humorous situations, alliterations, appeals to the imagination, justice, fair play, and anything that deflates pomposity. Subtlety is too complex for kids. Read with overt attention to all performance aspects and let yourself be as uninhibited as the children in your audience. As you analyze a children's literary text, adjust your performance choices to this younger, more demonstrative audience.

Children do not know the social graces of being an audience. They have not yet learned that audiences behave a certain way. They may interrupt a performance with questions or long laughter periods. Encourage any responses and stop the performance to answer them.

Children love enthusiastic performers. They love distinct character voices with funny inflections and gestures. If you have an illustrated book, you may have to read to the side as you show each new picture in the book. Reading from the actual book may require that you be even more familiar with the text than you would normally. Do not let the presence of a book detract or minimize the level of energy you must bring to this type of reading.

You must remember to keep the pace of delivery moving and brisk, but not too fast. Let the kids say repeating lines chorally if they learn the pattern. Let them join in with you with your encouragement to do so. When you perform a text for children, you want them to learn to think for themselves. They may jump right in with you and say all the lines. This joint performance effort may stir up an interest in performing later on in their lives.

As much as they may be reticent to admit it, adults like to hear some children's literature also. They may enjoy it and absorb aspects of a text at a more mature level. As a performer you may have to ask adults to act, imagine, or respond to your story as if they were a certain age. Some classic children's stories have messages for adults and messages for children in the same context. For example, Norton Juster's classic children's novel, *The Phantom Tollbooth,* has droll characters and situations for children and a message of the importance of education for adults:

from *The Phantom Tollbooth*
Norton Juster

Things began to change as soon as he left the main highway. The sky became quite gray and, along with it, the whole countryside seemed to lose its color and assume the same monotonous tone. Everything was quiet, and even the air hung heavily. The birds sang only gray songs and the road wound back and forth in an endless series of climbing curves.

Mile after

mile after

mile after

mile he drove, and now, gradually the car went slower and slower, until it was hardly moving at all.

"It looks as though I'm getting nowhere," yawned Milo, becoming very drowsy and dull. "I hope I haven't taken a wrong turn."

Mile after

mile after

mile after

mile, and everything became grayer and more monotonous. Finally the car just stopped altogether, and hard as he tried, it wouldn't budge another inch.

"I wonder where I am," said Milo in a very worried tone.

"You're. . . in. . . the. . . Dol. . . drums," wailed a voice that sounded far away.

He looked around quickly to see who had spoken. No one was there, and it was as quiet and still as one could imagine.

"Yes. . .the. . . Dol. . . drums," yawned another voice, but still he saw no one.

"WHAT ARE THE DOLDRUMS?" he cried loudly, and tried very hard to see who would answer this time.

"The Doldrums, my young friend, are where nothing ever happens and nothing ever changes."

This time the voice came from so close that Milo jumped with surprise, for, sitting on his right shoulder, so lightly that he hardly noticed, was a small creature exactly the color of his shirt.

"Allow me to introduce all of us," the creature went on. "We are the Lethargarians, at your service."

Milo looked around and, for the first time, noticed dozens of them—sitting on the car, standing in the road, and lying all over the trees and bushes. They were very difficult to see, because whatever they happened to be sitting on or near was exactly the color they happened to be. Each one looked very much like the other (except for the color, of course) and some looked even more like each other than they did like themselves.

"I'm very pleased to meet you," said Milo, not sure whether or not he was pleased at all. "I think I'm lost. Can you help me please?"

"Don't say 'think,'" said one sitting on his shoe, for the one on his shoulder had fallen asleep. "It's against the law." And he yawned and fell off to sleep, too.

"No one's allowed to think in the Doldrums," continued a third, beginning to doze off. And as each one spoke, he fell off to sleep and another picked up the conversation with hardly any interruption.

"Don't you have a rule book? It's local ordinance 175389-J."

Milo quickly pulled the rule book from his pocket, opened to the page, and read, "Ordinance 175389-J: It shall be unlawful, illegal, and unethical to think, think of thinking, surmise, presume, reason, meditate, or speculate while in the Doldrums. Anyone breaking this law shall be severely punished!"

"That's a ridiculous law," said Milo, quite indignantly. "Everybody thinks."

"We don't," shouted the Lethargarians all at once.

"And most of the time *you* don't," said a yellow one sitting in a daffodil. "That's why you're here. You weren't thinking, and you weren't paying attention either. People who don't pay attention often get stuck in the Doldrums." And with that he toppled out of the flower and fell snoring into the grass.

To find suitable children's literature, visit your local public library or a nearby bookstore. If it has been years since you visited the children's books section, you are in for a treat. Ask your professor if the performance of children's literature could serve as an alternative option for an in-class assignment. Re-discover (or maybe "discover" for the first time) the humorous worlds of Roald Dahl and Shel Silverstein, the fairy tale visions of the land of Narnia in the C.S. Lewis books, the sounds and rhymes of Dr. Seuss, the classic tales of Mark Twain, Robert Louis Stevenson, and The Brothers Grimm and so many others.

Multicultural Interpretation

We understand more about a different culture when we are compelled to read about it and even orally perform the literature of a culture. As Gamble and Gamble remind us, "In studying a variety of works, you can come to appreciate the ideas, beliefs, customs, and attitudes that characterize each group of people. . . . Such attitudes, as well as the behaviors through which these attitudes are manifested, reveal themselves in the literature of that culture."[4]

As an optional reading assignment, your professor may request that you choose to perform a literary text from diverse cultures within the United States, Africa, South America, Asia (including Japan, China, Korea, India), Russia, Israel, Europe (including England, Scotland, Wales, Ireland, France, Spain, Norway, Sweden, Denmark) and Micronesia. The text may be primarily written in English, but accents, dialects, structure of text, and occasional foreign phrases in the native tongue will be a challenge for you as your attempt to empathize with the other culture. A program on the Holocaust would be incomplete without poetry from survivors, such as Yuri Suhl's Yiddish and English poem, "The Permanent Delegate."

You will have to listen to accent tapes or talk to people from a distinct culture if the text itself is written with the sounds of the culture. You do not want to caricature the cultural voice, but you do need to represent it as best you can. The following text by Scottish poet Robert Burns requires a "wee bit of the Scottish brogue" to present it fairly and accurately:

"A Red, Red Rose"
Robert Burns

O my luve is like a red, red rose,
    That's newly sprung in June;
O my luve is like the melodie
    That's sweetly played in tune.

As a fair thou art, my bonie lass,
    So deep in luve am I;
And I will luve thee still, my dear,
    Till a' the seas gang dry.

Till a' the seas gang dry, my dear,
    And the rocks melt wi' the sun;
And I will luve thee still, my dear,
    While the sands o' life shall run.

And fare thee weel, my only luve,
    And fare thee weel a while;
And I will come again, my luve,
    Tho' it were ten thousand mile!

Here is another excerpt from a multicultural text written by a young African American male for the 1995 Essence Awards and performed by Oprah Winfrey at the annual Essence Awards ceremony. You may not have the dialect or accent to duplicate, but you can create a buoyancy with the pride and sense of accomplishment:

Excerpt from "Essence 25"
Khephra Burns

Forgive me if I boast a bit, but I am an
Emmy-winning, Oscar-copping, Grammy-grabbing,
Pulitzer Prize poet and Nobel Laureate,
beloved. My word, yes, I'm bookish. On
everybody's best-seller list. Seems like all
my best conjure comes out in words. Words
that cast spells like the songs of Solomon,
like jazz. Words that possess the secret of joy.
I know you know me. I was that sass-mouthed
colored girl on Broadway who couldn't just
sing a nice somewhere-over-the-rainbow song. . .
My by-line alone would fill a volume or two.
I'm Toni Morrison. I'm Maya Angelou. I'm
Ntozake Shange and Rita Dove. I'm Terry
McMillan and Alice Walker and Gwendolyn
Brooks. Look me up sometime. I'm in the book.

Religious Scripture Interpretation

The Bible and other religious scriptures are classic examples of the world's great literature. Allusions in world literature make references to these scriptures and an educated person needs to be familiar with the original literary texts. Fear of mixing church and state in public education creates an aversion to studying the Bible as literature occasionally, but the performance of religious scriptures does not need to be sectarian or merely a religious worship opportunity. These religious works are filled with great prose selections, epic tales, stirring poetic images, and deep philosophical ponderings. All too often some well-meaning readers present these texts as though

[Excerpt from "Essence 25" by Khephra Burns. *Essence Magazine* (October 1995): 96–97; 142–143]

they were "a series of dead quotations." As Charlotte Lee states, "It is they [readers of scripture] who make one yearn to hear [scripture] read fully."[5]

When you read the Bible or other scriptures aloud in a performance opportunity or even as part of a religious practice, bring to the reading the same skills and attention you would bring to any other type of literary performance. Audiences used to the drone of uninvolved readers will listen with renewed interest to stories and truths as if for the first time. "It is refreshing to listen to a reader who makes a conscious effort to help the audience catch the biblical writer's thought."[6] Scriptures with plot and characters and imagery need credible voices for personae, ranges of vocal patterning, attention to subtextual tone, and consistent nonverbal qualities. Poetic references need to be read with sensitivity to parallelism and rhythmic features.

English translations of the Bible vary from the classic King James Version to the modern paraphrased idioms of The Living Translation Bible. Other excellent reading translations include: The Torah, The New English Bible, The Jerusalem Bible, The New American Standard Version, and The New International Version. Choose a version that accommodates your presentational choices.

Some students may prefer to perform other religious scriptures. For example, *The Book of Mormon* has a similar biblical mode recounting a pre-historic American culture in a prose style. *The Mahabharata* is a two-thousand-year-old Indian poem and serves as the basis for Indian religion, history, and philosophy. Composed of one hundred thousand Sanskrit couplets, this massive work has several English translations and narrative elements with dialogue suitable for performance. *The Koran,* the holy book of Islam, also has narratives and pronouncements that could be presented in an effective oral reading format.

Each of these specialized forms for the performance of literature has unique features. Your previous training will assist you in bringing these special forms to the performance arena with energy, enthusiasm, and insight. Now we turn to outlets and opportunities to demonstrate your performance skills outside the classroom.

Performance Outlets

You signed up to take this beginning oral interpretation course for several reasons. Now as you reach the end of the course and the end of this text, you may well ask, "So where do I go from here?" There are numerous contexts available for you to improve your performance skills as well as use them to benefit others.

FESTIVALS AND FORENSIC CONTESTS

Oral Interpretation festivals are extra-curricular "celebrations" of literature. Intercollegiate participants agree to come to a campus location for noncompetitive sharing and appreciation of literary performance. Formats vary but usually interpretation scholars lecture on aspects of performance, followed by individual and group performances. A reaction and response time ensue after the presentations and the appreciation and analysis of a performance text results.

No matter what part of the nation you live in a festival occurs nearby. Festivals usually take place over a two- or three-day weekend. The focus of the festival experience is on learning, developing evaluative and analytical insights, and interactive discussion.[7] The casual atmosphere that surrounds the festival environment has the capacity to enhance your understanding of performance and analysis because gifted professors and experienced performers can dialogue about the activity in a comfortable setting. Festivals may have a keynote address by a prominent academic who specializes in performance. The schedule frequently has opportunities for students to perform as soloists and groups with a follow-up period for discussion and interaction.

Forensics (a term connected to ancient Greek legal communication and more recently applied to argumentative debate and public address competitive situations) began to expand to encompass diverse oral interpretation events at contests in the early 1970s. Most contests no longer offer a single "oral interpretation" event category, but divide the performance of literature into such event categories as prose, poetry, drama, duo drama interpretation, program oral interpretation, and Readers Theatre. Forensic contests offer competitive settings to perform and be ranked for purposes of award presentation. Approximately eight hundred colleges and universities compete in forensic tournaments during an academic season. Many of these schools have an active contingent of oral interpreters involved with the competition.

Typically, a student performer will enact the same program a minimum of three times before three critics and audiences. Judges use ballots to rank order the competitors and the top five or six competitors perform in a final round with multiple critics present. The winners receive trophies or plaques to commemorate their success.

Invitational and regional contests abound in every region of the country. National organizations sponsor tournaments at the end of the academic year that bring outstanding student performers together. Prestigious contests are sponsored by the American Forensic Association, National Forensic Association, Phi Rho Pi (the community college forensic association), and the fraternal honorary forensic organizations Pi Kappa Delta and Delta Sigma Rho-Tau Kappa Alpha (DSR/TKA).

While forensics tournaments can provide outlets for excellence, the competitor needs to be aware of basic rules for the interpretive events. Time limits generally run from eight to ten minutes and many judges penalize student competitors who go overtime by a significant amount (e.g., more than thirty seconds). Event categories are specific to genres of literature (except when combined in events such as POI). You must be sure that the text you have chosen to present fits in the proper genre/event category. Many speech tournaments divide competitors by level of experience and offer divisions for novices (beginners) and experienced performers.

If you are observing or competing in a forensic tournament for the first time, you will also notice some clear differences between the contest performances and your class presentations. The forensic competitor has usually practiced the selection more than the class participant has. The forensic competitor has the text virtually, if not completely, memorized. The demeanor of the forensic competitor at times seems to be quite "slick" and very professional.

While certainly there are basic rules for competitive events, the novice competitor discovers something the teacher or "coach" sometimes neglects to say. There are a wide variety of "unwritten rules" at forensic tournaments for the oral interpreter. One would wish that tournaments would not be so structured that they force these "rules" on competitors, but only the brave and the innovative venture outside their boundaries. These rules usually emerge from highly successful and talented performers who attempt to innovate, yet stay within conventions of the competitive atmosphere. The "unwritten rules" become somewhat codified at national tournaments and endorsed by returning graduate students or coaches who approve of the technique. The very fact that these "unwritten rules" are written down here is a wonderful example of an oxymoron, but Daniel Cronn-Mills and Alfred Golden offer a lucid, somewhat "tongue-in-cheek" listing of some of the important "unwritten rules"[8] for forensic tournament interpreters:

1. *Teasers are mandatory.* Even though the convention for introductions allows a direct presentation, the tournament setting seems to reward those who begin with a portion of the text;
2. *Know how to use a manuscript.* This means that you must use a three-ring binder notebook, colored black and measuring 6 1/2" x 8 1/2" x 1". You must purchase and use plastic sleeve holders to encase your pages. You should load in two pages front to back so that you have fewer page turns. Any transitions you make from one text to another text (especially in POI) should be made by "snapping" the pages across the rings. There are numerous opportunities to learn "book work" (e.g., how to hold the black notebook, how to use it as a prop, even how close to hold it to your chest while reading). Some performers have an almost military precision in handling their black notebook, snapping it into position from down at their sides;
3. *Movement and blocking depend on solo or group performance.* Solo performers tend to be somewhat constrained. Duo interpreters tend to be allowed much more latitude for movement (e.g., turns, shifts, walking, dancing, bending, kneeling, etc.) Different regions of the country tend to be more liberal or more conservative about movement and blocking;
4. *Minimum time is relative to genre.* A specific minimum-time limit is rarely stated for oral interpretation events, but eight minutes is generally assumed to be the minimum. Poetry program are allowed to go "7:30," but never shorter;
5. *Literature should "fit" interpreters.* Your text should reflect your physical and social characteristics (e.g., same sex, ethnicity, sexual orientation, etc.). The one exception to this rule seems to be that a gifted non-impaired interpreter who chooses to portray characters who are physically, cognitively, or emotionally challenged is allowed room to explore and develop a credible persona. Virtually all forensics texts use a first-person narrative approach to establish the close connection between performer and text;
6. *Literature should be new/undiscovered.* Forensic tournament judges tend to vote against the "classics" or what they perceive to be "overworked" or "overfamiliar" texts. Avoid any texts performed by any other performer. The statute of limitations runs out on this rule when no one can remember the piece, usually four to six years later. Forensic competitors have to dig around to find texts that are created by contemporary authors, but authors that no one recognizes. Many judges have a bias against hearing "rhyming" poetry, so it is better to stick with "prosaic" free verse texts;

7. *Program oral interpretation needs to be a compiled collage script.* Splicing of segments and intercutting of pieces seems to be the norm. Any opportunity to show off how fast you can read, how many different character voices and how fast you can turn pages tends to enhance your chances for success;

8. *No transitions should be used.* Transitions break the continuity of a program performance, even though they might help connect textual messages. A listing of all of the program pieces (in multiple program texts) or the single text listing is made following the teaser and never repeated in the program;

9. *Do not announce that you are the author of your piece.* Although self-authored or coach-composed texts are rarely prohibited, a judge that believes you or your coach wrote the piece may be predisposed to vote against you because the quality of the text cannot possibly match a published text from another competitor. Truth is that many competitors write their own texts, but they use pen names to level the playing field with judges;

10. *Duo interpretation should not have too many characters.* Two characters, one per competitor, are preferred in duo interpretation. However, if the piece is somewhat avant-garde you may experiment with more than one persona. Moving to a new location may help the audience understand that you are a different character, but too many characters become confusing.

This kind of "prescriptiveness" and "narrow" binding rule-making is the greatest criticism from the festival academics. It has much validity, unfortunately. Forensic tournaments frequently reinforce the "incestuous" evaluative criteria when graduate students return to coaching after a successful competitive career. ("This worked for me. Why don't you try doing it this way?") Those competitors who reached the pinnacle of success at national tournaments tend to be cloned by would-be competitors vying for the ultimate prizes. Forensics does not have to be so "prescriptive," but it requires periodic "rebels" to push the envelope of the "unwritten rules" to invigorate the activity. Evidence exists that this does indeed happen from time to time.

Though festivals and forensic tournaments have co-existed for some time, the proponents of each activity seldom dialogue. Some festival supporters oppose forensic competition, claiming that the competitive atmosphere of tournaments reduces literary performance to "product" only. Critics at forensic tournaments are not scholars in the performance studies discipline generally and make evaluative comments that are rigid and technique-oriented. The "process" of sharing ideas and reaction to literature occurs best at a festival; at a tournament rules, limitations, and award-orientation focus on winning to the exclusion of sensitivity to the study of text.[9]

A beginning dialogue between these two groups began in the early 1980s. Symposium personnel discovered that forensic coaches trained in performance studies graduate programs were mentoring their students in "process" sessions.[10] An independent study revealed that a cross-section of forensic coaches stressed analysis and pedagogy above competitive results in poetry interpretation.[11]

Into the next century, a new spirit of cooperation and mutual respect should emerge between the festival and forensics camps. The festival format allows sharing and appreciation of literature to occur in a low-key, supportive, and Socratic atmosphere. The freedom to explore and innovate in performance is not threatened by constraints of time or arbitrary rules. Forensic tournaments generate excellence in performance by competition. Though written and "unwritten" rules exist and untrained critics abound, the forensic contest still provides a meaningful educational experience. Rules do not need to stifle creativity and new coaches emerge each year with a new maxim:

> It is time for us in the forensic world to dissolve that gulf between performance studies and forensics, and to literally let the literature guide us.[12]

Both festivals and forensic contests have educational values. Both need to be supported and endorsed by educators from varying perspectives.

Consider involvement in either (or both) performance festivals and forensic contests. You will benefit from multiple performances and improve your skills. Seek out the director of performance studies or the director of speech and debate (forensics) and find out how you can participate on your school team. Both festivals and forensic contests are outstanding outlets for the performance of literature.

ORAL INTERPRETATION AND COMMUNITY SERVICE

Some college graduates take their experiences in oral interpretation and adapt the performance concepts to educating elementary and secondary school students. Oral Interpretation principles guide students to a greater appreciation of literature, strengthen reading skills, and provide performance opportunities within schools.[13] Today English and social science teachers, in particular, claim that performance-oriented methods are enhancing the education of youth everywhere.

Readers Theatre experiences have been used as performative persuasive devices. William Adams mentions that AIDS Awareness, Women's Rights, Gun Control, and other political movements have used group reading presentations "in such a way that attitudes will be changed without the stridency and hectoring that often mars attempts to alter the strongly-held attitudes, values and beliefs of others."[14]

Readers Theatre performances are instructing students to take steps to assure safe sex or "say no to drugs." Libraries, once the mere repository for books, have become performance arenas for solo and group oral reading presentations.[15] Senior citizen groups love to watch performance groups and participate in them as well. Local churches and religious centers are discovering the use of Readers Theatre and group performances to lead in worship or teach religious truth. Invalids in nursing homes appreciate the volunteer "readers" who come to share and care at their bedsides. Even deaf and blind schools open their doors to performances by literature groups who adapt presentations to the apparent limitations. A recent "party" approach to group reading involves the invitation of friends to a private home, with scripts mailed out in advance and a date and time for a "home performance."[16] This author compiled an original program of history and incidents to reflect a chronology for his own wedding ceremony with his former students reading the portions at a central part of the service. The truth of the matter is that the performance of literature has no limitations.

Outlets for Your Future

No matter what vocation you choose to pursue you will be involved with communication skills. A broadcasting or ministerial career requires a strong voice capable of reassuring others over a microphone or mediated channel. Oral Interpretation will help you. In sales or personnel work, confidence, poise, and just the right amount of the "dramatics" will seal a contract or insure a healthy and cooperative work environment.

You may choose to become a teacher. Good teachers use performance of literature skills to show enthusiasm and energize their students. A caring vocation such as nursing, medicine, counseling, or therapy relies on empathy, a quality gained through multiple chances to perform for audiences. You may be interested to know that graduate schools with theatre or speech communication emphases offer advanced degrees in performance studies, training you for the professional stage or the college teaching milieu.

Whatever outlets you pursue, remember that you bring to each new encounter a legacy of oral tradition, confidence, and sensitivity. The performance of literature experience provided the means to explore a universe of thought, philosophy, and human values. Oral Interpretation has a rich heritage and you will reap benefits because of it for the rest of your life.

Assignments

1. Your professor will give you an option for a class performance. Choose one of these specialized forms: program oral interpretation, original material interpretation, children's literature interpretation, multicultural interpretation or religious scripture interpretation. Follow procedures and time limits for each category. Apply the same standards of analysis, rehearsal, and adaptation to the audience that you did in previous readings.

2. Using the response form found in the appendix, evaluate or participate in a local oral interpretation festival or forensic contest. This experience may be a portion of your contract grade for this course. Talk to the professor in charge of extra-curricular performance outlets. If you enjoy oral interpretation, join the festival interest group or the forensics team to perform on a regular basis.

References

Adams, William. *Institute Book of Readers Theatre: A Practical Guide for School, Theater, & Community.* San Diego: Institute for Readers Theatre, 2003.

Bennett, Gordon C. *Readers Theatre Comes To Church.* Colorado Springs, CO: Meriwether Publishing Ltd., 1985.

Gateley, Gardner. "Does Training in Oral Interpretation Help Speech Therapists?" *Southern Speech Journal* 33 (Winter 1967): 140-142.

Lee, Charlotte I. *Oral Reading of the Scriptures.* Boston: Houghton Mifflin Company, 1974.

Levinson, Helen J. "Choral Speaking for the Severely Handicapped," *Speech Teacher* 5 (September 1956): 226-230.

Lewis, Todd V. *RT: A Readers Theater Ministry.* Kansas City, MO: Lillenas Publishing Company, 1988.

Lewis, Todd V. *RT Two: Two Scripts for Readers Theater.* Kansas City, MO: Lillenas Publishing Company, 1990.

McComiskey, Thomas Edward. *Reading Scripture in Public: A Guide For Preachers and Lay Readers.* Grand Rapids, MI: Baker Book House, 1991.

Nutial, Mark. "Readers Theatre for the Deaf," *Readers Theatre News* 5 (Fall 1977): 10-11.

Ratliff, Gerald Lee. *Introduction to Readers Theatre: A Guide to Classroom Performance.* Colorado Springs, CO: Meriwether Publishing Ltd., 1999.

Rickert, William. "Readers Theatre on Wheels: Casting Handicapped Performers," *Readers Theatre News* 7 (Spring/Summer 1980): 7-8, 34.

Notes

1. See: Keith D. Green, "Original Material in Forensics Oral Interpretation: A Violation of Integrity," *National Forensic Journal* 6 (Spring 1988): 69-72 and Thomas G. Endres, "Maintaining Integrity in Forensics Interpretation: Arguments Against Original Literature," *National Forensic Journal* 6 (Fall 1988): 103-111.
2. Todd V. Lewis, "The Performance of Literature at Forensics Tournaments: A Case for the Use of Original Material," *National Forensic Journal* 6 (Spring 1988): 63-67.
3. Interview with the author, February 25, 1988.
4. Teri Gamble and Michael Gamble, *Literature Alive! 2nd Edition.* Lincolnwood, IL: NTC Publishing Group, 1994, 339.

5. Charlotte I. Lee, *Oral Reading of the Scriptures.* Boston: Houghton Mifflin Company, vi.

6. Thomas Edward McComiskey, *Reading Scripture in Public: A Guide for Preachers and Lay Readers.* Grand Rapids, MI: Baker Book House, 1991, 16-17.

7. Alan Wade, Ted Colson, William E. McDonnell, and Isabel M. Crouch, "Interpretation Festivals in Colleges and Universities: Eastern, Southern Central, and Western States," in *Performance of Literature in Historical Perspectives,* edited by David W. Thompson. Lanham, MD: University Press of America, Inc., 1983, 359-391.

8. Daniel Cronn-Mills and Alfred Golden, "The Unwritten Rules in Oral Interpretation." Paper presented at the National Communication Association Convention (Chicago, IL), November 19-23, 1997.

9. Wade, Colson, McDonnel, Crouch, 371.

10. Todd V. Lewis, David A. Williams, Madeline M. Keaveney, Michael G. Leigh, "Evaluating Oral Interpretation Events: A Contest and Festival Perspectives Symposium," *National Forensic Journal* 2 (Spring 1984): 19-32.

11. Carolyn Keefe, "Verbal Interactions in Coaching the Oral Interpretation of Poetry," *National Forensic Journal* 3 (Spring 1985): 55-69.

12. Peter Pober, "The Conventions of Oral Interpretation in Individual Events: Closing the Binder on the Past," an unpublished paper presented at the Speech Communication Association Convention (Chicago, IL), November 3 1990, 12.

13. See: Thomas L. Fernandez, editor. *Oral Interpretation & the Teaching of English.* Champaign, IL: National Council of Teachers of English, 1969.

14. William Adams, *Institute Book of Readers Theatre: A Practical Guide for School, Theater, & Community.* (San Diego: Institute for Readers Theatre, 2003), 280.

15. Ibid, 280.

16. Ibid, 288.

Appendix

Evaluation Critique Sheets

Oral
Interpreter: _____ Selection: _____

Date _____ OI Type: Prose   Time _____ Grade _____

Preliminary Preparation   Comments
    Introduction/Transitions

    Effectiveness of CUTTING
    and CLARITY of Script

    Choice of Material
    (Suitable, Appropriate, etc.)

Delivery/Presentation
    Volume/Emphasis/Projection

    Familiarity With Script

    Use of Focus Points

    Phrasing/Use of Pauses/Pacing

    Attention to "Subtext"/Literary
    Cue Decisions

    Rate and Tempo Variables

    Vocal Variety/Use of Pitch Range

    Articulation/Pronunciation

    Comments on Persona(e)

    Narrative Functions
    (Sympathetic/Antagonistic/Objective)

Nonverbal Communication
    Poise/Confidence/Control

    Use of Body Movements
    (Gestures/Posture/Moves)

    Use of Facial Expressions

General Comments
    Overall Impressions

    Areas of Greatest Success

    Areas for Improvement

Oral
Interpreter: _____ Selection: _____

Date _____ OI Type: Prose   Time _____ Grade _____

Preliminary Preparation   Comments
    Introduction/Transitions

    Effectiveness of CUTTING
    and CLARITY of Script

    Choice of Material
    (Suitable, Appropriate, etc.)

Delivery/Presentation
    Volume/Emphasis/Projection

    Familiarity With Script

    Use of Focus Points

    Phrasing/Use of Pauses/Pacing

    Attention to "Subtext"/Literary
    Cue Decisions

    Rate and Tempo Variables

    Vocal Variety/Use of Pitch Range

    Articulation/Pronunciation

    Comments on Persona(e)

    Narrative Functions
    (Sympathetic/Antagonistic/Objective)

Nonverbal Communication
    Poise/Confidence/Control

    Use of Body Movements
    (Gestures/Posture/Moves)

    Use of Facial Expressions

General Comments
    Overall Impressions

    Areas of Greatest Success

    Areas for Improvement

Oral
Interpreters: _____ Selection: _____

Date _____ OI Type: Duo Drama Time _____ Grade _____

Preliminary Preparation   Name: Name:

    Shared Introduction/Transitions

    Effectiveness of CUTTING
    and CLARITY of Script

    Choice of Material
    (Suitable, Appropriate, etc.)

Delivery/Presentation

    Volume/Emphasis/Projection

    Familiarity With Script

    Clear Use of Focus Points

    Phrasing/Use of Pauses/Pacing

    Attention to "Subtext"/Literary
    Cue Decisions

    Rate and Tempo Variables

    Vocal Variety/Use of Pitch Range

    Continuity in Dialogue Portions

    Distinct Character Portrayals

    Credibility of Personae

Nonverbal Communication

    Poise/Confidence/Control

    Use of Body Movements
    (Gestures/Posture/Moves)

    Use of Facial Expressions

    Facial Reactions

General Comments

    Overall Impressions

    Areas of Greatest Success

    Areas for Improvement

Oral
Interpreter: _____ Selection: _____

Date _____ OI Type: Solo Drama   Time _____ Grade _____

Preliminary Preparation
Introduction/Transitions

Effectiveness of CUTTING
and CLARITY of Script

Choice of Material
(Suitable, Appropriate, etc.)

Delivery/Presentation
Volume/Emphasis/Projection

Familiarity With Script

Clear Use of Focus Points

Phrasing/Use of Pauses/Pacing

Attention to "Subtext"/Literary
Cue Decisions

Rate and Tempo Variables

Vocal Variety/Use of Pitch Range

Continuity in Dialogue Portions

Distinct Character Portrayals
(Credibility of Persona(e))

Monologue Depth and Variety

Nonverbal Communication
Poise/Confidence/Control

Use of Body Movements
(Gestures/Posture/Moves)

Use of Facial Expressions

General Comments
Overall Impressions

Areas of Greatest Success

Areas for Improvement

Oral
Interpreter: _____ Selection: _____

Date _____ OI Type: Shakespeare   Time _____ Grade _____

Preliminary Preparation
Introduction/Transitions

Effectiveness of CUTTING
and CLARITY of Script

Choice of Material
(Suitable, Appropriate, etc.)

Delivery/Presentation
Volume/Emphasis/Projection

Familiarity With Script

Clear Use of Focus Points

Phrasing/Use of Pauses/Pacing

Attention to "Subtext"/Literary
Cue Decisions

Rate and Tempo Variables

Vocal Variety/Use of Pitch Range

Consistency with Shakespeare's Rhythms

Distinct Character Portrayals
(Credibility of Persona(e))

Monologue Depth and Variety

Consistency with Accent or Attitude

Nonverbal Communication
Poise/Confidence/Control

Use of Body Movements
(Gestures/Posture/Moves)

Use of Facial Expressions

General Comments
Overall Impressions

Areas of Greatest Success

Areas for Improvement

Oral
Interpreter: _____   Selection: _____

Date _____ OI Type: Poetry   Time _____ Grade _____

Preliminary Preparation
     Introduction/Transitions

     Choice of Material
     (Suitable, Appropriate, etc.)

Delivery/Presentation
     Volume/Emphasis/Projection

     Familiarity With Script

     Clear Use of Focus Points

     Phrasing/Use of Pauses/Pacing

     Attention to "Subtext"/Literary
     Cue Decisions

     Rate and Tempo Variables

     Vocal Variety/Use of Pitch Range

     Attention to Rhythmic Portions

     Portrayal of Emotional Range

     Sensitivity to Imagery/Figures
     of Speech

Nonverbal Communication
     Poise/Confidence/Control

     Use of Body Movements
     (Gestures/Posture/Moves)

     Use of Facial Expressions

General Comments
     Overall Impressions

     Areas of Greatest Success

     Areas for Improvement

Oral
Interpreter: _____ Selection: _____

Date _____ OI Type: Program Interp.   Time _____ Grade_____

Preliminary Preparation
    Introduction/Transitions/
    Clarity of Theme

    Effectiveness of Cuttings and
    Combination of Materials

Delivery/Presentation
    Volume/Emphasis/Projection

    Familiarity With Script

    Clear Use of Focus Points

    Phrasing/Use of Pauses/Pacing

    Attention to "Subtext"/Literary
    Cue Decisions

    Rate and Tempo Variables

    Vocal Variety/Use of Pitch Range

    Attention to Rhythmic Portions

    Persona(e) Distinctiveness/
    Credibility

    Articulation/Pronunciation

Nonverbal Communication
    Poise/Confidence/Control

    Use of Body Movements
    (Gestures/Posture/Moves)

    Use of Facial Expressions

General Comments
    Overall Impressions

    Areas of Greatest Success

    Areas for Improvement

Oral
Interpreter: _____   Selection: _____

Date_____   OI Type: Children's Lit.   Time _____   Grade_____

Preliminary Preparation
Introduction/Transitions/
Clarity of Theme

Indication and Consistent
Adaptation to Ages 4 -12

Delivery/Presentation
Volume/Emphasis/Projection

Familiarity With Script

Clear Use of Focus Points

Phrasing/Use of Pauses/Pacing

Attention to "Subtext"/Literary
Cue Decisions

Rate and Tempo Variables

Vocal Variety/Use of Pitch Range

Attention to Rhythmic Portions

Persona(e) Distinctiveness/
Credibility

Narrative Elements (if any)

Nonverbal Communication
Poise/Confidence/Control

Use of Body Movements
(Gestures/Posture/Moves)

Use of Facial Expressions

General Comments
Attention to Child-like Elements

Areas of Greatest Success

Areas for Improvement

Oral
Interpreter: _____ Selections: _____

Date_____ OI Type: _____ Time _____ Grade_____

Preliminary Preparation
    Introduction/Transitions/
    Clarity of Theme

    Effectiveness of Cutting
    and Clarity of Script

Delivery/Presentation
    Volume/Emphasis/Projection

    Familiarity With Script

    Clear Use of Focus Points

    Phrasing/Use of Pauses/Pacing

    Attention to "Subtext"/Literary
    Cue Decisions

    Rate and Tempo Variables

    Vocal Variety/Use of Pitch Range

    Attention to Rhythmic Portions

    Persona(e) Distinctiveness/
    Credibility

    Narrative Elements (if any)

    Articulation and Pronunciation

Nonverbal Communication
    Poise/Confidence/Control

    Use of Body Movements
    (Gestures/Posture/Moves)

    Use of Facial Expressions

General Comments
    Overall Impressions

    Areas of Greatest Success

    Areas for Improvement

Readers Theatre Evaluation

Title of Script: _____ Date: _____

Performers: 1. _____ 2. _____ 3. _____
                4. _____ 5. _____ 6. _____

Performance Comments:

     Meaning of the Script Projected

     Effective Flow and Pacing (Progression and building to high peak of interest)

     Narration (Vivid with clear point of view)

     Characterization (Distinct/Believable)

     Aliveness (Projective Energy)

     Facial Expressions/Reactions

     Clear Entrances/Exits to Scenes

     Focus Point Consistency

     Psychological Closure

Script Evaluation Comments:

     Wholeness (Complete Experience)

     Clear Story Line/Identifiable Theme(s)

     Logical Divisions of Lines to Cast

     "Close-Up" Scenes (Scenes that reveal details of emotion, motivations, environment, characterization, etc.)

Staging Variables:

     Arrangements/Blocking

     Movement and Timing

     Use of Accouterments (Clothing, Music, Props, etc.)

General Effectiveness:

     Projection of Intellectual Content

     Projection of Emotional Content

     Audience Responsiveness:

Individual Comments on Performers Found on the Reverse Side

Communicating Literature   Name: _____

Literature Listening Report Form #1

Title of Tape/Program: _____

1. The performer's use of VOCAL RANGE was: Excellent/Moderately Effective/Limited.

2. The performer's use of RATE VARIABLES was: Excellent/Moderately Effective/Static.

3. The performer's sensitivity to RHYTHMS and TONE of the selection was:

    Excellent/Moderately Effective/Insufficient Generally.

4. If the tape included "narrative" portions:
    a. Did the performer create a clear "persona" for the narrator? _____

    b. Did the narration further the story as performed? _____

    c. Was the "narrator" vocally distinct from other "personae"? _____

5. For "dialogue" portions:
    a. Could you tell a difference in character distinctions? _____

    b. How did the performer make these character voices distinct? _____

    _____

6. For "monologues" or "multi-personae" portions:
    a. Did the character(s) seem credible/true-to-life/believable? Why so? Why not? _____

    _____

7. If you watched a "videotape",
    a. What were the strengths of the performance in nonverbal skills and blocking/movements?

    b. Weaknesses?

8. Performance DISTRACTIONS included these areas:

9. Performance STRENGTHS included these areas:

10. I thought the greatest value in listening to this tape was . . .

Communicating Literature   Name: _____

Literature Listening Report Form #2

Title of Tape/Program: _____

1. The performer's use of VOCAL RANGE was: Excellent/Moderately Effective/Limited.

2. The performer's use of RATE VARIABLES was: Excellent/Moderately Effective/Static.

3. The performer's sensitivity to RHYTHMS and TONE of the selection was:

    Excellent/Moderately Effective/Insufficient Generally.

4. If the tape included "narrative" portions:
    a. Did the performer create a clear "persona" for the narrator? _____

    b. Did the narration further the story as performed? _____

    c. Was the "narrator" vocally distinct from other "personae"? _____

5. For "dialogue" portions:
    a. Could you tell a difference in character distinctions? _____

    b. How did the performer make these character voices distinct? _____

        _____

6. For "monologues" or "multi-personae" portions:
    a. Did the character(s) seem credible/true-to-life/believable? Why so? Why not? _____

        _____

7. If you watched a "videotape",
    a. What were the strengths of the performance in nonverbal skills and blocking/movements?

    b. Weaknesses?

8. Performance DISTRACTIONS included these areas:

9. Performance STRENGTHS included these areas:

10. I thought the greatest value in listening to this tape was . . .

Communicating Literature   Name: _____

Literature Listening Report Form #3

Title of Tape/Program: _____

1. The performer's use of VOCAL RANGE was: Excellent/Moderately Effective/Limited.

2. The performer's use of RATE VARIABLES was: Excellent/Moderately Effective/Static.

3. The performer's sensitivity to RHYTHMS and TONE of the selection was:

      Excellent/Moderately Effective/Insufficient Generally.

4. If the tape included "narrative" portions:
    a. Did the performer create a clear "persona" for the narrator? _____

    b. Did the narration further the story as performed? _____

    c. Was the "narrator" vocally distinct from other "personae"? _____

5. For "dialogue" portions:
    a. Could you tell a difference in character distinctions? _____

    b. How did the performer make these character voices distinct? _____

      _____

6. For "monologues" or "multi-personae" portions:
    a. Did the character(s) seem credible/true-to-life/believable? Why so? Why not? _____

      _____

7. If you watched a "videotape",
    a. What were the strengths of the performance in nonverbal skills and blocking/movements?

    b. Weaknesses?

8. Performance DISTRACTIONS included these areas:

9. Performance STRENGTHS included these areas:

10. I thought the greatest value in listening to this tape was . . .

Communicating Literature   Name: _____

Performance of Literature Journal Report Form #1

Author(s) of Article: _____

Journal Article Title: _____

Date of Article: _____ Pages Read: _____ Name of Periodical: _____

Summary of Article (In Your Own Words):

The most valuable information I gained from reading this article consisted of:

_____

_____

_____

Communicating Literature   Name: _____

Performance of Literature Journal Report Form #2

Author(s) of Article: _____

Journal Article Title: _____

Date of Article: _____ Pages Read: _____ Name of Periodical: _____

Summary of Article (In Your Own Words):

The most valuable information I gained from reading this article consisted of:

_____

_____

_____

Communicating Literature   Name: _____

Festival or Tournament Report Form #1

Name of Festival/Tournament: _____ Date: _____

Location: _____ Time Spent: _____ Hours

Number of Rounds Observed: _____ Categories Observed: _____

Participation as Performer: Yes   No   _____

The biggest difference I noticed in "festival/forensics performances" from our class was:

Indicate which performance was the best in your estimation and why you thought so:

Indicate which performances had weaknesses and what you thought needed to be done to correct such weaknesses:

The greatest value of observing or participating in this activity for me was:

Communicating Literature   Name: _____

Festival or Tournament Report Form #2

Name of Festival/Tournament: _____ Date: _____

Location: _____ Time Spent: _____ Hours

Number of Rounds Observed: _____ Categories Observed: _____

Participation as Performer: Yes   No   _____

The biggest difference I noticed in "festival/forensics performances" from our class was:

Indicate which performance was the best in your estimation and why you thought so:

Indicate which performances had weaknesses and what you thought needed to be done to correct such weaknesses:

The greatest value of observing or participating in this activity for me was:

Index

(This index lists authors and subjects and literary selections.)